REGIONAL DEVELOPMENT AGENCIES AND BUSINESS CHANGE

For our friends and colleagues
working in economic development

Regional Development Agencies and Business Change

Edited by

GILL BENTLEY and JOHN GIBNEY
Centre for Urban and Regional Studies
The University of Birmingham
England

Ashgate

Aldershot • Burlington USA • Singapore • Sydney

Published by
Ashgate Publishing Ltd
Gower House
Croft Road
Aldershot
Hants GU11 3HR
England

Ashgate Publishing Company
131 Main Street
Burlington, VT 05401-5600 USA

Ashgate website: http://www.ashgate.com

British Library Cataloguing in Publication Data
Regional development agencies and business change. - (Urban
    and regional planning and development)
    1.Regional planning - England 2.Regional planning - Wales
    3.England - Economic conditions - 20th century 4.Wales -
    Economic conditions - 20th century
    I.Bentley, Gill II.Gibney, John
    307.1'2

Library of Congress Control Number: 00-109868

ISBN 0 7546 1271 6

Printed and bound by Antony Rowe Ltd, Chippenham, Wiltshire

Contents

PART II: BUSINESS CHANGE AND REGIONAL DEVELOPMENT IN THE WEST MIDLANDS

CONCLUSION

List of Figures

List of Tables

List of Contributors

Gill Bentley is Lecturer in Urban and Regional Economic Development at the Centre for Urban and Regional Studies, University of Birmingham, England.

Dr Philip Boland is Lecturer in Industrial Development and Regional Planning at the Department of City and Regional Planning, University of Cardiff, Wales.

Chris Collinge is Senior Lecturer in Regional Economic Change at the Centre for Urban and Regional Studies, University of Birmingham, England.

Dr Margareta Dahlström is Lecturer in Urban and Regional Studies at the Centre for Urban and Regional Studies, University of Birmingham, England.

Dr John Gibney is Senior Research Fellow at the Centre for Urban and Regional Studies, University of Birmingham, England.

John Lovering is Professor of Urban Development and Governance at the Department of City and Regional Planning, University of Cardiff, Wales.

John Mawson is Professor of Public Policy and Management at the Aston Business School, Aston University, England.

Peter Roberts is Professor of European Strategic Planning at the Geddes Centre for Planning Research, School of Town and Regional Planning, University of Dundee, Scotland.

John Shutt is Eversheds Professor of Regional Business Development at the Leeds Business School, Leeds Metropolitan University, England.

Barbara Smith OBE is a former Senior Lecturer at the Centre for Urban and Regional Studies, University of Birmingham, England.

Alan Srbljanin is Lecturer in Urban and Regional Studies at the Centre for Urban and Regional Studies, University of Birmingham, England.

Dr Barbara Tilson is Honorary Research Fellow at the Centre for Urban and Regional Studies, University of Birmingham and Research Director at BCT Research Associates.

Preface

Regional development agencies across Europe are in hot pursuit of the 'holy grail' of sustainable economic development. But sustainable economic development is an aspiration which is proving particularly difficult for economic development professionals to realise. The dilemma is not new, however, as successive generations of policymakers and practitioners have found themselves wrestling with the fundamental challenge of how best to 'facilitate' the developmental aspects of their respective regional economies.

After some delay in comparison with mainland European, Scottish and Welsh experience, the English regions are finally in the process of setting in place new regional development agencies (RDAs). Not surprisingly, much is expected of this new regional initiative.

This book is essentially a practical look at the strategic, organisational and resource challenges faced by the new English regional development agencies at the beginning of the year 2000. This examination of the emerging agendas around the RDAs looks at one region – the West Midlands – in more detail, in order to illustrate some of the key issues which are being faced in relation to business change and transition.

In recent years, there has been a considerable if perhaps not a wholly unpredictable revival of interest across academic, political and journalistic circles regarding the institutional, economic and cultural underpinnings of regional economic development. This book is the outcome of the joint editors' and individual chapter authors' shared and longstanding curiosity about the nature of regional economies and the regional institutions charged ambitiously with helping to 'make them work'.

What follows is undoubtedly a modest contribution to the evolving body of literature on regional economic development. We hope, however, that the work will provide useful insights and informative reading for all of those (students, researchers and practitioners alike) with an interest in the topic. This work draws partly on various ongoing research and consultancy projects on the West Midlands regional economy being undertaken by the Centre for

Urban and Regional Studies (CURS), at the University of Birmingham, England. As part of our own learning process we would be pleased to receive views, observations and critique from readers.

Gill Bentley and John Gibney
Centre for Urban and Regional Studies
The University of Birmingham
England

Acknowledgements

In preparing this edited work over the past 18 months, we are indebted to a great number of friends and colleagues.

In particular, we are grateful to Alan Murie for helping us to shape the project at the outset and for his helpful comments and encouragement throughout. Since 1996, hundreds of individual West Midlands based firms have spared scarce time to be interviewed as part of the ongoing research into the regional economy undertaken by the economic development and planning research group at CURS. Practitioners and policymakers in many business support agencies and local authorities have been consulted. We are grateful to all of the people in these firms and the region's public sector agencies and authorities for taking time out from busy agendas to talk to us and to share their concerns and aspirations. We have also benefited from the astute advice of the chapter authors on the overall scope of the book. They have also delivered their own work to tight timetables and without protest.

In addition, we owe thanks to colleagues at CURS, including Pat Cam, who have provided research assistance throughout both the writing of the book and on earlier research projects which have informed the sector chapters in Part II.

Credit is also due to Anne Keirby and Claire Annals at Ashgate Publishing Ltd for helping us with the printing and publishing arrangements. Karen Kings had the unenviable task of formatting the final draft of the book, Susan Leather the exacting task of proof-reading and Pauline Thorington-Jones the job of preparing the CRC. Many thanks indeed to them each for their efficiency and infinite patience.

Finally, we are grateful to the Office of National Statistics for the use of their economy data in Part II of the book and for the English RDAs for their logos.

List of Acronyms and Abbreviations

ABS	Anti-lock braking system
AOL	America Online
AWM	Advantage West Midlands
BCC	British Chambers of Commerce
BCIS	Birmingham City Information System
CBI	Confederation of British Industry
CLECs	Competitive local exchange carriers
CLES	Centre for Local Economic Strategies
CNC	Computer numerically controlled
CRM	Customer relations management
CURS	Centre for Urban and Regional Studies, the University of Birmingham
CWC	Cable and Wireless Communications
DCMS	Department of Culture, Media and Sport
DETR	Department of the Environment, Transport and the Regions
DfEE	Department for Education and Employment
DoE	Department of the Environment (now DETR)
DTI	Department of Trade and Industry
EAI	Enterprise Application Integration
EC	European Commission
EEDA	East of England Development Agency
EMDA	East Midlands Development Agency
EMU	European Monetary Union
EP	English Partnerships
EPSRC	Engineering and Physical Sciences Research Council
ERA	English Regional Association
ERDF	European Regional Development Fund
ERP	Enterprise Resource Planning
ESF	European Social Fund

ESRC	Economic and Social Research Council
EU	European Union
FDI	Foreign direct investment
FE	Further education
GDP	Gross domestic product
GLA	Greater London Authority
GORs	Government Offices for the Regions
GOWM	Government Office for the West Midlands
GOYH	Government Office for Yorkshire and the Humber
GVA	Gross value added
HC	House of Commons
HMG	Her Majesty's Government
ICT	Information and communications technologies
IDB	Industrial Development Board
ILGS	Institute of Local Government Studies
IT	Information technology
ITEC	Information technology, electronics and communications
IWA	Institute of Welsh Affairs
JIT	Just in time
LETS	Local exchange trading systems
LG	Lucky Goldstar
LGA	Local Government Association
LQ	Location quotient
LSC	Learning and Skills Council
MAFF	Ministry of Agriculture, Fisheries and Food
MITI	Ministry of International Trade and Industry (Japan)
NDPB	Non-departmental public body
NEB	National Enterprise Board
NWDA	Northwest Development Agency
OECD	Organisation for Economic Co-operation and Development
OEM	Original equipment manufacturer
ONE	One NorthEast
PFI	Private Finance Initiative
R&D	Research and development
RD	Regional director
RDA	Regional development agency
RDC	Rural Development Commission

REPC	Regional Economic Planning Council
RES	Regional economic strategy
RPC	Regional Planning Conference
RPG	Regional Planning Guidance
RSA	Regional Selective Assistance
RTD	Research and technological development
RTPI	Royal Town Planning Institute
RTS	Regional Transport Strategy
SBS	Small Business Service
SEEDA	South East England Development Agency
SIC	Standard Industrial Classification
SMEs	Small and medium-sized enterprises
SPDs	Single Programming Documents
SRA	Strategic Rail Authority
SRB	Single Regeneration Budget
SWERDA	South West of England RDA
TEC	Training and Enterprise Council
TUC	Trade Union Congress
ULSAB	Ultra-light steel automotive body
WDA	Welsh Development Agency
WMCC	West Midlands County Council
WMDA	West Midlands Development Agencies
WMEB	West Midlands Enterprise Board
WMEPC	West Midlands Economic Planning Council
WMPAC	West Midlands Planning Authorities Conference
YF	Yorkshire Forward

Map

INTRODUCTION

1 Regional Development Agencies and Business Change

GILL BENTLEY AND JOHN GIBNEY

More than ever and driven by rapidly evolving technologies, lifestyles and markets, the pace of change is quickening in key industry and service sectors of regional economies. For policymakers and practitioners working to build dynamic and sustainable regional economies, and faced with a myriad of often conflicting political and economic demands, these are certainly testing times.

Living and working in the West Midlands at the beginning of 2000, it is hard for us to ignore the feverish political tumult unfolding in 'real time' around the BMW/Rover issue and the prospect of local economic disruption. At times like this, scholars are naturally drawn to consider to what degree national and regional institutions charged with helping to 'make the regional economy work better' can ever hope to offset what in a time of crisis can appear to be economic inevitability. Clearly, to surrender to economic inevitability and do nothing is not an option. The regional development community as a whole (politicians, academics and practitioners) shares an almost moral obligation to do what it can to facilitate improvements in employment and the quality of life for local people or, at the very least, to try and improve the odds of this happening. However, the world is changing apace and the regional development 'job' promises to be ever more frustrating, fraught and challenging in the future. Any comfortable notion of 'business as usual', at least from the point of view of the work of regional development agencies (RDAs), can be confined to the past, and with the sure knowledge that the talent and ability of policymakers and practitioners will be tested to the full.

Contemporary developments in the manufacturing sector in the West Midlands provide much food for thought (e.g. Bentley in chapter 6 on the automotive sector). The German car manufacturer BMW may have moved quickly and impulsively in early 2000 to divest itself of the Rover 'issue', although this was perhaps not necessarily so unpredictable. Perhaps the UK government did manage to be wrong-footed and ill-prepared at one and the same time. No doubt academic colleagues will in time provide more searching analysis on the topic than is being offered by the welter of confusing and often contradictory journalistic commentary. More importantly, however, what these contemporary developments in the West Midlands serve to underline is that regional economies are complex, dynamic and increasingly fast moving. Some would say that to attempt to forecast or predict their future trajectory is dangerous. Yet our ability to anticipate and plan for change should not be underestimated either. It may not be a question so much of finding and analysing information about change and transition in regional economies that is the issue. Rather it may be our inability over time to ensure continuity of the economic research and intelligence effort, coupled with the lack of propensity to deploy policy and organisation effectively as a result of what we discover. Rapid business change should be seen as an everyday aspect of the RDA operating environment in developed regional economies. Politicians and practitioners need to get 'smarter' if they are to stay in touch and ultimately plan for change. This means making available the necessary time, space and resources for genuinely inclusive, non-partisan and open-minded reflection about future regional scenarios.

Over recent years, as a result of the work of a number of scholars, it has become common parlance that regions require to set in place appropriate and robust organisational arrangements, in order to better respond to the challenges of the 'modern economy'. This view is found in the notion of 'institutional thickness' (Amin and Thrift, 1999). Amin and Thrift argue that what is needed is a strong institutional presence, in the form of a range of organisations (firms, employers organisations, unions, and local and central government agencies concerned with economic development); that these organisations interact to a high degree with each other; that there are mechanisms to ensure collective responsibility; and that these organisations work in partnership to arrive at a set of shared goals to achieve a sense of common purpose which will stimulate action.

The desire to try and manage an ever more 'unpredictable' global economy has always proved difficult to resist for politicians at local and national level. Regions need to be organised to improve their ability to respond over the short and medium term to the inevitable ups and downs of increasingly globally driven economic cycles. Regional institutions involved to varying degrees in the economic development process (including RDAs) can at certain times and in certain places make a significant contribution to the well-being of the regional economy, particularly in terms of their aggregate impact. However, as the consultation on the regional economic strategies (RES) showed, there was a plethora of demands from local authorities and agencies for action to tackle local-level problems rather than those at a regional strategic scale.

Map 1.1 Map of the regions and logos of the English RDAs

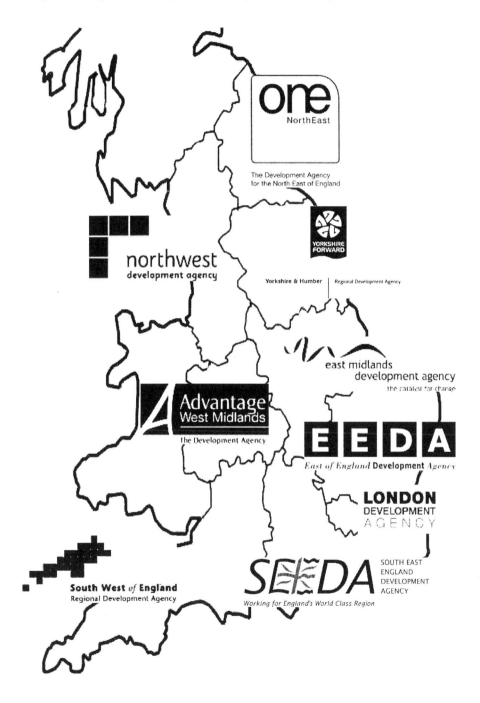

The English RDAs, which became operational in April 1999, are setting out their stalls at a time when the pace of business change and transition poses some critical public policy challenges (Jones and MacLeod, 1999). We are still in the early days of the English 'regional project', but it is hardly uncharted territory given the longstanding experience of development agencies in Wales, Scotland and to varying degrees other regions of mainland Europe (see Boland and Lovering in chapter 5 on Wales). It is timely and legitimate therefore to pose general questions about strategy and organisation and to offer up an initial prognosis. Even at this early stage, one of the critical issues faced by the English RDAs is how they can effectively connect strategy and organisation – which have been largely influenced by pre-existing notions and sets of interests surrounding the development of regional economies – with the modern reality of constantly shifting regional circumstances. It is still too early to offer definitive views. Yet the chapters that follow tend to suggest that the RDAs set in place to facilitate regional development in England must ensure that they more neatly fit with economic development needs as this new 'regional experience' unfolds. Furthermore, we would advance the related notion that the ability to recognise and interpret key local/global economy trends and subsequently to *fundamentally* reconfigure policy and organisation, ideally in advance of crisis, is a vital component of any regional economic strategy. This becomes increasingly true as the RDA operating environment becomes more complex.

Bearing in mind the pace of contemporary business change, the English RDAs have to be able to source, absorb and deploy substantive, good quality and timely economic intelligence which can enable policy formulation to occur within the context of a thorough understanding of local and global economic prospects. Economic insight of this kind should be regarded as an asset enabling practitioners to counteract the 'engrenage infernal' of local and national vested interests ever threatening to impose the short-term view. In the cut and thrust of national/local politics, economic intelligence, as the BMW/Rover story perhaps indicates, seems often be relegated to an afterthought. It leads us to ask whether the architects of the English 'regional project' are giving fundamental consideration to the requirements and dynamics of regional economies with varied and differing needs before new policy and organisational solutions are proffered. For in many ways each regional economy is unique, and different regional circumstances will require bespoke and flexible action.

This book, then, has a simple intention. It sets out to address the core surmise that the RDAs, as presently constituted, may not be able to provide a robust connection between policy and organisational capacity and the complex multifaceted requirements of the developed English regional economies. In essence, we suggest that the RDAs may not be presently in the right shape or indeed have the full set of attributes to, in their own words in the regional economic strategies, secure 'sustainable development', 'build competitive economies', or 'create advantage'.

The book is divided into two discrete parts which seek to connect the debate on the emergence of the RDAs with concerns around aspects of the regional economy brought to the fore through an examination of the localised experience of key industry and business sectors in the West Midlands. It is not our intention in this book to investigate the specific policy and organisational parameters of the RDA for the West Midlands (Advantage West Midlands (AWM)) since the organisation has been in existence for only some 12 months or so. Rather, we have chosen to look at the more general economic trends in the West Midlands via sector case studies for a broader view of the challenges faced by the RDA.

Organising for Regional Development

In Part I, *Organising for Regional Development in England and Wales*, and through the eyes of five leading academics, we are presented with informed analysis and consideration of the lessons to be drawn from the experience of regional development policy and practice in England and Wales over the past two decades. The first three chapters move from exploring the strategic origins of the regional revival in England to a very practical examination of the roles, responsibilities and prospects of the English RDAs. For comparative purposes, the final chapter in Part I of the book provides a valuable and timely perspective on the Welsh 'model' of regional development.

In chapter 2, John Mawson sets the scene by tracing the recent history of the regional revival in the UK within the context of the changing relationships between Whitehall and the English regions. He considers the ideas which have influenced the debate on regional development in England, and provides a strategic overview of the core policy and political processes at work. Key issues which continue to influence regional governance, central-local relations, local democracy and accountability are exposed, and the longer-term prospects for the English regional project are assessed.

In chapter 3, Peter Roberts combines comment on the theoretical context of the processes in play with valuable insights into how the work of the RDAs integrates with other aspects of regional planning and economic development.

In taking stock of progress to date with the setting up of the RDAs, he underlines the difficulty faced by those engaged in delivering the regional project within the 'congested regional environment' in England. The chapter outlines a number of essential policy and organisational challenges and proffers a set of organisational models to assist with our appreciation of the evolution of regional governance in England.

John Shutt draws our attention in chapter 4 to the set of very practical 'wicked issues' being faced by the RDAs as they tackle a range of local economic development matters. The chapter outlines the core functions of the RDAs and provides a critique of the design, content and aspirations of the various regional economic strategies (RES). Critically, Shutt suggests that the RES exercise has tended to favour regional consensus at the expense of more considered approaches to local economic development within the context of contemporary business change and transition at the beginning of the 21st century. The chapter underlines the potential importance of the RDA's role in stimulating genuine experimentation and debate about regional economic 'futures'.

In chapter 5, Philip Boland and John Lovering place the earlier discussion of the progress of the English RDAs alongside the experience of the Welsh Development Agency (WDA). Compared to England, Wales has relatively longstanding experience of both the strategic and tactical 'fall out' of RDA activity. The authors provide a valuable and thought-provoking assessment of the mixed success story of the WDA. The chapter serves to remind us of the very real danger that new powerful economic institutions in England may come to preclude genuinely open reflection upon economic development options, and are no guarantee in themselves that entrenched or partisan views can give way to boundary-breaking originality or creativity.

Within the context of the emerging strategic and operational agendas of the English RDAs and equipped with observations drawn from the model of regional development in Wales, Part II of the book considers the recent experience of business change and transition in the West Midlands.

Business Change and Regional Development

In Part II, *Business Change and Regional Development in the West Midlands*, we have chosen to set the previous discussion about the nature and role of the RDAs alongside an investigation of some of the key economic challenges faced by the West Midlands. Chapter authors have followed a similar approach in addressing different sectors of the economy. But given that individual business sectors reflect very different sets of circumstances, authors have been allowed considerable leeway in deciding on the particular slant of the sector case study. The four principal chapters in Part II take the reader through a range of economic development challenges via the study of business change in four sectors of the regional economy. The sector appraisals draw on a number of research projects undertaken between 1996 and 1999 by the economic development and planning research group in CURS on behalf of a number of local and regional agencies and local authorities in the West Midlands. These research projects have aimed to provide local policymakers with a better understanding of business change in the region and the implications of this change for economic development policy and programmes. For this book, we have chosen to focus on two 'traditional' sectors, the automotive sector and the rubber and plastics sector, for reasons of their strategic importance in the West Midlands region. Two further sectors, the business services sector and the information and communications technologies (ICT) sector, have also been chosen because they have generally been identified in the region as 'emerging' sectors. The discussion and assessment of change and transition across the four sectors take account of international, national and West Midlands's circumstances.

In the preface to Part II, Barbara Smith and Chris Collinge provide a brief but important scene-setting description of the West Midlands economy, focusing on the performance of the regional economy over recent time. Key trends and drivers are identified, and the general outlook for the West Midlands at the beginning of 2000 is presented.

In chapter 6, Gill Bentley scopes out the current state of play for the automotive sector in the region, in discussing the major changes which are occurring across the industry. She shows that while there is a cluster of firms within the West Midlands, developments in the industry threaten to break this up. This is demonstrated not least in the case of the takeover of Rover by BMW, which led to changes in sourcing strategy that meant the loss of business for firms in the supply chain. The subsequent sale of Rover poses the bigger question of what might happen when a firm at the heart of a cluster disappears. The chapter highlights the limits to actions by regional development agencies to secure sustainable regional economic development.

In chapter 7, Barbara Tilson highlights the upheaval brought about in the rubber and plastics processing sector in the West Midlands by the combination of fierce international competition and rapid technological change. The author examines the inter-related characteristics of change in the sector by focusing on the automotive and packaging industries in terms of environmental drivers, product and process development, skills and training, materials and new technology. Continual innovation is seen as a fundamental requirement of firms if they are to survive and grow in the West Midlands. The chapter flags up issues faced by economic development actors at regional level as they seek to enhance the innovative capacity of this sector, and underlines the importance of their stimulating genuine and value-added collaboration between firms.

In chapter 8, Margareta Dahlstrom places a discussion of change and developments in the business services sector within the context of the emerging regional agenda in the West Midlands. Business services are generally regarded as providing for a degree of local and regional economic growth and diversification in the West Midlands. Dahlstrom outlines the key drivers of change in the sector and reviews the importance of business services at international, UK and regional level. The chapter provides a helpful assessment of the potential contribution of business services to the West Midlands economy, and identifies a key role for the region's development agency in bringing forward economic development opportunities.

In chapter 9, Chris Collinge and Alan Srbljanin point out the complexities of the ICT industries, and focus on the notion of competing and complementary products, to argue that ICT industries cannot be treated as one amorphous activity. In looking at the various strategies firms are adopting in the fast-moving worlds of communications and computers, they show that, despite the importance of new small firms in ICT, the resurgence of predatory behaviour by companies in order to enhance their opportunities or defend established positions (through horizontal and vertical integration) is the reality which policymakers in the regions must come to terms with.

Finally, in the concluding chapter of the book, we seek to identify a number of critical issues which will impact upon the future success of the English RDAs.

References

Amin, A. and Thrift, N. (1999), 'Living in the Global', in A. Amin and N. Thrift (eds), *Globalization, Institutions, and Regional Development in Europe,* Oxford University Press, Oxford.

Jones, M. and Macleod, G. (1999), 'Towards a Regional Renaissance? Reconfiguring and Rescaling England's Economic Governance', *Transactions of the Institute of British Geographers,* vol. 24, no. 3, pp. 295-313.

PART I
ORGANISING FOR
REGIONAL DEVELOPMENT
IN ENGLAND AND WALES

2 Whitehall, Devolution and the English Regions

JOHN MAWSON

Introduction

Since coming to office, New Labour's devolution and regionalisation programme has led to a fundamental reshaping of UK territorial politics, public policy and administration. This chapter considers the changing relationships between various parts of the UK and between Whitehall and the English regions, and the implications for emerging regional development structures in England. It is clear that the economic, political and administrative forces that led to the return of the regional and devolution agenda are deep-seated and their persistence may well lead to pressures for further changes. In this dynamic, the English regions are in a pivotal and evolving situation. The failure of the Callaghan administration to fully recognise concerns about the impact of devolution on the North East and other parts of England led to parliamentary opposition and the wrecking of the Devolution Bill, and ultimately set in train events leading to the fall of the government in 1979 (Bogdanor, 1999). This time around it is important that as the devolution project unfolds it is viewed in its totality, taking into account the complex interactions between different parts of the UK.

In pursuing these issues part one of the chapter looks at the factors underlying the re-emergence of the regional agenda in England and how the previous Conservative administration responded. Attention then focuses on New Labour's evolving approach in opposition and the subsequent adjustments following the 1997 election. A critique of the new governance structures is presented against the background of constitutional reforms elsewhere in the UK. Based on these comparisons it is suggested that present arrangements in England are inherently unstable and will lead to pressures for further change.

The Re-emergence of the Regional Agenda

During the course of the 1980s, Conservative governments dismantled Labour's regional economic planning machinery and adopted a strong 'pro- Union' status quo position in regard to the constitution. It was in this period, however, that new pressures came about which were to lead to the re-emergence of the regional agenda in England (Mawson, 1996). The fragmentation of the public realm arising from privatisation, the establishment of arms-length agencies and the marketisation of public services, when taken together with a limited and poorly co-ordinated presence of government departments, highlighted the need to improve management of the regional level. The business support structure and institutional capacity for handling regional development and inward investment was widely seen as inadequate in comparison with that of other European Union (EU) countries and Scotland, Wales and Northern Ireland. Moreover, the need for civil servants to manage the implementation of European Union Structural Funds programmes at regional level and prepare regional strategies to access European funding resulted in pressures from the Treasury. Added to these administrative and policy considerations there were those outside government circles who expressed political concerns about the accountability and openness of government agencies and quangos at the regional level. A further significant factor in shaping Labour's attitude to regionalisation was the growth of the nationalist vote in Scotland and Wales, which potentially presented a serious challenge in Labour's traditional heartlands. Hence the party in opposition resurrected its commitment to devolution which had been abandoned after the collapse of Jim Callaghan's government in 1979 (Mawson, 1998).

While not wishing to respond to this regional democratic agenda, John Major's government recognised the need to tackle the issue of co-ordination. In 1994 the Conservative government launched its network of 10 Government Offices for the Regions (GORs) (Mawson and Spencer, 1997). Regional civil servants in the Training, Enterprise and Employment Division of the Department of Employment and the Departments of the Environment (DoE), Transport and Trade and Industry (DTI) were made accountable to a single senior civil servant, the Regional Director (RD). Subsequently in 1995 the Department of Education was merged with the Department of Employment to form the Department for Education and Employment, (DfEE) adding a further significant dimension to the work of the GORs.

Reporting to the relevant Secretaries of State, the RDs were made responsible for all staff and expenditure routed through their offices and for ensuring that the necessary co-ordination and links were established between main programmes and other public monies at the regional level.

Early successes of the GORs included the introduction of the Single Regeneration Budget Challenge Fund, securing greater integration of the management of European funding, the establishment of the network of Business Links, introducing a regional dimension to the competitiveness White Paper, and facilitating local and regional partnerships to secure policy development and implementation. However, there were significant areas of public policy with a regionally specific impact which remained outside the immediate sphere of influence of the GORs. Moreover, there was reluctance by Conservative ministers to allow the GORs to engage in any form of open forum or debate with the key regional players on the development of various regional strategic priorities. The RDs became subject to criticism that they were powerful unaccountable bureaucrats who were in a position to pick and choose regional opinions and play off one group of regional actors against another in the exercise of their policy discretion.

Labour's Developing Regional Agenda

The Labour Party's consultation document, *A Choice for England,* published in June 1995, argued the case for making the GORs, quangos and other agencies more open and accountable to the regions (Labour Party, 1995). The emergence and development of local authority joint working at the regional level was seen as one potential basis for developing a more accountable democratic regional structure.

The solution proposed was a two-stage process with the creation of indirectly elected regional chambers or assemblies made up of a relatively small number of nominated councillors (40 was suggested) in the first phase. Nominations would come from an electoral college based on a formula reflecting a geographical and political balance. The chambers would co-opt other regional partners (Confederation of British Industry (CBI), Chambers of Commerce, Trades Union Congress (TUC), voluntary organisations).

A Choice for England stated that the assemblies would not have tax-raising or legislative powers but consideration would be given to transferring certain functions held by the GORs and quangos, or at least sharing responsibility with the GORs. They would have the responsibility for establishing the elected regional authorities.

As to the timescale, Jack Straw stated that it would vary from region to region and would be dependent on three safeguards:

1. The plan for the chamber should be drawn up by democratic representatives in the region.
2. Parliamentary approval.
3. Popular consent tested through a referendum.

In June 1996 the Labour Party launched the second key component of its proposals for the English regions in the form of the report of the Regional Policy Commission (Regional Policy Commission, 1996). Central to the Commission's thinking was the establishment of a regional development agency for each region under the remit of the relevant chamber or assembly.

To some observers the package offering the establishment of chambers throughout England and the prospect of moving to elected assemblies in a second unspecified period was a pragmatic response to the political reality of varying enthusiasm for regionalism and the need to avoid more costly local government reorganisation. The promise of early legislation to establish the RDAs was seen as securing the passage of devolution legislation by gaining the support of the powerful North East block of Labour MPs as well as others from the North of England (Condon, 1996). Moreover, it would be argued that those regions which took early steps to establish elected assemblies would set in train a 'domino effect' with other regions following quickly behind, not wishing to lose comparative advantage. Straw's staged approach was therefore interpreted as a robust strategy fitting in with the short-term 'low cost' priorities of New Labour, addressing immediate political pressures arising from devolution, while at the same time providing the scope for a more ambitious form of English regionalism in the longer term.

The Regional Stakeholders

As the debate surrounding devolution came increasingly to the fore, so other key actors with a stake in the regional scene also began to address the agenda (Davies, 1996). During the course of 1994 and 1995 a number of these issues were aired during the House of Commons (HC) Trade and Industry Committee review of regional policy under the chairmanship of the Labour regional spokesman, Dick Caborn (HC Trade and Industry Select Committee, 1995). The British Chambers of Commerce argued, in evidence to the Select

Committee, that a stronger regional voice was needed if Britain's views on regions were to be properly represented in Europe and that this could be best accomplished by a regional forum which also provided an advisory and co-ordinating remit in economic development. Concerns about regional co-ordination and the transparency and accountability of government were also raised by the CBI.

The CBI's report, *Regions for Business*, published in the run up to the 1997 election, confirmed the growing consensus surrounding a new form of regional governance involving the establishment of formal regional partnerships based on all the main public and private sector organisations (CBI, 1997). The report argued that there was a need for better resourcing of these nascent partnerships, which had sprung up in most regions and had the potential to guide policy-making by establishing regional priorities for action as well as advising the GORs on land use and transport issues, and EU and Single Regeneration Budget (SRB) funding. It was felt that regional partnerships should also achieve greater co-ordination of the work of agencies such as English Partnerships and the Highways Agency as well as inward investment and business support services. Similar proposals were set out by the British Chambers of Commerce (BCC) in its *Regional Policy Brief* (1997), which advocated the establishment of regional strategic fora based on 'regional partnerships' comprising the key stakeholders: trade unions, Chambers of Commerce, the CBI, Training and Enterprise Councils (TEC)s, local authorities and educational bodies (BCC, 1997). The TEC National Council also supported this approach in its *Regional Development Principles* paper (TEC National Council, 1997).

It was not just the business community, however, which was to recognise and respond to the new regional agenda. Regional issues have always been a key matter of concern for local government in relation to matters such as transport, planning, environmental issues, regeneration, economic development and European funding. Over the years the need to engage in policy development and advocacy, and to implement various strategic initiatives at this geographical scale has necessitated the creation of regional joint machinery, though much of this type of work has been undertaken through the county councils. With the restoration of a comprehensive geographical coverage of regional working by the early 1990s, and an increasing recognition of the need to articulate local authority interests at the regional level, a decision was taken to establish English Regional Associations (ERAs) in 1993 (ERA, 1995). Further pressures leading in the same direction were the strengthened presence of central government in the regions as represented in the work of the GORs and the establishment of a single Local Government Association (LGA) in April 1997, with an electoral college organised on a regional basis.

English Regions Under New Labour

It is clear from the developments described above that at the time when Labour took office, there had emerged a degree of consensus as to the way forward in the regions concerning partnership working or 'governance' as distinct from formal elected regional government. Labour moved swiftly to establish a new Department of the Environment, Transport and the Regions (DETR) under the Deputy Prime Minister. A Bill to establish regional development agencies was announced in the Queen's Speech (Her Majesty's Government (HMG), 1997). However, there was no direct reference to taking forward the 'Straw component' of the package, despite the fact that in a number of regions steps had been taken to establish regional chambers and/or regional partnerships and in others plans were well advanced in anticipation of a Labour election victory.

Ministers stated that they were not able to take the English proposals any further forward. This was because of the lack of time available to bring forward a complex constitutional issue against the background of a crowded first-year parliamentary timetable (*The Scotsman*, 27 June 1997). Furthermore, there was the absence of a consistent demand for elected regional assemblies across the English regions. It was also argued that there was no stomach for a further round of local government reorganisation, which would be necessary in order to remove the remaining strategic tier of county councils.

Behind the scenes the Prime Minister and a number of other senior ministers were known to be sceptical about a move to democratic decentralisation to the English regions, and the Cabinet's only powerful advocate, John Prescott, even struggled to secure the commitment to early introduction of the RDAs. With a large parliamentary majority it is clear that the Prime Minister no longer felt under any short-term pressure to deliver significant decentralisation to the English regions as the price for parliamentary support for the Devolution Bill. Instead the strategy was to be one of waiting to see if regional development agencies would prove sufficiently successful to build up regional awareness and a momentum for political decentralisation.

Setting up the RDAs

The philosophy and rationale for the establishment of RDAs was set out in the White Paper *Building Partnerships for Prosperity: Sustainability, Growth, Competitiveness and Employment in the English Regions* (DETR, 1997a). This followed a wide-ranging national and regional consultation exercise on an 'issues' paper, undertaken between June and September 1997 (DETR, 1997b). The RDA programme was seen as part of the government's agenda to

> Modernise Britain's economic performance, to bring it to and above the average in Europe... The problems are well known. Poor skills, lack of investment and an inheritance from having been the first country to industrialise mean that the English regions are underperforming compared to equivalent regions elsewhere in Europe. This is even more marked within regions and shown in low wages, firms driven out of business, the waste of unemployment. The results are physical decay and social exclusion. (DETR, 1997a, p. 7)

The government's approach to tackling these issues was based on four principles

- that power should not be centralised in Whitehall, but that **local, regional and national structures are needed for decision making** and for action to put those decisions into effect;
- that **regional structures must be based firmly on partnership** with each local or regional interest being able to contribute effectively towards an integrated and coherent strategic programme which commands general support;
- that issues should not be tackled in isolation but **that much greater integration and co-ordination of effort is necessary** to deal with the pressing needs of economic and social decay and to promote the successful regional economies vital to our future prosperity; and
- that **some regional tasks such as economic development and spatial planning need clear leadership and the experience in action** which the business community can contribute; but that they must also look to a wider circle of partner organisations and to the views of communities through their elected representatives. (Ibid., p. 14)

In operational terms this meant that much of the RDAs' added value was to derive from a partnership and co-ordinating approach rather than direct delivery

The Regional Development Agencies will therefore have a wide remit. In part this will be met through developing a strategic programme, in part through monitoring and advising other bodies and in part through direct delivery... (Ibid., p16)

In respect of other relevant areas of central government activity, RDAs were to have a

Major consultative and advisory role particularly through the RDA-led regional economic strategies. RDAs will therefore contribute to transport and infrastructure planning, though with a direct role in the provision of infrastructure for investment projects; to protecting the environment and promoting sustainable development; they will also through their work on economic and social regeneration contribute to objectives on crime prevention, housing, health and social cohesion. (Ibid., p. 16)

The consultation paper, which was launched in the summer of 1997 (DETR, 1997c), indicated that for each region there would be a single RDA based on existing GOR boundaries (nine RDAs in total if London is included). The government stated that it did not wish to impose a blueprint from Whitehall; it wanted to allow each region to have arrangements which fitted local circumstances, building on the work of existing organisations.

As to accountability, the RDA boards would be formally appointed by the Secretary of State, after taking into account regional views. RDAs would have small boards of directors, private sector led, but with other regional stakeholders from public, private and voluntary sectors. Ministers indicated their willingness to acknowledge non-statutory regional chambers as a mechanism to provide some regional guidance over the board's priorities. In the consultation phase a focus of much concern was the extent to which the RDAs would be accountable to the full range of regional interests given the government's stated preference for small private sector led boards. This concern was compounded by a lukewarm attitude towards the idea of chambers having any statutory rights to establish regional priorities for the GORs and RDAs. Needless to say this was a view held more strongly by the local authority and voluntary sectors while opposed by the business representative bodies (Mawson, 1997).

In the event, the Act encouraged the regions to establish voluntary chambers which would have the right to be consulted by the RDAs in the development of their strategy and priorities. The composition of the chambers was to be approved by the Secretary of State. No central government funding was to be forthcoming to assist the work of the chambers and while RDAs would be required to take account of chambers views, there was to be no requirement to act upon them.

The eight RDAs were established under the 1998 Regional Development Agencies Act and began operation in April 1999. Each RDA has five statutory purposes:

- to further the economic development of its area;
- to promote business efficiency, investment and competitiveness in its area;
- to promote employment in its area;
- to contribute to the achievement of sustainable development in the UK where it is relevant to its area to do so;
- to enhance the development and application of skills relevant to employment in its area.

RDAs operate with existing powers and responsibilities transferred from central government with only limited additional public funding provided. Their roles include the preparation of a Regional Economic Strategy and advising and commenting upon other areas of government policy and expenditure where relevant (e.g. training, education and business support). In relation to the task of implementation, RDAs have taken over the powers of English Partnerships and the Rural Development Commission largely in respect of land and property development, as well as responsibility for inward investment and the promotion policies of the English regional development organisations. They oversee the Single Regeneration Budget and are in due course to have a role in determining the direction of European Union Structural Funds policies. Other responsibilities include preparing skills and regional technology action plans and managing the DTI's former Regional Supply Offices (supply chain development). With an ultimate staff target of around 150-200, the RDAs' budgets are dwarfed by those of their equivalents in Scotland, Wales and Northern Ireland which are between two and three times as large.

Planned expenditure for the first year of operation (1999-2000) is summarised in Table 2.1 (Cabinet Office, 2000). As the table shows, expenditure varies considerably across the regions, with the largest absolute spend in the North West (£176 million) and the lowest in the Eastern Region (£31 million). On a per capita basis, the North East has the highest planned expenditure at £47 per head, while once again the Eastern region is lowest at £6 per head. Single Regeneration Budget expenditure is the largest component of the overall budget, followed by land and property.

The RDA Board and the Voluntary Chamber

RDAs are non-departmental public bodies (NDPBs) and may have a board of between 8 and 15 members (most have 12 members). The government recognised that the success of RDAs would be heavily dependent on the skills, experience and background of their board members. They were not in any way to be delegates representing a particular organisation or locality, rather their perspective was to be one of taking into account the views of the region as a whole.

The Chairpersons were to have a business background and there was to be a predominance of board members from the private sector. The philosophy, however, was not to stick to a set composition of sectoral interests, but rather to draw widely from business, co-operatives and community enterprise bodies, education, rural areas, voluntary sector and wider business and employee perspectives. The one exception to this approach was in the case of local government where it was recognised that while RDAs were ultimately accountable to ministers, they should also be responsive to their local communities. To that end local government was to be given four board seats, to reflect broadly the spread of types of authority and their political balance across the region. However, given the reaction in the consultation exercise to concerns about the imposition of another top- down quango on the regions, the government considered that an additional means of more formal consultation was desirable. It was therefore decided to build on the arrangements being put in place by local authorities and their regional partners to form voluntary regional chambers defined in the White Paper as

> A body that includes councillors from the local authorities in the region and representatives of the various stakeholders with an interest in the region's economic, social and environmental success. (DETR, 1997a)

The government's guidance on regional chambers indicated that before they could be designated by the Secretary of State as a formal consultation body, non-local government members should comprise no less than 30% of the chamber (DETR, 1998). In the event all were designated in time to comment on their RDA's regional economic strategy with local authorities comprising 70% of representation and 'social and economic' partners making up the remaining 30% (e.g. private sector bodies, the voluntary sector, education and statutory organisations). In some cases the chambers have built on existing arrangements, while in others they have started from scratch, this means there

Table 2.1 Funds – Regional Development Agencies: planned expenditure for 1999-2000 (£ million)

Programme	NE	NW	Y & H	WM	EM	E	SW	SE	Total
Land and Property	11.66	17.29	11.16	22.75	7.37	4.89	19.93	23.21	118.27
Derelict Land Grant	1.94	1.62	7.23	0.75	1.03	0.08	0.18	0.03	12.87
Single Regeneration Budget	91.58	137.48	102.18	75.93	36.78	14.59	21.68	37.49	517.71
Rural Development	2.60	1.17	3.07	1.72	3.08	2.82	6.02	1.64	22.13
Skills Development Fund	1.72	4.76	3.28	3.72	2.53	3.05	3.04	4.66	26.77
Competitiveness Fund	0.25	0.25	0.25	0.25	0.25	0.25	0.25	0.25	2.00
Inward Investment	1.66	1.39	1.41	1.31	0.98	0.90	1.55	0.90	10.12
Administration	9.77	12.13	8.04	7.68	7.15	4.80	7.49	5.22	62.29
Total	121.20	176.10	136.63	114.11	59.18	31.40	60.14	73.41	772.17

Source: Cabinet Office, (2000).

are variations in their stages of development and how wide they have defined their regional role. In general, the chambers are poorly resourced through subscriptions (mainly from local authorities) with small secretariats and a reliance on secondments and in-kind support. The dominant role played by local government in the chambers and in their resourcing and servicing has inevitably raised question marks among other stakeholders.

Devolution 2000 – an English Perspective

Since the publication of the RDA White Paper (DETR, 1997a) and the passing of the Act in 1998 there have been various Select Committee enquiries and much debate about the roles and likely effectiveness of the RDAs and chambers (HC Environment, Transport and Regional Affairs Select Committee, 1998; 1999). At the political level within the regions there is a desire on the one hand to ensure that the RDAs prove successful in order to give their advocates in government the ammunition to argue for the transfer of more powers and responsibilities from central departments. On the other hand, there remains concern about their accountability and sensitivity to regional issues, the comparatively limited powers and resources vis-á-vis development agencies elsewhere in the UK, and the apparently ambiguous and overlapping roles and responsibilities in many areas of policy with GORs and central government departments and their agencies.

Against the background of these issues and concerns it is instructive to reflect on how the government's evolving devolution agenda is being viewed from an English perspective at the turn of the millennium.

The English regions are now surrounded by a range of new democratic and regional development structures, and inevitably comparisons are being made with the powers and responsibilities of chambers and RDAs (Mawson, 1999). In the case of Scotland, the Parliament has taken responsibility for Scottish Office functions and has the ability to shape domestic policy and pursue primary legislation outside reserved areas. It now has a potentially powerful political voice to articulate Scotland's interests in the economic and European spheres and the means to execute policy through a cohesive economic development network. This is achieved through Scottish Enterprise and its network of Local Enterprise Companies. The new Parliament offers local government and other public, private and voluntary sector stakeholders the opportunity of a partnership role in shaping national legislation through various policy forums. There is the scope to reorganise, scrutinise and democratise the quangos, thereby opening this important area of the public domain to local democratic engagement. In the event of the peace process coming to fruition, similar advantages will be available to the Northern Ireland Assembly in terms of taking over the Northern Ireland Office, the ability to pass primary legislation in the domestic sphere, and the inheritance of an economic development infrastructure boosted by substantial international funding and encouragement to inward investment.

While the Welsh Assembly has inherited the Welsh Office, it does not have primary legislative capacity, but nevertheless is able to exercise considerable powers over Welsh affairs, including local government, through secondary legislation. The Assembly has responsibility for the Welsh Development Agency and benefits from a regionalised business development structure incorporating the Business Links/TEC network. The Welsh Assembly itself has regional committees to oversee its work through the country and this, together with a powerful policy partnership, presents local government and other stakeholders with a major opportunity to influence and shape the emerging domestic agenda.

In the case of London, the Mayor and Greater London Authority have inherited funding earmarked for the key services of police, fire and transport as well as responsibilities for strategic planning and economic development. The Mayor has a powerful elected mandate to devise a unique form of strategic and land-use plan for the capital, provide a leadership and co-ordination role for the public sector, and work in partnership with private and voluntary sectors towards agreed London-wide agendas. Unlike the situation elsewhere in England, the London Development Agency is accountable directly to the Mayor and Greater London Assembly. Elected by the largest single constituency in the country it will be difficult for Whitehall departments to ignore the powerful political voice of the Mayor. This is an advantage not available to the other English regions.

Territorial Comparisons and Momentum for Further Changes?

Taken together, the various forms of devolution and the associated powers and responsibilities set out above are leading to unfavourable comparisons with what is on offer to the English regions (Mawson, 1999). Increasingly, elected politicians, business leaders, representatives of key regional institutions and other regional stakeholders are questioning whether the regions possess the necessary clout to articulate their interests, and whether the RDAs have sufficient powers and resources to be an effective counterweight. In border regions particularly there are concerns about a 'shadow effect' from powerful neighbours with a perceived advantage in attracting inward investment or European funding.

Resentments at the regional level are also fuelled by the inbuilt financial advantage that Scotland, Wales and Northern Ireland secure from the so-called Barnett formulae which influence the distribution of public expenditure among the separate parts of the UK. The issue has been the subject of a Treasury Select Committee inquiry in which members from the north of England and London were vociferous in their complaints about the perceived unfairness of the system (HM Treasury Select Committee, 1997). Indeed, more widely it seems likely that those aspects of public policy which have an explicit territorial dimension will be subject to increasing public scrutiny – not least because the new Scottish and Welsh Assemblies will see such matters as being at the heart of their concerns.

To take one example, the processes of demarcating assisted area boundaries and determining eligibility criteria for national and European funding, which historically were negotiated and resolved behind closed doors by senior officials and ministers in Whitehall and Brussels, will now be subject to far greater openness and transparency. The hidden geographical trade-offs between different parts of the UK which were made in the past to secure the greater national interest will now be exposed, making the resolution of these matters far more difficult from both an administrative and a political point of view. While guidelines have been established about how such matters will be dealt with, and the primacy of a single UK government position in Brussels has been emphasised, nevertheless the stages leading up to an agreed position will prove far more difficult to handle. Similarly in the case of inward investment policy, the UK government has introduced a concordat covering the work of the various development agencies to ensure a more coherent national approach and avoid wasteful competition in the post-devolution era. However, the complaints from the business community in the North East about poaching of inward investment projects by Scottish Enterprise, which has a greater level of discretion over the application of regional selective grants, suggests how difficult this task may prove to be in a climate of enhanced territorial competition (House of Commons Trade and Industry Select Committee, 1998).

In formal political terms, feelings of comparative disadvantage are likely to be increasingly articulated through concerns about the so-called 'West Lothian' question. This issue was originally posed by Tam Dalyell MP at the time of the previous devolution debate when he highlighted the anomalous situation that Scottish MPs would have the right to vote on English affairs, but the equivalent right would not be available to English MPs (Bogdanor, 1999). Some have advocated the creation of an English Parliament, while the government has recently resurrected the Select committee on English Affairs. The reform of the House of Lords presents a further opportunity to tackle the issue of the English democratic deficit through the introduction of a regional dimension in an elected second chamber. While all these proposals are designed to introduce an explicit English dimension into this new context, there will be those from the regions who will be sceptical as to how far such structures will seriously challenge the centralising tendencies of London and the South East unless they are paralleled by elected regional assemblies.

Whitehall, Devolution and the Regions

The above discussion has sought to highlight some of the tensions and pressures arising from the current devolution settlement. In the light of these concerns, the chapter now turns to consider some possible steps which could be taken at both central government and regional level to tackle the problems.

Since coming to office the Prime Minister has been keen to tackle the problem of departmentalism, which is endemic in the civil service. From the beginning of the last century the machinery of government in Britain has been organised on a hierarchical and functional basis through powerful government departments (Stewart, 1994). As a consequence, interdepartmental working has always proved problematic both at the centre and regionally. This has presented problems for those aspects of public policy which have a geographical or territorial dimension. Nationally devised programmes, for example, have different rules and regulations which make co-ordination at the local level very difficult. The public service management reforms of the 1980s and early 1990s compounded the difficulties. They sought to decentralise management responsibilities to single-purpose executive agencies and quangos as the traditional multipurpose local authority was stripped of roles (Clarke and Stewart, 1994). However, the new devolved structures have remained wedded to a hierarchical functional tradition. They are accountable upwards to Whitehall, which controls them and sets targets, leaving limited scope for local policy discretion. These structures may have strengths in focusing on service delivery, but are less helpful when it comes to building integrative policy mechanisms at regional and local levels. This has become a major weakness in an era of accelerating technological, social and environmental change in which problems are becoming increasingly complex and inter-related. The dilemmas are no more starkly evident than in the spheres of regional and rural development, area regeneration and social exclusion.

Historically, block funding to the Scottish, Welsh and Northern Ireland Offices and the drawing together of domestic policy responsibilities under a single cabinet minister has meant that the issue has been less of a problem in these countries than is the case in England. It was not until 1994 when John Major's government established the GORs (drawing together environment, transport, education, employment and industry functions under a single senior civil servant) that there was any semblance of an identifiable and cohesive central government presence in the English regions. Even then, key departments such as agriculture did not have a presence within the GORs and there was no direct line management relationship with key Next Step Agencies and statutory agencies such as the Housing Corporation. This weakness of the limited number of government activities overseen regionally by the GORs was compounded at the centre by the absence of structures capable of receiving integrated regional solutions (Mawson and Spencer, 1997).

Co-ordination of GOR roles at the centre through the Government Office Management Board (comprising senior officials from the GORs' parent departments) has tended to focus on routine administrative matters rather than on cross-cutting policy concerns (exceptions being competitiveness, regeneration and sustainability) and there have been limited connections with the processes of cabinet decision-making. Annually, the GORs have submitted operational plans as part of the public expenditure planning process, but the integration achieved regionally is not taken forward easily at the centre since the parent departments negotiate their GOR elements separately with the Treasury. These weaknesses are compounded by the fact that the Treasury itself does not engage in any detailed disaggregation or analysis of the distribution of public expenditure among or within regions.

At a time when the government is engaging in such a fundamental reshaping of the geography of British politics and public administration it is surprising that there has been apparently so little strategic thinking in government about the implications. The closest has been the Cabinet Committee chaired by the Lord Chancellor, which has overseen constitutional reforms. Its remit has focused on legal and constitutional matters rather than on the political and policy consequences of devolution and regionalisation.

However, there are signs that the issue has now been recognised and steps are gradually being taken to develop a more coherent approach. The Prime Minister's increasing concerns about 'joined-up' government in various policy areas, for example has led to the establishment of the Social Exclusion Unit and its report on a national strategy for neighbourhood renewal: an interdepartmental co-ordination unit on Area Based Initiatives based in the DETR; and the Cabinet Office's various studies of the organisation of central government and central government's presence in regions and localities (Hall and Mawson, 2000). There is much work still to be done to achieve a genuinely corporate approach to decision-making at the centre, although if the recommendations in these various reports are vigorously carried through they will serve to clarify and strengthen the co-ordination role of the Government Offices at a regional level and greater interdepartmental co-ordination in Whitehall.

Following publication of the Cabinet Office report *Reaching Out: The Role of Central Government at Regional and Local Levels* (Cabinet Office, 2000), the government has moved swiftly to accept its main recommendations and set in train their implementation over a 12-month period. A central conclusion is that changes at regional level are not sufficient to improve the effectiveness of government and that changes are also needed in Whitehall. As a consequence, a new Cabinet Office co-ordination unit has now been established under Lord Falconer, reporting in turn to the Deputy Prime Minister. It has superseded the Government Office Management Board, and the Interdepartmental Support Unit for Area Based Initiatives and will be responsible for (i) managing the GORs, (ii) ensuring better co-ordination of policy initiatives with a regional or local impact and (iii) ensuring better collective consideration of proposals to change regional or local structures of government departments and agencies. This will include facilitating the establishment of public service agreements between GORs and Whitehall departments, including cross-departmental activities and budgets.

Regionalisation – Where Next?

The 1999 cabinet reshuffle which saw the transfer of Dick Caborn, the architect of New Labour's regionalisation programme, from the DETR to the DTI was widely interpreted as a set-back for those wishing to see a continuation of the momentum towards elected regional government. Sources close to the Prime Minister at the time were quoted as saying he was becoming increasingly sceptical about regional government in England given recent experiences in Scotland, Wales and the low turnout at the European elections. However, government ministers continue to emphasise that the issue remains on the agenda and will be addressed after the next election (Whitehead, 2000). While the situation remains unclear, it would be a mistake to assume that further significant changes in the political and administrative framework are unlikely. There may be resistance to further decentralisation within Whitehall, but it has to be remembered that devolution has set in train significant economic and political imbalances between the English regions and Scotland, Wales and Northern Ireland which will require resolution. There are also significant structural weaknesses and ambiguities surrounding the current regional framework which are bound to lead to further changes. Moreover, it is increasingly being recognised in central government that the regional tier (RDAs, GORs) presents one important organisational mechanism for achieving improvements in the delivery of public policies through more 'joined-up' government.

In responding to the various pressures which the devolution and regionalisation programme has unleashed it will be necessary to address some of the present weaknesses in the machinery of central government which have been identified in recent Cabinet Office reports (Mawson, 2000).

In administrative terms there is a need to develop a more corporate approach and explicit territorial perspective in the work of all relevant Whitehall departments, Next Step Agencies and quangos. The use of public service agreements between departments is one way in which the Whitehall machine can tackle cross-cutting issues at regional and local levels. It will also be necessary to address the way in which departmental policies, procedures, financial management systems etc. could be harmonised and budgets pooled to facilitate joined-up working at regional and local levels. Whitehall needs to allow greater flexibility and administrative discretion among government agencies to facilitate integration with regional and local partnerships. Moreover, the development of a far greater capacity to analyse the distribution of public expenditure among and within the regions and nations of the UK is a sine qua non of devolution. Given the tensions that are bound to arise over public expenditure distribution, the government could consider developing a regional 'needs assessment process' linked to the longer term public expenditure planning process to which the GORs, RDAs and regional chambers might have an input.

In political terms there is a need to develop a more strategic oversight of the evolving constitutional agenda and the reshaping of the geography of public policy. This could be achieved by establishing a powerful cross- cutting cabinet committee to cover the nations/regions, chaired by a senior government minister such as the Deputy Prime Minister. It would help to tackle some of the increasingly sensitive policy issues (e.g. student fees, subsidies to farmers) which are surfacing as a result of the current partial and disjointed perspective on territorial policy (Robinson P, 2000). Two pertinent examples of this difficulty include a statement by the Governor of the Bank of England that increased unemployment in the north arising from higher interest rates was a price worth paying in respect of tackling inflation in the south, and the problems the Prime Minister has experienced in trying to shift the debate away from the north/ south divide, to within region differences.

The establishment of the RDAs covering eight English regions has led for the first time to the emergence of specific and agreed regional development priorities, however, there is currently no policy framework at the centre capable of addressing what the sum of the parts means in terms of national spatial priorities and how cross-cutting and conflicting priorities are resolved. The government's response to the RDA strategies, for example, claimed that they would 'address the imbalances that exist within and between all regions of the country' (DETR, 2000). However, this seems unlikely given the emphasis on encouraging each region to maximise its economic potential, thus further widening the gaps between the economic powerhouse of the south and other parts of the country. One solution might be to further consolidate the role of the Cabinet Office Co-ordination Unit by giving it responsibility not only for GORs and Area Based Initiatives but also the RDAs.

Turning to the question of regional government, after the next election there are a number of options which could be pursued to tackle the perceived democratic deficit, including a regional element in the reformed House of Lords and/or an enhanced scrutiny role over the work of RDAs, GORs and other relevant public bodies by an indirectly nominated chamber. The arrival of elected mayors could add a complication to attempts to develop a coherent view across the regions on regional priorities and partnership working, given that they will inevitably adopt an aggressive stance in relation to their area interests. Thought will need to be given as to how, if at all, this partial coverage of elected representatives can be accommodated within a strengthened regional chamber. One solution might be to take the agenda a step further and have elected regional mayors operating with a cabinet appointed from the ranks of the chambers.

Setting in train the *Choice for England* 'staged approach' (Labour Party, 1995) might ultimately lead to elected regional assemblies across the country with a strong scrutiny and oversight role over the regional priorities of central government, an appointments role in relation to relevant quangos and the fostering of a regional partnership approach with local government and the voluntary and private sectors. It seems unlikely that consideration would be given to powers of primary legislation for such assemblies along the lines of the Scottish Parliament, although a block budget together with secondary legislative responsibilities and oversight of some regional civil service functions along the lines of the Welsh Assembly might be more realistic. However, at this juncture it is difficult to foresee how the political question surrounding regionalisation in England will ultimately be resolved. The next section therefore considers how present government arrangements could be improved.

GORs and the Regional Chambers

Until the recent Cabinet Office report on the role of central government at regional and local levels, the work of the GORs and regional chambers has received scant attention. In following through the recommendations of *Reaching Out*, it is clear that GORs will play an increasingly important pivotal role in the new governance structures (Cabinet Office, 2000). It is the obvious vehicle to facilitate collaboration between RDAs, chambers and regional stakeholders prior to any move to elected regional government. The GOR provides a point of access to enable regional stakeholders to tie central government down to a single clear regional position, and if given the necessary support at the centre, should help to avoid too many crossed wires. In its enhanced role the GOR will be in a position to ensure that those government departments, Next Step Agencies and quangos not currently giving the regional dimension sufficient priority do engage positively in the work of the RDAs and chambers. This will be essential if RDAs are to successfully fulfil their wider co-ordination and advisory roles in those areas of public policy where they do not have a direct implementation role.

As far as the chambers are concerned, they have been left to address various policy uncertainties at regional level as well as the practical difficulties of resourcing their role. In particular they have been faced with one critical question: namely, how far they should limit their activities to a narrowly proscribed regional economic development agenda scrutinising the RDAs, or seek to establish a strategic framework for public policy covering wider economic, social and environmental issues. In the case of regions such as the East Midlands, the North West and Yorkshire and Humber, the chambers have adopted a broader vision of regional development and have undoubtedly encouraged their RDAs to adopt a similar perspective. There are also at least two regions where chambers have entered into concordats with their RDAs and GORs to clarify roles and relationships (LGA, 1999). However, the capacity of the chambers to draw together and secure the involvement of all relevant government departments and agencies into the process of determining regional priorities is strictly limited by their willingness to co-operate. It is here that the GORs could play a key role in assisting the chambers to develop integrated regional strategies covering, for example, transport, planning, environment, health education and economic policy (Roberts, 2000). Without the GOR facilitating the appropriate links and co-operation of government departments and agencies it will be difficult to deliver the 'joined-up' regional strategies required.

There remains the danger that GOR officials could end up exercising far too much power and influence in the new structures if regional stakeholders do not rise to the challenge and opportunities offered by the new RDA chamber framework. A more locally accountable and transparent policy framework can only be achieved by the active participation of local authorities and other regional stakeholders in the current albeit imperfect structures. However, the government's unwillingness to provide the necessary level of resources to build up organisational capacity and technical expertise to enable the new 'stakeholders' to play their part in the regional chambers makes this task more difficult (Robinson, 2000). It is surely a matter of concern that the government is able to find some £18 million per annum to finance the administration of the Scottish Parliament and £15 million to fund the Greater London Assembly election, yet it cannot offset some of the costs which local government is incurring in voluntarily running the chambers, nor can it provide adequate support for other regional stakeholders to enable them to participate in the new governance structures (Mawson, 1999). In the absence of a move to elected assemblies, aside from resourcing the chambers, there are a number of other actions which central government could take to strengthen their present role.

One significant step forward would be to require the Regional Director to attend the chamber three or four times per annum to explain the developing regional priorities of the GOR and other significant government agencies in the region. A stage further would be for ministers to require the GORs, Next Step Agencies and quangos, to work jointly with the chamber in developing regional policies and give it rights of appointment to some or all of the regionally relevant quangos, including the RDA. The government could also give the chambers responsibility for a Spatial Development Strategy along the lines of that of the Greater London Authority (GLA) with statutory rights to determine regional priorities covering a broad range of economic, social and environmental policy fields.

Regional Development Agencies

In comparative terms the English regions are at a disadvantage when it comes to the resourcing and organisational capacity of their RDAs relative to equivalent agencies elsewhere in the UK (Robinson, 2000). Since RDAs establishment in April 1999 there has been mounting pressure on central government, both from the RDAs themselves and from the regions to address some of their perceived structural weaknesses (Falk, 2000). Effectively only very limited new monies have been made available with the bulk of resources coming from existing funding regimes. The RDAs have not been given a block budget enabling them to fully shape policies to local circumstances, and have to negotiate separately with each parent department in relation to the funding regimes they have inherited. As NDPBs they remain somewhat hide-bound by the Treasury's financial constraints which limits their abilities to operate directly in financial and commercial markets and in investment.

It is significant that the key budgets and responsibilities transferred to RDAs came in the main from the DETR (reflecting the championing of RDAs by the Deputy Prime Minister) while there has been resistance from the DTI and the DfEE to giving up some very obvious regional economic responsibilities, for example control over Business Links and TEC budgets and greater influence over Regional Selective Assistance (Wighten and Kamptner, 1997). There remain uncertainties surrounding the RDAs' future role in respect of European funding and strategies and concerns about the splitting of regeneration activities between RDAs and GORs.

In the rush to establish RDAs it could be argued that there was a failure to take an overview of all the relevant elements of public policy which are undertaken at the regional and sub-regional levels and in what ways the RDAs' role might fit into this wider picture (Mawson, 1997). Vague statements in the 1999 statutory and supplementary guidance about co-ordination have left the RDAs' leadership and implementation role still to be resolved in a number of key policy fields such as rural development (DETR, 1999a; 1997b). A survey undertaken for the Cabinet Office has highlighted prevailing uncertainties about the roles and responsibilities of RDAs in relation to GORs, government departments and their agencies. The issue has been highlighted in the recent updating and development of various regional strategic documents, including regional planning guidance, regional transport, housing and cultural strategies; the regional sustainability framework; and EU strategies covering the Structural Funds and Agricultural Support. It has also surfaced in the preparation of RDA action plans, particularly in those policy areas where the RDA has a limited direct implementation role but rather is dependent on the activities of partners through, for example, contracting arrangements, or where the RDA has to exercise influence/persuasion over the working of other partners in order to implement the RES priorities.

Conclusion

This chapter has charted the re-emergence of the regional agenda in England over the past decade and how central government has responded to the challenges. The impetus for change has come from pressures to improve economic performance to address administrative and democratic failings in the management of public policy at the regional level, and the need to provide some form of political and economic counterbalance to devolution. Reflecting the historic diversity of the UK, the demands for decentralisation have been articulated in different forms across the country and are at different stages in their development. Given this background it was inevitable that central government should adopt an asymmetric approach and one in which solutions are more clearly charted in Scotland, Wales and Northern Ireland than is the case for England. As the consequences of the new devolved settlement become ever more evident it seems likely that there will be pressures for further changes from the English regions. In formal political terms much will depend on the outcome of the next general election, the extent of the pressure and how far an incoming government would be willing to devolve real political power, resources and administration in response. It is clear that the government machine has already embarked on significant administrative decentralisation, which if unchecked could serve to further strengthen the power of central government within the regions.

Irrespective of the outcome of post-election decisions as to the future form of regional government in England there are a number of steps which could be taken to improve the efficiency and effectiveness of current arrangements, which in themselves might serve to address some of the perceived unfairness of the present devolution settlement and provide a building block for moves to a more formal tier of government in due course.

Significantly, research undertaken for the Cabinet Office report *Reaching Out* (2000) found that there was no inherent criticism of the roles of RDAs, GORs and chambers per se in the regions, but rather a desire to see far greater clarity as to their relationship with each other, with other regional partners and with central government. There is a fairly widely held view in the regions that there needs to be a review of the functions of RDAs so that they have a clear responsibility for the key regional development functions. There is also a recognition that RDAs need to be given far greater budgetary discretion and significant additional resources if they are to make an impact on national competitiveness and regional problems. Further strengthening of the RDA's role, however, is seen as being accompanied by increased engagement with and accountability to the region and key regional stakeholders in the public, private and voluntary sectors. One way forward would be to give the regional chamber rights to appoint to the RDA board and enhanced rights of scrutiny and approval of RDA strategies.

The ambiguities surrounding the wider remit of the RDA could be addressed in part by giving the lead responsibility for the setting of regional strategic priorities to the chamber and developed in partnership with the GOR and RDA. Roles and relationships could be clarified through the signing of concordats. If the chambers were to play an enhanced role, they would need some limited resourcing from central government to fulfil that role and to provide technical support to the stakeholders (e.g. voluntary, local authority and private sectors) to enable them to fully engage in regional work. The GOR would play a key role in ensuring that all relevant parts of central government and its agencies (including the GOR itself) actively participated with stakeholders in setting the regional agenda. At the end of the day, however, unless there are changes in the way decisions are taken at the centre, such that the government machine is capable of comprehending the territorial aspects of public policy across the country and taking on board 'joined-up' solutions emerging from regional structures and agencies, the devolution project is doomed to failure.

References

Bogdanor, V. (1999), *Devolution in the United Kingdom,* OPUS, Oxford.

British Chambers of Commerce (1997*), Regional Policy Brief,* BCC, London.

Cabinet Office (2000), *Reaching Out. The Role of Central Government at Regional and Local Levels,* Performance and Innovation Unit, HMSO, London.

Clarke, M. and Stewart, J. (1994), 'The Local Authority and the New Community Governance', *Regional Studies,* vol. 28, no. 2, pp. 201-19.

Confederation of British Industry (1997), *Regions for Business,* CBI, London.

Condon, T. (1996), 'Blair buys off Home Rule rebels', *Scotland on Sunday, 12* May.

Davies, H. (1996), 'Regional Government', paper delivered at regional newspaper editors' annual lunch, Newcastle, 6 January.

Department of the Environment, Transport and the Regions (1999b), *Supplementary Guidance to Regional Development Agencies*, DETR, London.

Department of the Environment, Transport and the Regions (1997a), *Building Partnerships for Prosperity, Sustainability, Growth, Competitiveness and Employment in the Regions,* CM 3814, DETR, London.

Department of the Environment (1997b), *Regional Development Agencies. Issues for discussion,* DoE, London.

Department of the Environment (1997c), 'Regions Invited to Have Their Say?', *DoE News Release,* 214, 11 June.

Department of the Environment, Transport and the Regions (1998), *Regional Development Agencies, Guidance on the General Principles of Designation of Voluntary Regional Chambers,* DETR, London.

Department of the Environment, Transport and the Regions (1999a), *Guidance to RDAs on Regional Strategies,* DETR, London.

Department of the Environment, Transport and the Regions (2000), *Response to Regional Strategies,* DETR, London, 12 January.

English Regional Associations (1995), *A Survey of the English Regional Association,* ERA, London.

Falk, J. (2000), 'Resourcing Regional Development', M. Nathan (ed), *The New Regionalism,* Centre for Local Economic Strategies, Manchester, pp. 15-8.

Hall, S. and Mawson, J. (2000), 'Joining it up locally? Area regeneration', *Regional Studies,* vol. 34, no. 1, pp. 67-79.

Her Majesty's Government (1997), *Regional Development Agencies Bill,* Bill 100, 10 December, HMSO, London.

HM Treasury (1997), *The Barnett Formulae,* Treasury Select Committee, HC 341, HMSO, London.

House of Commons (1995), *Regional Policy,* Fourth Report, Trade and Industry Select Committee, Session 1994-95, HC 356, HMSO, London.

House of Commons (1998), *Regional Development Agencies,* First Report Environment, Transport and Regional Affairs Select Committee, Session 1997-98.

House of Commons (1998), *Co-ordination of Inward Investment,* Trade and Industry Select Committee, First Report, 1997-98, HC 355, HMSO, London.

House of Commons (1999), *Regional Development Agencies,* Tenth Report Environment, Transport and Regional Affairs Select Committee, Session 1998-99, HMSO, London.

Labour Party (1995), *A Choice for England: A Consultation Paper on Labour's Plans for English Regional Government,* Labour Party, London.

Local Government Association (1999), *Regional Chambers – State of Play,* April and November, LGA, London.

Mawson, J. (1996), 'The Re-emergence of the Regional Agenda in the English Regions: New Patterns of Urban and Regional Governance?', *Local Economy,* vol. 10, no. 4, pp. 300-26.

Mawson, J. and Spencer, K. (1997), 'The Government Offices for the English Regions: towards Regional Governance?', *Policy and Politics,* vol. 25, no. 1, pp. 71-84.

Mawson, J. (1997), 'New labour and the English Regions: a Missed Opportunity', *Local Economy,* vol. 12, no. 3, pp. 194-202.

Mawson, J. (1998), 'English regionalism and New Labour', *Regional and Federal Studies,* vol. 8, no. 1, pp. 158-75.

Mawson, J. (1999), 'The English Regions and the Wider Constitutional and Administrative Reforms', J. Dungey and I. Newman (eds), *The New Regional Agenda,* Local Government Information Unit, London, pp. 85-98.

Mawson, J. (2000), 'Joined-Up Government and the Democratic Region', in J. Dungey and I. Newman (eds), *The Democratic Region,* Local Government Information Unit, London, pp.33-54.

Regional Policy Commission (1996), *Renewing the Regions. Strategies for Regional Economic Development*, Sheffield Hallam University, Sheffield.

Roberts, P. (2000), 'Strategic Connectivity' in M. Nathan (ed), *The New Regionalism,* Centre for Local Economic Strategies, Manchester.

Robinson, J. (2000), 'Participation in Chambers and Regional Development Agencies by Voluntary Organisations' in J. Dungey and I. Newman (eds), *The Democratic Region,* Local Government Information Unit, London, pp. 85-89.

Robinson, P. (2000), 'Does the Government really have a regional policy?', M. Nathan (ed) *The New Regionalism,* Centre for Local Economic Strategies, Manchester, pp. 5-8.

TEC National Council (1997), *Regional Development Principles,* produced by the Economic Strategy Group, TEC National Council, London.

The Scotsman, 27 June 1997, 'Blair faces English Home Rule Revolt'.

Stewart, M. (1994), 'Between Whitehall and town hall: the realignment of urban regeneration policy', *Policy and Politics,* vol. 22, no. 2, pp. 133-46.

Whitehead, A. (2000), 'Regions and the Modernisation Agenda', M, Nathan (ed), *The New Regionalism,* Centre for Local Economic Strategies, Manchester.

Wighton, D. and Kamptner, J. (1997), 'Beckitt Beats off Prescott over the Regions', *Financial Times,* 16 July.

3 The New English Regional Project: Integrating the Work of the RDAs with other Elements of Regional Planning, Development and Management

PETER ROBERTS[1]

Introduction

The present government has placed great emphasis on the design and delivery of 'joined-up' policy, including 'joined-up' spatial policy. The Regional Development Agencies represent one of the major components of the new territorial institutional framework, which is charged with the task of achieving integrated planning, development and management. However, in creating the RDAs, it is questionable as to whether the introduction of an additional element onto an already crowded, and some would argue over-complex, regional platform is a step forward or a recipe for future confusion. Answering this question involves a consideration of the progress of the technical-professional, administrative and governance dimensions of the new regional agenda.

This chapter discusses a number of the key issues related to the introduction of RDAs into what a number of observers consider to be a generally supportive and welcoming, albeit somewhat congested, regional environment (Benneworth, 1999a; Roberts and Lloyd, 1998). However, in presenting this assessment, the chapter calls into question the wisdom of establishing the RDAs as non-departmental public bodies rather than as executive agencies directly accountable to elected regional government. The chapter also considers a number of other fundamental matters of theory and history, before shifting attention to a discussion of the main components of the regional 'project' and an assessment of the key challenges facing the new regional arrangements. This section of the chapter also offers an initial evaluation of the early stages of the operation of these new policy systems and institutions. The final section presents some tentative conclusions on the performance to date of the new English regional 'project' and indicates the key areas for future consideration and action. Throughout the chapter attention is focused on questions of territorial competence, integration and coherence, although a number of other accompanying issues are discussed.

Theory and History

The two themes discussed in this section are closely interwoven. Theory has served to inform and influence the processes of policy development and implementation that are subsequently reported in the history of regional planning, development and management, while the experiences reported and evaluated in this history, from within and outwith the UK, have helped to forge new elements of theory. Both parts of this section of the chapter are eclectic in form and content; they draw upon the theory and practice of regional planning, economic development, regional politics and governance, public administration and spatial analysis. Furthermore, neither of the discussions can be considered to be final or closed; they are both simply reports at a particular staging point in the evolution of territorial planning, development and governance.

At the outset, it is essential to position the English regional project within the wider context of the various regional economic, social and political changes that have taken place in the UK during recent decades. This attempt at contextualisation is made all the more difficult by the absence of a fixed point from which the changes can be observed. Indeed, attempts to establish integrated regional land-use and economic planning have been characterised by Baker et al (1999, p.763) as facing a succession of 'continual efforts to define and redefine its content and scope'. In such a situation it is difficult to present a series of snapshots of arrangements at particular moments in time, although a number of authors have attempted to track the longer-term evolution of regional structures (Mawson, 1997; Roberts and Lloyd, 1999; Wannop, 1995).

An important aspect of the wider context for the English regional project is provided by the changes that have occurred in the interpretation and application of the role of the state. While at one time the central state was seen as the dominant source of policies concerned with what can be broadly described as 'spatial intervention', in recent years this role has diminished. At the same time as the central state having been subject to both ideological and financial shifts and challenges, other actors have emerged. These new participants – from the private, voluntary and community sectors – now work alongside the state as partners. In addition, within the public sector the role of the central state itself has been transformed, with the European Union and local or regional authorities playing an increasingly active role. Overall, collaboration, networking and partnership are now the dominant modes of organisation associated with the design and discharge of spatial intervention policy. This process, which started in the 1970s, has been observed and assessed at both an intermediate (Stöhr, 1990) and a more advanced state (Fordham et al, 1998; Audit Commission, 1999) in the UK and elsewhere. The major characteristics of the old and new models of regional planning, development and management are illustrated in Figure 3.1.

A second element of the context is provided by the wider changes that have occurred in the structure of economies, and in the nature, pace and scale of the transformation which has taken place. No longer can a local or regional economy be insulated or buffered from the effects of external change - not that many regional economies were, in reality, in such a position in the past. If anything, the vulnerability of a local or regional economy to the influence of external forces is increasing rather than decreasing. This greater economic openness is a product of internationalisation and globalisation, and the consequences can be seen in the disengagement of production from place and the breakdown of the relationship between the characteristics of a regional economy and the 'individual nation's delimitations' (Nordström, 1996, p. 47).

The third component of the changed context for spatial intervention at regional level relates to the transformation which has occurred in the type of instruments that are employed to deliver policy and in the mechanisms used for their implementation. State investment, in the main, is no longer concerned with direct intervention or with the use of, for example, nationalised industries as leading activities which can attract or guide regional development. Rather, the current approach employs tax breaks, performance-related payments, private investment and a wide range of other instruments and mechanisms in order to achieve the stated objectives, including the promotion of sustainable development through environmental taxation and social justice (Roberts et al, 1999). Furthermore, these objectives are now generally claimed to be the product of extensive consultation, collaboration and partnership working, although some authors have called into question the extent and depth of partnership capability, arguing that 'despite a lot of rhetoric and some good practice, in most parts of the UK cross-sectoral partnerships still lack depth, substance and long term stability' (Geddes and Martin, 1996, p.31).

The final element of the context is European in origin, and is concerned with the gradual acceptance of the desirability of organising the institutions

Figure 3.1 Models of regional planning, development and management: changing policies and styles

Feature or characteristic	Traditional model	New model
Dominant direction of policy	Top-down	Bottom-up /top-down
Model of government	Centralised	Devolved
Method of approach	State-dominated	Partnership
Organisational paradigm	Fordist	Post-Fordist
Key objective	Maximum promotion of regional economic growth	Balanced regional development
Major target of policy	Large mobile manufacturing firms	Mix of size and types of firm
Policy instruments	Bureaucratic regulation, financial inducements, advisory services and general public provision	Greater autonomy, some financial assistance, advice and support service and mixed public/private/ voluntary provision
Key competitiveness factors	Economic scale	Innovation, networking and partnership
Economic focus	Public sector investment	Balance of public and private investment
Social content	Low and paternalistic	Higher with emphasis on role of community
Environmental approach	Greening in order to attract investment	Broader ideas of sustainable development and ecological modernisation

Source: Roberts and Lloyd (1999).

and conventions of government and governance in a manner which reflects the new challenges facing territorial planning, development and management. In the debate on the meaning and substance of subsidiarity it has now been accepted that the true intention of this process is the establishment of a direct relationship between an appropriate level of territorial governance and the discharge of a particular set of 'basic tasks'. These tasks reflect, on the one hand, many of the traditional functions associated with a particular level of government; an obvious example is the defence function undertaken by the nation state. On the other hand, the new perspective on the definition of 'basic tasks' places emphasis on territorial rather than functional integration (Friedman and Weaver, 1979) and on the redefinition of what bundle of functions might most appropriately be discharged at a particular level of government. It is in this context that the region cum small nation has been identified as an appropriate level of territorial government and governance which is capable of undertaking a wide range of tasks, including all of the major functions associated with the implementation of sustainable development – environmental, social and economic – and the provision of many community services. Indeed, the region-cum-small nation can be said to represent a unit of territorial planning, development and management which is the governance equivalent of the small and flexible unit of production in the manufacturing sector.

In addition to these elements of context, it should be noted that until recently the UK could be described as the only large member state in the European Union that lacked a directly elected and powerful level of sub-national government. Although this situation has now changed as a consequence of the devolution of powers to Scotland, Wales and Northern Ireland, and the establishment of the Greater London Authority, the situation in the other regions of England has not improved as substantially or as quickly. As a result, the English regions outside London continue to suffer from a democratic deficit that, in the opinion of Wiehler and Stumm (1995, p.249), presents 'an obstacle to the economic development of these regions'. The key explanatory factor, which underpins the relationship between the absence of an elected regional tier of government and underperformance in terms of economic development, can be found in a consideration of the extent to which national policy 'fits' the requirements of individual regions. Benneworth (1999b), for one, questions the appropriateness of a 'one-size-fits-all' policy as a basis for effective regional planning and development.

Moving to the history of the English regional project, many of the concerns that have already been expressed are confirmed. However, a number of other issues should be considered, including the longstanding difficulties that have been experienced in integrating land-use and economic policy at a regional level, the continuing dominance of functional over territorial concerns in the design and administration of central government policy, and the major problems that have been, and still are, experienced because of the switchback progress of arrangements for local and regional government.

The first of these issues can be traced back to the late 1940s. Ignoring the recommendations contained in the Barlow report, the arrangements that were put in place for the management of national and regional spatial policy divided responsibilities among a number of ministries. As a consequence, the administration of regional land-use and planning policy was divorced from regional industrial and economic policy, while other important elements of the spatial policy portfolio were either retained by, or distributed to, other departments of state. This division of function, which has endured in a more or less rigid form for 50 years, has led to the entrenchment of views in Whitehall and the creation of 'the problem of departmentalism which is endemic in the civil service' (Mawson, 1999, p.8). Prior to the creation of the GORs in 1994, the pattern of departmental separation at the centre was replicated in the arrangements that were evident in the regions (Roberts and Lloyd, 1999). Since 1994 a number of initiatives have been introduced in order to reduce departmentalism at regional level, but even these reforms have had little impact on policy formulation at the centre or on the overall pattern of distribution of public expenditure. At the heart of the matter, the major obstacle to reform is the absence of any real support in either Whitehall or Westminster for the provision of regional budgets that can be allocated as a block grant and then deployed in a flexible manner in pursuit of specific regional policy objectives. To this day, many policy matters that traditionally were included within the territorial functional portfolios of the Scottish and Welsh Offices are still absent from the list of topics and areas of activity that fall within the competence of a GOR. The creation of the regional development agencies has not resolved this matter, especially given the status of RDAs as NDPBs which are accountable upwards to the sponsoring DETR, rather than horizontally to elected regional authorities.

A second issue drawn from the history of regional governance in England is related to the transformation of the regional project from a comprehensive overhaul of the constitutional arrangements in the UK, including the establishment of elected regional authorities in England alongside devolved government to Wales, Scotland and Northern Ireland, to a more restricted, fragmented and patchy transfer of certain powers. The original 'project' proposed the creation of regional economic development agencies alongside a number of other regional agencies (for education, transport, planning, social policy etc.); it was intended that all of these agencies would be accountable to an elected regional authority. These proposals formed the core of the regional project that was developed by a Labour Party Parliamentary Spokesman's Working Group, and published in 1982 as the *Alternative Regional Strategy*. In the view of the *Alternative Regional Strategy*, the key reform was to establish an elected authority in each region. This authority would possess considerable powers to devise and implement specific policies relevant to its individual region and to adjust the balance of distribution within a block granted regional budget in pursuit of these policies (Parliamentary Spokesman's Working Group, 1982). This policy position was maintained for some years, and even in the 1995 consultation document, *A Choice for England* (Labour Party, 1995), a two-staged approach envisaged an indirectly nominated regional chamber evolving into a directly elected assembly. Equally, the report of the Regional Policy Commission recommended that 'regional development agencies be established separate from the regional chambers, but responsible to the chambers and acting as their executive arm in the field of economic development' (Regional Policy Commission, 1996, p.33). However, what has now been put in place is a considerably diluted and fragmented set of arrangements which separate the RDAs from the regional chambers/ assemblies, with the GORs continuing to administer a partial portfolio of regionally relevant functions. This situation has been described by one observer as 'a part-work' that does not 'represent a real constitutional settlement' (Benneworth, 1999b, p.4).

The third and final issue from the history of the English regional project elaborates the point made at the end of the preceding paragraph. This issue reflects the continuing constitutional difficulties that are associated with both the operation of the traditional system of governance whereby local and regional government is closely controlled by the centre, and the establishment of new constitutional arrangements. On the first of these two topics, it is evident that the switchback progression of local and regional government during the past 30 years, especially when coupled with the very real erosion of the powers and budgets of local and regional authorities, has done little to address the fundamental problems that result from the continued presence of the ultra vires principle (Roberts, 2000). The instability which results from the absence of constitutional certainty and specification of the rights and roles of the various levels of government has disabled regional and local government, causing regional planning, development and management to be regarded as mercurial phenomena which have waxed and waned over time (Wannop, 1995). The second topic reflects the consequences of the characteristics and behaviour just described; as can be seen from the present arrangements, the process of constitutional change in the UK as a whole, and especially in the English regions outside London, has proceeded in a piecemeal fashion. This process has resulted, for example, in the establishment of non-elected regional chambers (now generally called assemblies) in eight of the English regions and the introduction of an elected authority for Greater London. In parallel, other institutions and agencies associated with regional government have been, or are, the subject of scrutiny, review and reform. Two such examples are the reform of the House of Lords (one option was to introduce members who represented the regions) and the continuing review of local government boundaries and functions – the two-tier system of local government is considered by some to represent an obstacle to the introduction of regional government (Mawson, 1997).

What can be detected from these three issues reflecting the history of the English regional project is the presence of a number of underlying forces and tensions. The first of these can best be described as the 'pro-Union status quo position' (Mawson, 1999, p.4). This position represents the strengths of centralism and the traditional reluctance of the centre to concede powers and resources to the regions; this is a reflection of the traditional 'colonial administration' model described by Kellas (1991) in his evaluation of the Scottish and Welsh Offices. A second tension has already been alluded to; this is the divide within central government between individual departments, the result of which is the continuing compartmentalisation of functions and policies. Third, there are a number of varying assessments and differences of opinion regarding the implications and consequences for local government of the introduction of elected regional authorities; some see such a move as further eroding local powers, while others argue that devolution from the centre has the potential to strengthen local government and produce a more favourable policy regime (Stoker et al, 1996). This last point reflects the various options that exist for the future evolution of regional arrangements in England. These options, which are illustrated in Figure 3.2, include the evolution of 'regional administration' (from the 'colonial' model represented by the GORs) into either 'partial regional governance' (in which regional stakeholders and partners collaborate in the planning and management of a region, but direct political accountability is absent) or 'regional government' (where regional government governs, but does not attempt to involve the wider range of stakeholders). The final stage of evolution in this model is described as 'complete regional governance'; here, directly elected regional government collaborates with the full range of regional actors. This 'complete regional governance' can be defined as encompassing the 'formal machinery of government' together with the other regional partners and stakeholders who collaborate in order to 'manage aspects of the collective affairs or public realm' (Healey, 1997, p.8).

Figure 3.2 Alternative paths to complete regional governance

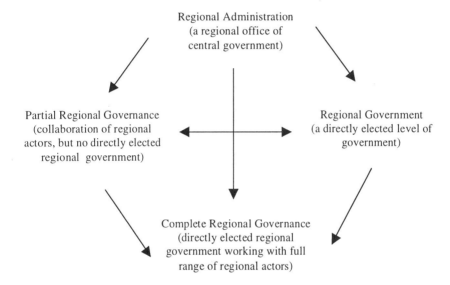

These arrangements of responsibility, political power and resources represent the fundamental parameters within which regional functions are organised, administered and discharged. Breheny (1996), in discussing the scope of regional planning, makes the point that there is little to be gained by attempting to develop policies or plans in the absence of the powers or influence necessary to ensure their implementation. Similar observations have been made in other academic and practice studies, including the report of the Royal Town Planning Institute (1986) and in the analysis provided by Wannop (1995) of containment by conference. Overall, one conclusion that can be drawn, is that an assessment of the ability to implement a strategy should form part of the strategy-making process itself. Strategies which sit on the shelf do little to further the cause of regional planning, development, and management.

Finally in this section of the chapter, it is important to consider the influence exerted by models of organisation that exist elsewhere. Some of these models of regional organisation and administration have already been noted, including the 'basic tasks' approach which is employed in Germany, but other examples are plentiful. A useful summary of the characteristics and features of alternative systems of regional management and government is provided by Wiehler and Stumm (1995), while Savy (1996) provides a wider assessment which includes an evaluation of the various approaches that have been adopted in relation to a range of public policy tasks at the regional level. These assessments demonstrate the important role performed by elected regional government – working alone or as part of a more inclusive system of complete regional governance – in ensuring coherence overall and establishing the parameters within which individual strategic exercises can be developed. As can be seen in the existing literature (e.g. Roberts, 2000), the recent experience of Scotland may offer guidance to the English regions with regard to this issue.

The next section of the chapter builds upon the theories, experiences and lessons that have been discussed in the preceding paragraphs. These messages from the past and from elsewhere are used to help to inform an assessment of the new regional arrangements in England.

Ensuring Coherence and Promoting Integration

The modern history of the building of regional capacity in England starts with the abolition of the Regional Economic Planning Councils (REPCs) in 1979. This act, which resulted in the loss of a highly cost-effective and influential mechanism for the development and co-ordination of strategic policies at regional level and which swept away more than 15 years of steady achievement in the creation of regional administration, left most regions in a state of powerlessness and disorganisation. In part, this was because many public authorities and other organisations – what nowadays are called regional 'stakeholders' or 'partners' – had invested considerable effort and faith in the workings of the REPCs, but it also reflected a general shift in ideology, which resulted in what Breheny and Hall (1984, p.95) described as 'the strange death of strategic planning and the victory of the know-nothing school'.

The consequences of the destruction of the established apparatus of regional planning, development and management, which was represented by the REPC and its associated organisations (Roberts and Lloyd, 1999), were numerous and have been rehearsed elsewhere by the present author and others (Roberts, 1997a; Glasson, 1992; and Wannop, 1995). The most serious of these consequences were that:

- the links between regional land-use planning and regional economic planning, which had been forged by the REPCs, were destroyed, thereby allowing the traditional schism between these two areas of policy to re-emerge;
- it became difficult to ensure the co-ordination and integration of the full range of policy fields at a regional or sub-regional level; this difficulty was exacerbated as the regional strategies and plans prepared during the 1970s increasingly became time-expired;
- it proved difficult to accommodate new demands for the production of regional plans, strategies and programmes; as a consequence, this led to either a failure fully to respond to such demands or the establishment of a series of separate and often overlapping administrative structures.

As indicated in the previous section, one response to the needless destruction of the regional institutional capacity that had been established during the 1960s and 1970s was the production of even more ambitious proposals for regional governance in documents such as the *Alternative Regional Strategy* (Parliamentary Spokesman's Working Group, 1982). Other responses developed through the strengthening or reformulation of regional administrative capacity, including action taken by local authorities, trades unions, environmental and community groups, and business institutions to establish regional-level organisations and inter-working arrangements. It is somewhat ironic that further acts of institutional vandalism, including the abolition of the metropolitan county councils and the Greater London Council in 1986, reinforced the status of the new voluntary regional administration which had started to emerge during the early 1980s. Further reinforcement of these new regional arrangements included the establishment of partnerships responsible for the planning and management of the European Structural Fund regional programmes (Roberts and Hart, 1996; Bentley and Shutt, 1997) and the creation of regional conferences of local authorities charged with the preparation of Regional Planning Guidance (RPG) (Roberts, 1996; Baker, 1998).

Further additions to, and refinements of, the regional institutional landscape occurred during the late 1980s and early 1990s, including the formalisation of regional local authority conference arrangements and the networking of these conferences (or chambers or assemblies) through the establishment of the English Regional Associations, the creation of the GORs in 1994, and the introduction of a number of associated political reforms such as the European Parliament's Committee of the Regions. In addition to these changes at regional level, concepts and models of joint working, collaboration and partnership were elaborated (Carter, 2000), and new roles and functions which could most suitably be discharged at regional level were introduced, such as the operationalisation of the objectives of sustainable development.

The purpose in relating this tale of ever-increasing policy and organisational complexity at regional level is to illustrate the point that the RDAs did not enter a regional institutional 'desert' when they were established in 1999. Rather, the RDAs were introduced as new and potentially powerful actors into an established and rapidly evolving complex regional institutional landscape. Indeed, it can be argued that in one sense, the creation of the RDAs disrupted the organic development of regional governance and caused attention to be focused on the 'executive' arm aspect of the embryonic regional chambers, rather than on the desirability of upgrading the pre-existing voluntary regional arrangements into complete regional government or governance. The present author and others have argued the merits of the organic development model, noting that this was the pathway from partial regional governance to complete regional governance that has been followed elsewhere (Roberts, 1997b; Mitchell, 1998), and that the present settlement is unsatisfactory and represents unfinished business (Harman, 1998).

As can be imagined, the introduction of the RDAs was not greeted with universal acclaim. Indeed, some regional stakeholders argued that the new bodies were unnecessary and disruptive, while the Conservative Party indicated that RDAs would be abolished by an incoming Conservative administration. The objections and reservations regarding the political positioning and powers of the RDAs also reflect a number of technical and professional concerns. Chief among these concerns is the status of the regional economic strategy which the RDA is required to prepare in relation to the other strategies, plans and programmes that are prepared at regional level. In one sense this is the crucial factor, and it is likely to prove to be the real test of the strength of the current arrangements at regional level in England.

As can be surmised from the preceding paragraphs, the gradual accretion of regional functions and organisations over the past decade has led to the creation of a number of parallel systems of political representation and administration at regional and sub-regional levels. Thus, in most English regions it is likely that a range of strategic tasks will be in progress at any one point in time, including the preparation or management of:

- Regional Planning Guidance and Regional Spatial Strategy;
- RDA Regional Economic Strategy and Action Plans;
- Regional Transport Strategy;

- Regional Sustainable Development Framework;
- Regional Tourism Strategy;
- Plans prepared by TECs – and the new Learning and Skills Councils;
- Regional Cultural Strategy;
- Local Environment Agency Plans;
- European Structural Funds Programmes.

Not surprisingly, considerable difficulties are encountered in attempting to co-ordinate and integrate these various strategies. In some English regions more than a dozen regional strategy exercises are currently underway.

It has already been noted that in an ideal world a directly elected regional government, preferably working with the stakeholders and partners within a region, would be in a position to prepare and implement an authoritative corporate regional vision; however, in the absence of such a level of government it is more difficult to establish which strategy, if any, takes precedence. This matter has been debated by academics (Baker et al, 1999; Roberts, 2000) and by a number of parliamentary committees (House of Commons, 1999). The general conclusion of these academic and political investigations is that a regional spatial development strategy, which attempts to work within the parameters set by the objectives of sustainable development, should take precedence because it provides 'an over-arching strategy for the region' (House of Commons, 1999, p.xii). Thus, even though not all RPG is equally either up to date or comprehensive in terms of the spatial analysis and strategic prescription contained in the documents, the various RPG documents do provide a common spatial foundation and framework for other plans, programmes and strategies. However, the present government has decided not to nominate any of the exercises as superior or over-arching. Indeed, in the case of a dispute between RPG and a RES, it is anticipated by the government that the 'Secretary of State will be able to resolve any conflicts', however, this is considered to be a 'longstop and not something that we expect to happen' (Planning, 1999).

It might be helpful here to outline and discuss the alternative models of organisation that would appear to be available in order to achieve coherence between the various strategic territorial plans prepared at regional or other levels. The term 'territorial' is used here in order to suggest that other, more suitable areas may exist for the purposes of strategic planning, development and management than the present English (GOR) regions (Roberts, 2000). Indeed, one of the problems currently encountered in attempting to ensure co-ordination of the various regional plans and strategies is a reflection of the government's insistence that pre-existing bodies should abandon long-established arrangements for the planning and management of 'standard' regions and switch to new arrangements. For example, RPG for East Anglia has traditionally been prepared for a three-county region comprising Norfolk, Suffolk and Cambridgeshire. At the time of the introduction of the RDA for the East of England, the revision of RPG was at an advanced stage. However, the RDA for the East of England covers a six-county territory which also includes Bedfordshire, Essex and Hertfordshire. This change in territorial composition and boundary has necessitated a shift in spatial focus and organisational structure (Roberts and Lloyd, 1998).

The four organisational models on offer are:

- one based on a bi-lateral relationship between RPG and a RES;
- a multi-lateral model which creates a cat's cradle of network relationships between the various strategies, in the absence of an over-arching strategy or vision;
- a model in which retrospective co-ordination of the various regional strategies is attempted;
- a model based on the presence of an over-arching vision and spatial strategy which provides a common foundation for all other strategies and plans.

These models are illustrated in Figure 3.3.

In determining which, if any, of these models should be employed, individual regional organisations or agencies will wish to consider which of the functions for which they are responsible should be linked to other areas of activity. In part, such decisions will be informed by established practices and agreements, but will also be influenced by the presence of the new arrangements and may necessitate the creation of special administrative regimes at a regional or trans-regional level. One example of organisational innovation is the introduction of concordats in a number of regions. These documents specify the roles of two or more regional partners – the GOR, the RDA and the chamber/assembly – and spell out the responsibilities of each of the partners and the arrangements for collaboration and joint determination.

While concordats and other forms of regional-level agreement provide a means of establishing coherence and collaboration, other mechanisms can be seen in operation. One important element in the creation of collaborative and partnership structures is the presence of trust; however, the literature would appear to demonstrate that trust emerges from successful collaboration rather than existing at the outset (Cooke and Morgan, 1998). In addition, genuine collaboration can be identified as an outcome of permanent partnership working, including the experience of having to resolve disagreements and make difficult choices, rather than as an instant consequence of forming a partnership (Roberts and Hart, 1996). Reflecting these experiences, it is not surprising that in some regions emphasis has been placed on sub-regional working and collaboration, thereby attempting to promote coherence 'from below' rather than imposing it 'from above'. A variation on the sub-regional model is the sector-based approach, but this method lacks the spatial organisational ability possessed by the sub-regional model.

An alternative perspective on how best to stimulate collaboration between regional partners, as a means of ensuring coherence between the various regional plans and strategies, is provided by assessments which argue that all attempts (including concordats, agreements and sub-regional arrangements) are likely to fail in the long run in the absence of the authority possessed by an elected regional government, which is necessary in order to act on behalf of a region. The advocates of elected regional government argue that such an approach has the twin merits of providing accountability at regional level with respect to the RDAs and other NDPBs (Morgan, 1999), and helping to ensure that an over-arching regional vision and strategy can be put in place in each region. Although this line of argument is not pursued further here, it is discussed at length elsewhere in this book, and it is a matter of concern in a number of regions.

The final topic considered in this section is the issue of how to ensure coherence at inter-regional level. As is almost always the case, an individual territory cannot stand alone, especially in a developed and densely populated nation. The regions of England are highly interdependent and the RDAs have much to gain from positive collaboration on matters such as the allocation of research and development funding and activity, the improvement of infrastructure and the attraction of inward investment. Inter-regional collaboration can assist in the promotion of policy coherence both within regions and at national level. The three northern RDAs have recently formalised their collaborative arrangements and have agreed to work together on a range of common issues.

Having reviewed the causes and consequences of the difficulties encountered in attempting to promote territorial coherence and ensure the integration of the various strands of regional working, the final section of this chapter develops some initial conclusions and presents a number of suggestions

Figure 3.3 Models of regional organisation in order to ensure co-ordination and coherence

Note: In order to avoid complexity, a limited number of examples have been used in cases b, c, and d.

a: Bi-lateral relationship

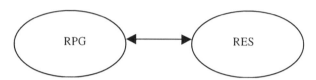

b: Multi-lateral relationship

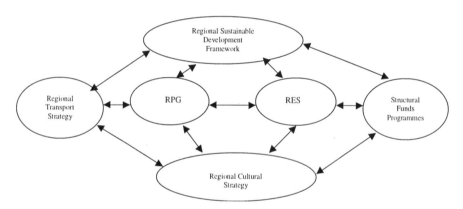

c: Retrospective co-ordination

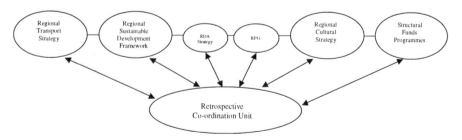

d: Corporate regional approach

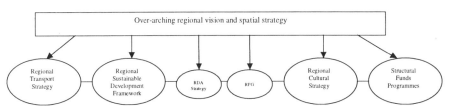

for further consideration and action. In offering these conclusions, the author is aware that it is far too soon to give an authoritative judgement on either the effectiveness of the arrangements that have been part introduced in order to promote coherence, or on the form and content of the various plans and strategies that have been prepared. However, an early comment on such matters may serve to highlight any areas that require additional consideration.

Taking Stock and Looking Forward

In offering an analysis of the evolution and present status of the arrangements for the administration and governance of the English regions, it is apparent that there are many variations between regions in terms of current practice and future ambition. These variations reflect the differences of history and economic geography which help to define the human, physical, environmental and financial resource base of regions, as well as the differences that exist in terms of the relative powers and significance of the various regional bodies. The former point is self-evident and can be seen in the varied inheritances that are reflected in the baselines from which the regions will now evolve. The latter point is less obvious or explicit, and reflects the relative, rather than absolute, power and influence of, for example, the RDA vis-à-vis the other regional stakeholders in the North East compared with the situation which obtains in the South East. This is not to suggest that the absolute powers exercised by an RDA are any more or any less in a particular region; however, quite clearly, the relative influence exerted by an RDA will not be the same in all regions. Furthermore, the status, power and significance of other regional bodies will also vary from region to region. This suggests that what exists, and will continue to exist, is asymmetric regional administration and governance, especially when London is brought into consideration. While there is nothing inherently wrong with asymmetric administration, devolution or regional governance (Keating, 1998), it runs counter to the dominant model that has been employed in the past and would also appear to offer little hope of the immediate evolution of the present arrangements into elected regional government. In simple terms, the evolutionary model of regional government which has operated in France (Roberts, 1997b) is unlikely to emerge in the English regions outside London in the near future.

Referring again to Figure 3.3, which demonstrates the four basic models that can be employed to encourage integration of the various regional plans and strategies, it is apparent that in the short to medium term emphasis is likely to be placed on achieving greater coherence and co-ordination through the establishment of a bi-lateral, multi-lateral or retrospective co-ordination model. This is the message conveyed by the establishment of concordats, inter-agency agreements and co-ordination units. The presence of such initiatives suggests that three aspects of coherence, collaboration and integration will be of particular importance in the future:

- political and organisational collaboration and agreement within a region;
- professional and technical co-ordination and integration both within and between regions;
- administrative collaboration and joint working at central government level, and between the GOR and other central government departments and agencies present in a region.

The first of these three aspects implies the extension of the present best practice of collaboration to all regions, and the general expansion of the scope of collaboration and co-operation in order to incorporate a wider range of functions. In parallel with these essentially organisational developments, it is likely that the search will continue for ways of introducing greater regional accountability, including perhaps the creation of a joint reporting arrangement for the RDAs so that they are required to report to regional chambers/assemblies as well as the DETR. This is at the heart of the calls for the regional project to develop to its logical conclusion, that is, the creation of directly elected regional chambers (Harman, 1998). Much depends on the speed at which the regional chambers/assemblies evolve (Local Government Association, 1999) and the confidence of central government to allow further devolution to proceed.

A second aspect of the future evolution of the current arrangements is likely to be concerned with the establishment of more comprehensive and elaborate arrangements for the co-ordinated design and delivery of key aspects of regional policy. This trend can be observed in the elaboration of the regional arrangements, as reported by the LGA in April and in November 1999, and in the specific actions proposed and taken in the various regions, including specific steps to, for example, co-ordinate analysis and policy-making at sub-regional level in the North East or the introduce collaborative arrangements for the preparation of an Integrated Regional Strategy in the East Midlands. Equally, arrangements now exist for inter-regional working on issues such as the attraction of inward investment and trans-national representation. This aspect of future development is likely to progress irrespective of political considerations (Roberts, 1999).

Finally, there is the question of how best to promote greater co-ordination and coherence within central government, and especially in the various regional 'outposts', including the GORs. This issue is at the heart of the arguments about the pace and scale of devolution. The Cabinet Office report, *Reaching Out* (2000), proposes that a central co-ordination unit should be established in order to promote and manage coherence both in terms of the policy stance of the methods of implementation employed by central government departments, and in relation to the operation of the GORs. This is an important step forward, but in one sense can be regarded as a form of retrospective co-ordination that is best avoided. However, this takes this chapter back into the realm of elected regional government, and as such is outside the subject under consideration here.

Irrespective of the precise level of support given to the presence of the RDAs and to the development of the Regional Economic Strategies. there is a noticeable desire in most of the regions of England to continue to argue in favour of an extended regional mandate. Even though the introduction of RDAs may have disrupted pre-existing working relationships in some regions, the overall impression is that the very presence of the RDAs has stimulated debate and action on a number of fronts. In the final analysis it is surely preferable to have to grapple with the problem of ensuring coherence across a number of possibly competing regional strategies, than not to have an active regional strategic arena. The important thing is to learn from experience and ensure that best practice becomes the norm.

Note

1 Disclaimer. The views expressed in this chapter are those of the author and should not be taken as representing the views, policies or opinions of any other organisation, agency or authority.

References

Audit Commission (1999), *A Life's Work*, Audit Commission, London.

Baker. M. (1998), 'Planning for the English Regions: A Review of the Secretary of State's Regional Planning Guidance', *Planning Practice and Research*, vol. 13, pp. 153-69.

Baker, M. et al (1999), 'Obscure Ritual or Administrative Luxury? Integrating Strategic Planning and Regional Development', *Environment and Planning B*, vol. 26, pp. 763-82.

Benneworth, P. (1999a), 'RDAs Update – The State of Progress', *Regions*, 219, pp. 10-8.

Benneworth, P. (1999b), 'Buying Them Like Shoes', paper presented at the 39th Annual Congress of the European Regional Studies Association, Dublin, August.

Bentley, G. and Shutt, J. (1997), 'European Regional Policy in English Regions', in J. Bachtler and I. Turok (eds), *The Coherence of EU Regional Policy*, Jessica Kingsley, London.

Breheny, M. (1996), 'The Scope of Regional Planning', paper presented at the RGS-IBC Conference, Glasgow, January.

Breheny, M. and Hall, P. (1984), 'The Strange Death of Strategic Planning and the Victory of the Know-nothing School', *Built Environment*, vol. 10, pp. 95-9.

Cabinet Office (2000), *Reaching Out. The Role of Central Government at Regional and Local Levels,* Performance and Innovation Unit, HMSO, London.

Carter, A. (2000), 'Strategy and Partnership in Urban Regeneration', in P. Roberts and H. Sykes (eds), *Urban Regeneration*, Sage, London.

Cooke, P. and Morgan, K. (1998), *The Associational Economy: Firms, Regions and Innovation*, Oxford University Press, Oxford.

Fordham, G. et al (1998), *Building Partnerships in the English Regions*, DETR, London.

Friedmann, J. and Weaver, C. (1979), *Territory and Function*, Edward Arnold, London.

Geddes, M. and Martin, S. (1996), *Local Partnership for Economic and Social Regeneration,* Local Government Management Board, London.

Glasson, J. (1992), 'The Fall and Rise of Regional Planning in the Environmentally Advanced Nations', *Urban Studies*, vol. 29, pp. 505-31.

Harman, J. (1998), 'Regional Development Agencies: Not the Final Frontier', *Local Economy*, vol. 13, pp. 194-7.

Healey, P. (1997), 'The Revival of Strategic Planning in Europe', in P. Healey et al (eds), *Making Strategic Spatial Plans*, UCL Press, London.

House of Commons (1999), *Tenth Report of the Environment, Transport and Regional Affairs Committee – The Regional Development Agencies,* IIC 232-1, The Stationery Office, London.

Keating, M. (1998), What's Wrong with Asymetrical Government?', *Regional and Federal Studies,* vol. 8, pp. 195-218.

Kellas, J. G. (1991), 'The Scottish and Welsh Offices as Territorial Managers', *Regional Politics and Policy*, vol. 1, pp. 87-100.

Labour Party (1995), *A Choice for England: A Consultation Paper on Labour's Plans for English Regional Government*, Labour Party, London.

Local Government Association (1999), *Regional Chambers – State of Play: April and November*, LGA, London.

Mawson, J. (1997), 'The English Regional Debate: Towards Regional Governance of Government?', in J. Bradbury and J. Mawson (eds), *British Regeneration and Devolution*, Jessica Kingsley, London.

Mawson, J. (1999), 'Devolution – The English Regions and the Challenge of Regional Governance', paper presented at the Annual Conference of the Regional Studies Association, London, November.

Mitchell, J. (1998), 'What Could a Scottish Parliament Do?', *Regional and Federal Studies*, vol. 8, pp. 68-83.

Morgan, K. (1999), 'The Economic Impact of the Scottish Parliament: Possibilities and Constraints', in J. McCarthy and D. Newlands (eds), *Governing Scotland*, Ashgate, Aldershot.

Nordström, L. (1996), 'European Developing Regions – Reality or Chimera?', in J. Alden and P. Boland (eds), *Regional Development Strategies*, Jessica Kingsley, London.

Parliamentary Spokesman's Working Group (1982), *Alternative Regional Strategy: A Framework for Discussion*, Labour Party, London.

Planning (1999), 'No Ranking for Strategies', *Planning*, 1343.

Regional Policy Commission (1996), *Renewing the Regions*, PAVIC Publications, Sheffield.

Roberts, P. (1996), 'Regional Planning Guidance in England and Wales: Back to the Future?', *Town Planning Review*, vol. 67, pp. 97-109.

Roberts, P. (1997a), 'Strategies for the Stateless Nation: Sustainable Policies for the Regions in Europe', *Regional Studies*, vol. 31, pp. 875-82.

Roberts, P. (1997b), 'Whitehall et la Désert Anglais: Managing and Representing the UK Regions in Europe', in J. Bradbury and J. Mawson (eds), *British Regionalism and Devolution*, Jessica Kingsley, London.

Roberts, P. (1999), 'From Here to Eternity: Future Prospects for the RDAs and Regional Governance', paper presented at the Annual Conference of the Regional Studies Association, London, November.

Roberts, P. (2000), 'Setting the Pace: Scotland and the UK Devolution Project', in A. Wright (ed), *The Scottish Parliament: The Challenge of Devolution*, Ashgate, Aldershot (forthcoming).

Roberts, P. and Hart, T. (1996), *Regional Strategy and Partnership in European Programmes*, Joseph Rowntree Foundation, York.

Roberts, P. and Lloyd, G. (1998), *Developing Regional Potential*, British Urban Regeneration Association, London.

Roberts, P. and Lloyd, G. (1999), 'Institutional Aspects of Regional Planning, Management and Development: Lessons from the English Experience', *Environment and Planning B*, vol. 26, pp. 517-31.

Roberts, P. et al (1999), *Environmental Taxation*, Local Government Association, London.

Royal Town Planning Institute (1986), *Strategic Planning for Regional Potential*, RTPI, London.

Savy, R. (1996), *Regions and Territories in Europe*, Assembly of European Regions, Limoges.

Stöhr, W. (1990), 'Introduction', in W. Stöhr (ed), *Global Challenge and Local Response*, Mansell, London.

Stoker, G. et al (1996), *Regionalism*, Local Government Management Board, London.

Wannop, U. (1995), *The Regional Imperative*, Jessica Kingsley, London.

Wiehler, F. and Stumm, T. (1995), 'The Powers of Regional and Local Authorities and their Role in the European Union', *European Planning Studies*, vol. 3, pp. 227-50.

4 New Regional Development Agencies in England: Wicked Issues

JOHN SHUTT

Introduction

This chapter discusses the establishment of the English regional development agencies and aims to identify the range of regional and local economic development issues which need to be addressed by government and regional actors, one year on. It does so through the prism of Yorkshire and Humber and reference to Yorkshire Forward, although many of the issues raised are not unique to one region or regional development agency.

Although strategic guidance from the DETR has been issued (DETR, 1998b), the Regional Economic Strategies which have been produced show that many issues facing the RDAs can only be tackled through greater regional discussion and additional support and clarification by central government. Following the first year of active development and submission of the first Regional Economic Strategies to the DETR, there is now a need to move on to examine the measures which can improve implementation and delivery over the next 10 years. The RDAs need to be considered in the context of the forthcoming Urban White Paper, the forthcoming White Paper on Rural England, and the government's vision for an 'Urban Renaissance' (DETR, 1998c; 1999e). A further review of economic development roles is required at regional, sub-regional and local levels with greater clarity about respective tasks.

While continuing developments in the motor industry, impacting within specific regions, serve to reinforce the central need for more vigorous RDAs within the English regions (see Bentley, chapter 6), there is still concern that the government is sending out too many mixed messages in relation to the regional agenda. Having been established, RDAs expected to be in the lead, co-ordinating policy and leading the economic regeneration effort in each region. But now the Cabinet Office report, *Reaching Out* (2000), has recommended that Government Offices in the Regions should have their role strengthened, and the Cabinet Office Central Co-ordinating Unit has been established to 'join-up' regional programmes and policy. The new Learning and Skills Councils (LSCs), which are to be set up by the DfEE, are seen as a counterbalance to the RDAs, and the new Small Business Service (SBS) by the DTI is interpreted by many as possibly weakening the RDAs' co-ordination role for economic development and regeneration in each region in the years ahead. This need not be the case.

The requirement now, one year on, is for RDAs, partners in the regions and government to take stock of RDAs' roles and implementation problems, and gear up the RDA regional economic development effort to be more effective. Each RDA must now achieve greater impact and bring new impetus and added value. Whether each region will make progress without further central government guidance and clarity on a range of regional governance matters remains a critical issue, but in the absence of further legislation, regional actors must show that progress is being made through 'internal' regional clarification.

Consideration of the key issues identified here raises many questions about the ability and effectiveness of the English RDAs to develop an integrated approach to regional economic development. The issues are 'wicked' in the sense that they are ones which can be difficult to address because they tend to cut across traditional policies, boundaries, funding streams and departments. They are wicked, too, in the sense that the identification, treatment and prioritisation accorded to dealing with them may well determine the philosophy, approach and mode of intervention of each RDA. To be effective, RDAs will need to put more effort into their training and capacity-building plans.

The 1998 legislation on RDAs has created a two-tier system of regional development and democratic accountability in the UK, and an imperfect and imprecise system in England for regional economic development and regional governance. Further measures to strengthen the RDAs are required in the 2000 Annual Spending Review, while within each region, the plans for English regional government will require elaboration following the next general election. One way of assisting the region-building process in the interim would be to provide further resources to assist the development of the regional chambers and the assemblies. The RDAs need to consider what is required to galvanise local economic development partnerships, particularly those operating at city, town and sub-regional levels.

The New Regional Agenda: Bringing Together a New Framework for the Regions

The government published its White Paper, *Building Partnerships for Prosperity'* in December 1997, setting out its plans to create a new RDA in each region (DETR, 1997b). A Bill was introduced in Parliament in December 1997, and the Regional Development Agencies Act 1998 received royal assent in November 1998. The Act provides for the English RDAs to be established as government-sponsored bodies, with boards that are business-led and reflecting a range of diverse interests in each region. The chairmen of the boards were identified in July 1998 (Table 4.1) and have remained in place through the first phase. The shadow boards were formed in the autumn of 1998 and have been fully operational from 1st April 1999. The exception is London, where the aim is to establish the RDA following the setting up of the new strategic Greater London Authority (GLA) on 3rd July 2000. The Welsh Development Agency has been made accountable to the new Welsh Assembly, and Scottish Enterprise to the Scottish Parliament. The Northern Ireland Assembly, when and if convened, will take charge of the Industrial Development Board for Northern Ireland (IDB Northern Ireland).

In Wales, Scotland, Northern Ireland and London, the RDAs will be responsible to directly elected regional authorities and regional governments. In England, they are new quangos responsible to the Secretary of State for the Environment and, to a certain extent, to new voluntary regional chambers, whose membership consists of a regional public-private partnership.

Each of the English regions now has four principal actors at the regional level developing the new regional agenda.

Building Partnerships in the Regions: The New Regional Governance

From their creation in 1994, GORs have evolved as regional administrations, bringing together the former regional offices of the Departments of the Environment, Trade and Industry, Education and Employment, and Transport. Regional directors are responsible for introducing a more co-ordinated approach across the civil service. Each region now has a regional assembly, often established with all-party support, bringing together all the local authorities in each region and building a new regional-level local government organisation. The assemblies often regard themselves as the forerunner of regional government. Separate and sometimes linked to these assemblies, there are

Table 4.1 Chairmen of the new regional development agencies

Region	Name	Private sector interests
Eastern	Vincent Watts	Vice Chancellor of the University of East Anglia
East Midlands	Derek Mapp	Chairman, Leapfrog Day Nurseries
North East	John Bridge	Chief Executive, Northern Development Company
North West	Lord Thomas of Macclesfield	Former Managing Director, Co-operative Bank
South East	Allen Willett	Chairman, Willett International Ltd
South West	Sir Michael Lickiss	Chairman, Edexcel Foundation (BTEC)
Yorkshire and the Humber	Graham Hall	Chief Executive, Yorkshire Electricity Group Plc
West Midlands	Alex Stephenson	Managing Director, Rover Group Power Train
London	To be announced	

Source: DETR (1998b).

now a range of voluntary regional chambers; these are public-private partnerships which have to be consulted by the new RDAs as part of their statutory obligations (Figure 4.1 and Table 4.2). It is not yet clear how regional assemblies and regional chambers will best work together, or how they are to focus and develop their respective work programmes. So far, their debates and actions are too distanced from the general public, who have little understanding of their roles.

Different arrangements are in place throughout England. In the North West region, the assembly and chamber have been combined. Both are focusing on the RDA formation and partnership process. It is the regional chambers that have the potential to bring together the range of key regional partners and stakeholders, not only from the public and private sectors, but also from further and higher education. The voluntary and community sector, faith communities, and environmental, health and rural interests are also members of regional chambers. Yet the chambers have sparse financial and human resources with which to build regional capacity and regional partnerships. Each RDA has to consult its regional chamber on its strategy and key documents, such as the annual report and corporate plan. The RDA in each region has to give an account of its actions to the chamber. The regional assemblies subsist on a subscription base of local authority funding and also require their functions strengthening.

Public understanding of this 'regional institutional architecture' is slim. Many are confused about the respective roles of GORs, assemblies, chambers and RDAs. Much greater clarification is required of lead responsibilities, and better communication strategies are needed from each of the key actors.

Table 4.2 Regional stakeholders: the example of Yorkshire and the Humber

The Regional Assembly for Yorkshire and Humberside	Inaugurated on 8th July 1996, marking the agreement of all 22 local authorities in the region on the need for a new regional level organisation representing local government in Yorkshire and Humberside. The regional assembly has all-party support.
Yorkshire and Humber Regional Chamber	Established voluntarily by the regional assembly and the Yorkshire and Humberside partnership, and launched by John Prescott MP, Deputy Prime Minister, on 27th March 1998. The chamber's purpose is to promote the economic, social and environmental well-being of Yorkshire and Humberside in the interests of all those who work in the region. As the region's main partnership, it will focus on policy co-ordination across the region, bringing together key regional partners, including the RDA, other public authorities, grant agencies and regional stakeholders. These include the CBI, the Association of Yorkshire and Humberside Chambers of Commerce, regional TUC, YHTEC, YHUA, Association of Colleges, Yorkshire and Humberside Regional Forum of Voluntary and Community Organisations, Environmental Agency, health organisations, faith communities and rural interests.

Source: ERBEDU (1999).

Figure 4.1 Regional governance in England from 1ˢᵗ April 1999

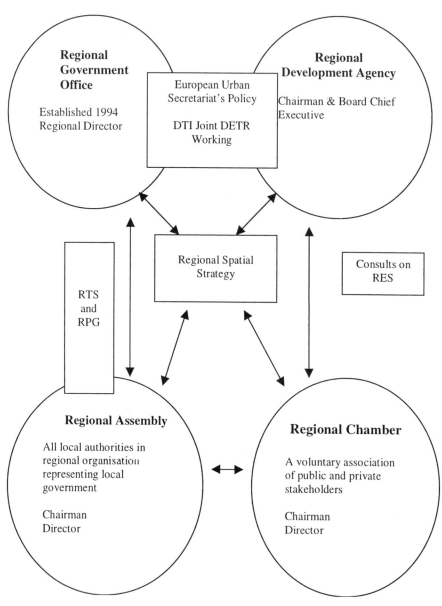

RDA Functions, Visions and Regional Economic Strategies

The statutory purposes of RDAs were set out in the Regional Development Agencies Act, 1998 (Table 4.3).

Table 4.3 Regional development agency functions

A	To further the economic development and regeneration of its area
B	To promote business efficiency, investment and competitiveness in its area
C	To promote employment in its area
D	To enhance the development and application of skills relevant to employment in its area
E	To contribute to the achievement of sustainable development in the United Kingdom where it is relevant to do so.

Source: Section 7 (1) Regional Development Agencies Act 1998.

Core Functions of RDAs

The DETR White Paper *Building Partnerships for Prosperity* (1997a), Regional Development Agencies Act 1998 and subsequent guidance define the core functions for the RDAs.

- The RDAs will provide **leadership** in developing and implementing a new Regional Economic Strategy for each region for the 21st century. They will build upon existing regional partnerships and develop a fuller understanding of regional economies, including research. They are to expand and develop regional economic intelligence.
- The RDAs have, from 1st April 1999, the lead role in the social, physical and economic regeneration of each region, seeking to maximise benefits and spread the benefits of economic development and investment. Each RDA will: (i) administer the SRB Challenge Fund; (ii) administer and combine the regeneration role of English Partnerships (EP) and the Rural

Development Commission; and (iii) absorb and integrate the activities of existing inward investment agencies.

- The RDAs must address both urban and rural issues, integrating town and country, and be responsible for the economic development and regeneration of rural areas.
- The RDAs will take a 'leading' role in the European Union Structural Funds programmes in each region for the 2000-2006 period. In the first instance, however, responsibility for delivering European programmes remains with Government Offices for the Regions and with the Department of Trade and Industry.
- The RDAs will provide advice to ministers on Regional Selective Assistance (RSA). The DTI has since reviewed RSA, which is seen as an important tool in attracting and retaining internationally mobile investment.
- The RDAs will monitor and provide a regional focus for the work of Business Links in promoting small and medium-sized enterprises (SMEs) and Enterprise programmes. The DfEE has reviewed the Training and Enterprise Councils (to be replaced by LSCs) and the DTI is establishing the Small Business Service.
- The RDAs will promote the reclamation and preparation of sites, including taking the role now played by English Partnerships through its regional offices. EP Regional Offices went into the RDAs, but EP has retained a central national role on key strategic programmes.
- The RDAs will facilitate investments, including projects encouraging public-private partnerships. New Regional Capital Funds are to be established.
- The RDAs will market their regions as business locations in conjunction with the Invest in Britain Bureau and regional partners.
- The RDAs will promote technology transfer, including maximising the benefits of the work of the higher and further education institutions (universities and colleges) in the region.
- The RDAs will make improvements to the skills base of the region, including developing a regional skills agenda, assessing the contribution of TECs towards regional objectives and promoting training for major investments. In April 2001, Learning and Skills Councils will become fully operational at sub-regional levels, and TECs and the Further Education Funding Council will cease to exist.

Regional Economic Strategies

Throughout England, the new RDA chairs and chief executives have been busy establishing new RDA teams and new boards, elaborating vision statements, and commissioning consultants to help them prepare the new Regional Economic Strategies. The strategies were submitted to the DETR in October 1999 and will provide the starting point for much of each RDA's work and, it is hoped, for the regional and local partners in the 21st century (Table 4.4).

The RES documents are the first comprehensive review of the economy of the English regions for over 30 years. Each RDA embarked upon a large-scale consultation process in its region with all the key regional stakeholders.

> The government will encourage RDAs to make this strategy a partnership document, with regional, sub-regional and local partners involved in producing and in delivering it. The strategy will provide an analysis of the needs of the region, and the RDA's approach to addressing these needs. It will provide a regional framework for the delivery of national government programmes, as well as providing an opportunity for the regions to influence the development of government policies. (DETR, 1998b)

Each RDA faces a range of issues, some of which are difficult to address because they cut across traditional boundaries (both geographical and professional) policies, programmes, funding streams and departments. Each RDA has a massive change management agenda to fulfil, bringing together the old inward investment agencies, English Partnerships, the Rural Development Commission and services from government agencies in each region. The fundamental purpose is to improve each region's economic performance, and enhance regional competitiveness, economic regeneration and business growth in each region. The new RDAs have taken responsibility for programmes such as the Single Regeneration Budget, and have resources of up to £200m per annum depending on the size of the region (Table 4.5). However, the bulk of the funding is for local area regeneration, rather than competitiveness and investment funding. This raises serious questions about RDA objectives and partner relationships at local economic development level. Area regeneration, local initiatives and neighbourhood strategies require different treatment to regional and sub-regional economic strategies related to competitiveness and inward investment. This issue is being explored further (see, for example, Robson et al, (2000), for the Joseph Rowntree Foundation).

The RES timescale (submission by October 1999) has brought together

Table 4.4   English RDAs: eight regional strategies

RDA	Title of strategy
AWM Advantage West Midland	Creating Advantage: The West Midlands Economic Strategy
EEDA East of England Development Agency	Moving Forward: A Strategy for the East of England
EMDA East Midlands Development Agency	Prosperity through People: Economic Development Strategy for the East Midlands 2000-2001
ONE One North East	Regional Economic Strategy for the North East; Unlocking Our Potential.
NWDA Northwest Development Agency	England North West: A Strategy Towards 2000
SEEDA South East England Development Agency	Building a World Class Region: An Economic Strategy for the South East of England
SWERDA South West of England RDA	Regional Strategy for the South West of England: 2000 – 2010
YF Yorkshire Forward	Advancing Together - Towards a World-Class Region

fresh 'State of the Region' assessments (e.g. ERBEDU, 1999) and three months of intense discussions with partners across the regions, providing new frameworks for economic development strategies for the next 10 or even 20 years. Invariably the strategies have been rushed, but the consultation processes have been large-scale and impressive in all regions. The process raised many expectations in 1999. The South East RDA proposes that the economic development strategy

Table 4.5 Planned programme expenditure by RDAs for DETR programmes: £ million

Region	1998-1999 Estimated out-turn	1999-2000 Plans	2000-2001 Plans	2001-2002 Plans
North West (including Merseyside)	0.3	211.6	224.1	226.9
North East	0.5	124.2	119.1	124.5
Yorkshire and the Humber	0.5	146.2	160.8	165.0
East Midlands	0.4	55.9	59.9	57.1
West Midlands	0.4	112.1	105.1	121.3
Eastern	0.4	25.4	22.2	26.9
South East	0.5	62.1	59.8	91.4
South West	0.4	70.1	59.7	51.9
London	-	246.0	264.5	274.5

Source: DETR, (1999a).

needs to follow the rigours of a good business plan. It should be grounded in specific proposals, with responsibility for delivery agreed with, and devolved to, the appropriate public, private or voluntary partnership, organisation or individual at the regional or more local level. Actions and strategies should be costed and timed and the assumptions underlying them set down. (SEEDA, 1999)

The business-like approach to delivery is welcome, but early readings of the submitted economic strategy documents show the pre-occupation with 'competitive advantage', and with wealth creation and world-class visions. The difficulties of addressing regional futures and the social inclusion and sustainable development objectives of the RDAs seep through a first reading of all the strategies (CLES, 1999). It is perhaps to be expected, given the starting points of the new RDAs, but it shows the complexities of implementing the original brief. The South East RDA, for example, proposes to prioritise 'Enterprise Hubs in a Wired Region',

> a network of enterprise hubs will cover the whole region. We will aim to have 25-30 hubs in place within five years. These hubs will provide focal points for inter-firm trading and networking, and the delivery of world-class business support services. However, they will particularly facilitate tailored support for those 'gazelle' companies (high-growth businesses) that have the ambition and potential to become leaders in their field and internationally. (SEEDA, 1999)

The RES statements so far appear to find it hard to question many existing local economic strategies and priorities because most RDAs have sought to build a regional consensus. Perhaps too often there is also a general acceptance of many long-standing economic development strategies and initiatives which are failing. The Yorkshire Forward strategy claims that its 10-year framework will allow for a rolling programme of priorities to be set every two years, focusing discretionary funding and resources on priority actions.

> Given the scale of challenges facing the region, we must truly prioritise, if we are to achieve our vision. The region must do the important few things well. (Yorkshire Forward, 1999)

The brave words mask the problems of focusing both on the priorities and on achieving discretionary funding on tightly restricted government funding programmes.

Yorkshire Forward's regional priorities are outlined in Table 4.6.

Table 4.6 Yorkshire Forward: regional priorities

YORKSHIRE FORWARD	
New Regional Economic Strategy (October 1999)	Key economic sectors focus on business-led support service
Create Yorkshire Business Birth Rate strategy	Image and tourism boost
Regional Skills Action Plan	Community-based regeneration in coalfields, cities and towns

Source: Yorkshire Forward (1999).

At regional level, Yorkshire Forward will be:

- increasing the competitiveness and innovation of business in six key economic sectors, utilising the Regional Innovation Strategy;
- creating new lasting competitive businesses through a Business Birth Rate Strategy, including setting up centres of excellence clustered around the region's universities (including a Virtual Business School), and a Yorkshire and Humber Venture Capital Fund;
- attracting inward investors by developing a better product and strong positive image;
- achieving a radical improvement in basic educational attainment linked to business needs by implementing a Skills Action Plan;
- implementing a programme of integrated community-based regeneration of the region's city and town centres in urban and rural areas including the former coalfields;
- establishing strategic development and trade zones, including a Humber Trade Zone and a Dearne Valley Development Zone, and developing market towns as centres of rural enterprise;
- developing an e-business region, by improving the use of information and communication technologies (ICTs) and connecting the strong service sector in Leeds, the regional capital, particularly to Bradford, York, Sheffield and Hull – and to the world!

The RES will require further development and consideration in the region as action plans are elaborated. The task of each RDA is to make sure that this takes place with the key partners within a region. For this to happen, both regional and sub-regional teams and priorities are required.

At sub-regional levels, there are some well-focused economic partnerships, for example, in Yorkshire, The Humber Forum and South Yorkshire Partnership; but in West Yorkshire or North Yorkshire, for example, partnerships may not be so well developed or hang together with the same coherence of purpose.

In terms of growth sectors and development strategies, it would be a healthy development to review existing commitments and priorities in order to devise a new set of regional priorities for the 21st century. The signs of the RES process are that this debate has only just begun. There are many weaknesses in necessary economic research and the knowledge base which require addressing, together with a thorough assessment of existing regional agency plans and those of the outgoing TECs, the local authorities and other actors. In Yorkshire, strategies that need to dovetail include:

- rural regeneration priorities;
- city and town futures;
- coalfield regeneration strategies;
- seaside resorts regeneration.

In each of these cases, the economic development partnership process is at different stages.

Integration with environment, transport and regional strategic planning guidance and the EU Structural Funds for 2000-2006 demands strategic co-ordination and cultural changes. So, too, does integration with new government policies for the Single Regeneration Budget, New Deal and other strategic initiatives (e.g. the new youth service, Connexions). To do this effectively will require training for board members as well as staff. The process of engagement of the RES with the planning, environment, transport and European arenas raises a particularly difficult set of issues, and requires a strategic partnership between the RDAs and GORs.

RDAs have been through their honeymoon period with the submission of the RES. There are fears that RDAs may now fail to:

- develop consultation with partners in a meaningful way;
- consult adequately on action plans;
- privilege urban areas above rural areas;
- resource properly the strategic regional priorities and actions;
- get to grips with the regional institutional architecture.

The RDAs must address these fears. The Department of the Environment, Transport and the Regions has produced its official response to each of the RES documents (DETR, 2000), submitted by the eight Regional Development Agencies outside London. The Department for Education and Employment is to hold detailed discussions with RDAs on Skills Action Plans. The DETR appears to have been disappointed by the limited attention paid to issues of social exclusion in many strategies

> There may be scope for improving the extent to which equal opportunities and the removal of racial disadvantage are embedded in the strategy. We expect that action plans will set clear priorities and targets to address this important issue. We will not achieve social inclusion unless we enable all of our people to realise fully their potential and contribute to the quality of life of our society. (DETR, 2000)

Next, it is useful to review the range of 'wicked issues' with which the RDAs are having to contend.

Organisation and Change Management

The RDA is charged with the integration of a range of agencies; each with its distinctive organisational culture. Each RDA will need to develop its own distinctive organisational culture, including establishing its own:

- personnel and employment policies;
- geographical organisation – with offices in the sub-region;
- regional philosophy;
- sub-contracting and partnership delivery arrangements.

One important question is whether the RDA demands a sub-regional strategy and organisation, with regional programmes which can be developed and maintained at a sub-regional level, while at the same time developing a firmer urban **and** rural regional strategic approach. The rural 'voice' fears over-domination by urban regeneration concerns, and RDAs need to guard against this.

The existing programmatic delivery of European and national government favours a strategic sub-regional approach and is difficult to avoid. In practice, however, many cultural problems within regions have arisen from too much parochialism, isolation of localities and insufficient joint working. There is a need to connect the prosperous and poorer parts of a region around a more determined economic strategy. Movement has already started with the work of the regional assemblies and the new RDAs can add greater impetus. If an RDA has its delivery focused on sub-regional partnership teams, however, a cross-cutting regional set of work teams focused around key strategic drivers at regional level and issues for the 21st century will also be needed. The question is, will RDAs have the resources to pursue and implement these strategic priorities at both regional and sub-regional levels? This is an issue on which RDA chairs have been lobbying hard throughout the first year in particular to achieve greater flexibility in central government budgeting procedures and additional funds for development. The RDA chairs are hoping that their lobbying will produce results in 2000.

Growth and Jobs

In developing any new sector strategy for a region, cognisance is required of the dilemma between capital investment and rising productivity in sectors still receiving RSA but producing relatively few jobs, and the predicted rise in employment in the service and knowledge sectors, demanding technology, literacy and softer management skills. More action is required to address the relatively low 'employment intensity of growth' in the regions. Jobs in poorer communities do not automatically follow economic growth, so further actions are required in a region to stimulate the connection between the two. The RDA boards need to think through their approach to industrial competitiveness and growth in the regions, and the policies required for job generation and employment targeted at specific deprived localities; they also need to examine the targeting of accelerated growth poles. One of the problems of the RES process has been the simplicity with which these processes are conceived.

**The Economic Development Partnership Process:
Establishing Priorities**

The economic development partnership process in each locality is in a process of transition. Each local authority has to bring forward its annual economic development plan; each TEC had its annual labour market plan. In some localities, TECs, Chambers of Commerce and Business Links are still separate, while in others, they are merging. On top of the patchwork quilt of economic development mainstream actors, a number of public-private regeneration partnerships exist at local and sub-regional levels. In Yorkshire, for example, the Bradford Congress, Wakefield Alliance, Leeds Initiative, Sheffield First Partnership, Dearne Valley Partnership and the Humberside and Calderdale Forums are just a selection. The localities no longer have a single voice. The new RDA will need to map out and build strong linkages with these economic development partnerships, and to understand their existing programmes. It may need to build and support new local partnerships and assist them through capacity-building measures, and will need to support and challenge visions and priorities already in hand. The RDA will need regular dialogue with these partnerships to discuss priorities and their connection to the regional strategy. This will necessitate considerable resources for communications and community development capacity if regular consultations are to be meaningful.

How will priorities be arrived at in terms of timing and resource allocation for programme areas? It will be crucial, in terms of legitimacy, to relate to the regional chamber and assembly and the locality partnerships as articulated in their own plans. But the production of a more coherent regional strategy will necessarily create conflicts and tensions, and it will be important to identify them. There is also a clear mismatch between resource availability, staffing and expertise on the one hand, and priorities on the other. Where are the expertise, resources and staffing on skills and labour markets, for example, to create the new regional skills strategies? One of the difficulties is the gap between strategic frameworks and implementation capacity.

In terms of training and small-enterprise policy, development is set for a further period of turbulence with the new Small Business Service, and Learning and Skills Councils entering the arena in 2001. The RDAs will need to build good relationships with these new bodies to ensure that fragmentation of effort does not take place. The DETR comments that in Yorkshire and Humber

> The Skills Action Plan helps to underpin all the objectives in the strategy. It provides a good balance of social inclusion issues, with a strong focus on basic structured development, workforce development, lifelong learning and higher skills development. The Skills Action Plan has commanded widespread support across the region and will be a good basis for early dialogue with the emerging Learning and Skills Councils. (DETR, 2000)

Priorities, Financial Packaging and Resources

European Matched Funding

The RDAs will need to review programme budgets and resources critically, and to establish lobbying and development priorities for the 21st century. Table 4.7 summarises the RDA programme budgets for 1998/99-2001/02, using Yorkshire Forward as the example. Each element requires critical review of existing priorities in the light of the RDA board's emerging corporate plan. In addition to the existing programmes, there will be the need to achieve better matched-funding programming with existing European funding sources. The RDA will also need to attract new private sector funding into the region, including examining Private Finance Initiative (PFI) project priorities and flagship PFI priorities and projects for each region.

The financing package will need to be considered in the light of the new priorities for European regional policies under Agenda 2000 and the matched funding required. While this new Structural Funds package has been finalised,

Table 4.7 Estimated Yorkshire Forward RDA programme budget 1998/99-2001/02 (millions)

Programme	98/99	99/00	00/01	01/02
SRB 1-4	79.0	89.0	79.0	59.0
SRB 5	-	11.0	34.0	63.0
RDC	2.5	2.8	2.8	2.8
EP	62.0	70.0	70.0	70.0
YHDA	2.4	2.5	2.5	2.5
TOTAL	146.0	175.0	189.0	197.0

Source: Government Office for Yorkshire and the Humber (1998).

and draft Single Programming Documents (SPDs) for the new Objective 1 and 2 areas are in the process of being finalised with the European Commission (EC), joining up the two processes of urban and European priorities can be difficult (see, for example, EC, 2000).

Directorate General (DG) Regio has announced that it wishes to see its new SPDs for European Objective 1 and 2 areas dovetailed into the new Regional Economic Strategy. The RDA and GOR have concentrated on seeking this type of joined-up policy and programming across the EU, UK and the new regional priorities. This will require critical decisions within the RDA in terms of achieving single planning horizons between EU and UK programmes. One of the difficulties here is that DTI European Secretariats are still to reside in GORs, not in the RDAs. This places a premium on effective collaboration between the two organisations at regional level.

Needs vs. Competitiveness

The RDAs will need to consider the balance of their work programmes in terms of community needs vs. inward investment and competitiveness agendas, and the relative weight which should be given to each of these priorities. While policies can be devised that both meet needs and raise competitiveness, in practice these policies often conflict. The needs agenda has to focus on community economic capacity-building, social inclusion and skills training. The competitiveness agenda needs to focus on technologies, and sectoral and world-class attainment. The RDA board needs to focus its debate on the search for 'value-added' additionality, which it can bring to both agendas in the region. Too many people in these two worlds still fail to see the interconnections between needs and competitiveness and the RDAs will be required to address this issue.

Rural vs. Urban

It is easy to see why the rural areas fear domination by urban actors and by urban deprivation in the regional economic development process. The new framework for European Structural Funds, however, will demand a new urban and rural plan for the region which rests inside the Regional Economic Strategy. Ensuring that rural and seaside regeneration priorities are recognised alongside the urban agenda must be a key RDA priority. Rural priorities, however, are of a different scale, and the RDA must deliver to both constituencies. Many rural regeneration issues require a wholly different approach to the competitiveness agenda.

Social Exclusion

Social exclusion is very much a strategic issue, after years of being virtually outlawed from official policy documents by previous governments. It is valuable to distinguish between poverty and social exclusion. Poverty exists in the short term, where we are unable to meet our basic survival needs. Social exclusion is a more long-term manifestation of social marginalisation, reflected in low incomes, inability to meet long-term survival needs, exclusion from participating in the mainstream economy because of a series of social and economic barriers, and an effective sidelining in the decision-making processes which affect people's everyday lives, including disengagement from local democratic processes. The RDA needs to consider its social exclusion approach in relation to its broader economic strategy. This requires a much bigger focus on social enterprise, community development and the third sector than many are prepared for. It is perhaps in this arena where RDAs could learn much from experience of urban regeneration in the United States (Shutt, 2000).

Reconciling Needs and Competitiveness: Economic Tiers

The RES process shows that it is easy for a RDA to get carried away with the rhetoric of competitive advantage and wealth creation. But it is only part of the story. Considerable work by the EU and the Organisation for Economic Co-operation (OECD) in recent years has sought to reconcile wealth creation and attempts to tackle social exclusion. Particularly influential is work which identifies three tiers in any national/regional economy. The first tier is a broad subsistence economy of self-help, reciprocal exchange and so on, which is often how many people still cope with domestic matters, such as cleaning and decorating, care of dependants and so on; also important here are credit unions, community trusts and enterprises, LETS (local and exchange trading systems) and so on. The second tier is the regional/local economy of interacting small and medium-sized businesses, providing largely for regional or national needs, and including complex local purchasing networks. At the top, there is a third tier of engagement with the international economy and key multinational enterprises and large companies.

By and large, policy has tended to focus on the politically visible 'big hits' to be got from focusing on the international trading sector. But in practice, attending to the other two tiers is equally important if we are to address social exclusion in the regions (DETR, 1998a). Aiming for reduced economic leakage of business and consumer spending, in order to move towards greater self-reliance, helps local businesses to survive and ride out troughs in the national and international economies. Similarly, trickle-down has not yet been proven to work. If we want to assist the socially excluded, then we need to address these issues directly, working with all tiers of the regional economy, not just the top.

In terms of promoting the social economy, the European Commission identified 19 'fields' in which it believed the potential existed to create new jobs, which could then be matched to the potentially available labour supply. These fields are: home-help services, childcare, new information and ICTs, assistance for young people facing difficulties, housing improvements, security, local public transport, revitalisation of urban public areas, local shops, tourism, audio-visual services, cultural heritage, local cultural development, waste management, water services, protection and conservation of natural areas, control of pollution, energy and sport. In establishing these fields, the EC committed itself to exploring new and radical ways of matching labour supply and demand at the local level, including supporting a new range of local players capable of acting as identifiers of unmet needs, as social entrepreneurs and as intermediaries advising in the job-placement process. The RDAs will need to examine these kinds of strategies, as well as the conventional attachment to property and inward investment and key sector policies; however, their capacity to do this remains unproven.

Integrating Economic Development, Transport and Environmental Planning

It is difficult to achieve a 'holistic' view when in each of these major areas of policy there has been too little regional practice. A new transport and planning strategy is to be prepared, following further DETR strategic planning guidance in 1999 (DETR, 1999b; 1999c). RDAs will not themselves have responsibility for strategic policy on land use and related planning matters at a regional level. They will, however, need to build effective working relationships with a host of central government and external agencies to effectively carry through a Regional Economic Strategy within the changing regional context. This relationship with public and private transport authorities, the Highways Agency, Railtrack plc, Passenger Transport Authorities and the Environmental Agency will be critical to enable the RDA to effectively contribute to these priorities. The RDA needs to be able to deal with the tensions and contradictions between these policy areas and to focus efforts on joined-up thinking. It is here that the Cabinet Office Performance and Innovation Unit and Cabinet Offices in the Regions need to steer the policy-making process into joined-up regional frameworks, rather than mirror central government departmental priorities.

With the entry of the Ministry of Agriculture, Fisheries and Food (MAFF), Home Office, and the Department of Culture, Media and Sport (DCMS) into the Government Office system, GORs will be able to represent a broader range of government agencies. Their role is changing from directly delivering services to becoming a contracting house for the wider regional planning and strategy development process. This can be a positive step.

Regional Planning Forum and Regional Planning Strategies

Joint working between the RDAs and Regional Planning Conferences (RPCs) of the assemblies and local authorities is thus envisaged, assisted not just by their common interest in economic regeneration, but also by the proposed directives on the RDAs, to have regard to sustainable development and improve the environment of their regions. In Yorkshire, the Regional Planning Forum has now been incorporated within the regional assembly. The evolving process of regional planning has been the subject of government consultation documents (DETR, 1999d; 1999e). *The Future of Regional Planning Guidance* was followed by *Planning for* the *Communities of the Future*, addressing the key issues of sustainable development and the need to move away from the 'predict and provide' approach to housing land identification. In February 1999, the draft Planning Policy Guidance Note 11 (PPG11) proposed a more **inclusive** process and that Regional Planning Guidance should provide the major regional spatial guidance to **all** regional strategies, not just to development plans.

Draft Regional Planning Guidance will be prepared by the RPCs (Table 4.8), and following wide public consultation and an examination in public, the Secretary of State will approve and publish a draft RPG for Yorkshire and the Humber in June 2000.

The Regional Planning Forum has an executive comprising two elected representatives per county area. It has a co-ordinating group of officers preparing the RPG.

The Government Office for Yorkshire and the Humber (GOYH) played a significant role in getting the joint sustainability appraisal of Regional Planning Guidance and the Regional Economic Strategy off the ground and has helped the Regional Planning Forum to evolve.

Table 4.8   Regional Planning Guidance June 1999

Region	Current RPG		Revised guidance issued (expected)
East Anglia	RPG 6	Jul 91	Early 2000
East Midlands	RPG 8	Mar 94	End 2000
London	RPG3	May 96	Awaits new Mayor of London – post-2000
Northern	RPG7	Sept 93	End 2000
North West	RPG13	May 96	Spring 2001
South East	RPG 9	Mar 94	Dec 1999
South West	RPG10	Jul 94	End 2000
West Midlands	RPG11	Sept 95	Summer 2002
Yorkshire and Humber	RPG12	Mar 96	End 2000

Regional Partnerships

The RDAs as NDPBs will be accountable to ministers for their policies, and through ministers to Parliament. The government has stated that it wants:

- RDAs to take the lead in developing and promoting public/private partnerships in the regions;
- RDAs to work closely with Government Offices for the Regions; GORs

will be key partners of RDAs – for example, in relation to planning and housing policies in the regions, and in relation to European policies and the regional Skills Action Plan and regional Trade Strategy.

It is extremely important that the Regional Economic Strategy, the Regional Transport Strategy and the Regional Planning Guidance fit together in each region.

It is also particularly important in these areas of activity that the RDA thinks through its strategic context in relation to other regions. One of the greatest difficulties of the new Regional Economic Strategies is that they have been prepared in advance in the absence of agreement on the new RPG and transport strategy frameworks.

Transport and Economic Development

The need for a new regional transport policy has already been recognised by the government and local authorities. The consultative paper, *Developing an Integrated Transport Policy,* published in August 1997, emphasised the need for major developments to take place in locations and ways which facilitate and encourage public transport rather than use of the car (DETR, 1997b). It also referred to the need to generate more strategic thinking about the transport effects of urban economic development and rural development policies within regions.

The Regional Transport Strategies will begin the process of establishing public transport priorities for the regions in the 21st century. In Yorkshire, the process is being financed by the regional assembly, GOYH and the Highways Agency. Once projects, priorities and a programme are agreed, then the RDA will be in a position to assess its own transport project investment priorities, and will be able to have a dialogue with the strategic actors in the region.

In May 1997, the government began a review of railway regulation and the proposed aims and detailed responsibilities of the Strategic Rail Authority (SRA). The SRA will lead and provide a clear strategic direction for rail transport in Britain, co-ordinating investment, integration and railfreight plans. The RDA will need to monitor developments in the SRA proposals and work closely with Railtrack on regional investment priorities of common strategic interest, including the practical issues of railfreight and railway modernisation.

There are clear gaps in the regional rail system. It will be important to examine improved provision of local stops to encourage rail commuting, in support of the broader regional requirements to alleviate congestion problems and contribute to the goals of sustainable development. Again the signs are that the RES process has so far failed to grapple with the complexities of transport policy and integration. Further work is required to ensure that a range of regional initiatives and investment programmes are adequately pulled together.

Sustainable Development

One of the five core objectives of the RDA is to have regard to promoting sustainable development in its activities. This is significant. At one level, the tone of the statement is that of 'having regard to', rather than being 'required to'; as such, the RDA can opt to treat it as a secondary concern. This would be unwise. All RDAs will find themselves subject to considerable scrutiny by pressure groups on their environmental performance, not simply in-house, but also on how their activities contribute to sustainable development on the regional and global scales. Equally important, there is a growing market for environmentally sensitive products and services, both within the regions and globally. Being a laggard rather than a leader in this field would ultimately increase regional spending leakage and weaken the regional economy.

There is an administrative and strategic imperative here, given the differing backgrounds of the RDA's inherited staff and the new board. It can be expected that awareness of sustainable development will be uneven, and a substantial education programme may be required for the RDAs, so that staff in particular are alert to the imperatives surrounding sustainable development. Key issues will include the re-use of brownfield sites, siting major employment generating activities close to good public transport links, the move within planning to promote mixed-use development, improved water conservation and re-use, and the energy efficiency gains to be had from improved building design, layout and use of building materials. Similarly, it will be important to be aware of good practice initiatives in terms of working with employers to reduce their waste production, find alternative uses for waste products (including recycling and repair) and ensure safe disposal. A particular issue will be to reduce pollution not only within the region, but also thinking more globally in terms of, for instance, acid deposition problems elsewhere in Europe and the post-Rio and Kyoto summit national government commitments to reduce greenhouse gas emissions. Reduced (air, land, water, noise) pollution can contribute to the broader goal of improving regional quality of life, which in turn can help to promote economic development in the region. The essential point is that sustainable development should be integral to the RDA's approach, not an add-on.

Evaluation

How the RDA chooses to evaluate itself will be critical. Experience shows that all too often performance indicators drive programmes and projects, often in undesirable directions. Choose tedious, conformist indicators and the RDA will nurture another generation of conformist slavish programmes and managers. If something more radical and innovative is called for, then evaluation and monitoring criteria also need to reflect this. The experience with EU-funded programmes for community economic development reflects this problem: the selection of conventional output measures allowed these innovative programmes to be initially subverted by mainstream players able to offer 'standard' products, which hit the stated targets, rather than the desired innovative projects. The EU commissioned another special study to push people towards greater innovation, including a wider range of evaluation criteria (Lloyd et al, 1996). The key point is that the selected criteria will need to be broad in scope, covering economic, social and environmental concerns, as well as clearly focused and targeted. The classic SMEs supported output measure, for instance, is now notoriously ineffective for a knowledge economy, which might require output measures such as anything from a two-minute phone call, to a two months' supportive engagement. RDA indicators focusing solely on job-creation targets and gross domestic product (GDP) per head are also inadequate for the task ahead.

Conclusions

The establishment of the English RDAs has been generally welcomed by academics and policy-makers (e.g. Jukes, 1998; Dungey and Newman, 1999), but there is considerable speculation as to whether the arrangements will endure or turn into 'fragmented temporary arrangements or a series of experiments' (Roberts, 1999). Mawson (1997) criticises the RDA legislation as a missed opportunity, and many others hope that the RDAs are not just an economic departure but a first step on the road to further regional government for the English regions (e.g. CLES, 1997). There is some anxiety that the break in the Prescott-Caborn axis in the summer of 1999 weakened the voices in the Labour

Cabinet arguing for further democratic decentralisation legislation for the English regions. However, events throughout 1999 with regard to the Welsh, Scottish and Greater London Assemblies kept the regional agenda in focus.

Others argue that two of the key building blocks for developing regional government are now in place, with the Regional Development Agencies delivered by ministers and approval now in place for all eight regional chambers, with the RDAs required to consult them on strategy and account for their work. Now the Cabinet Office is turning its attention to joined-up programming by central government departments. In the regions, partners and organisations are keen to see the RDAs begin to deliver on the promise of a new approach to regional regeneration. The campaigners in the regional assemblies and chambers often argue that the shift towards further devolution is inevitable and will remain a key priority for a second-term Labour government. Whether or not a commitment to English regional government will be made depends on a complex interplay of forces inside and outside the Parliamentary Labour Party, and also on the experience of the Scottish Parliament, Welsh Assembly and Greater London Assembly. The difficulty now in England is how to manage the new regional arrangements in ways which strengthen the case for regional devolution, and how to handle the process leading to referendums on elected regional government. As Groom (1999) observed, the establishment of the RDAs 'marks the start of the process by which England will determine its future governance. No one, including the government, knows where it will end'.

The RDAs themselves have the opportunity to take regional economic development further and move regionalism forward in a positive and dynamic way. However, further attention is now required to equip them with the appropriate resources to develop the new Regional Economic Strategies and focus their regional and sub-regional priorities. The regional assembly and regional chamber in each region need to make the case more clearly for regional devolution and undertake further work on regional financing and structures.

In the UK for the past 20 years we have been dominated in our approach to the regional agenda by a focus on institutional structures and power devolution and the quest for European funding. We are now moving into a new regional building 'era' which demands a new focus. What is now required is the building of regional research and intelligence capabilities, business development for the knowledge industries, strategic public-private partnerships and alliances, and new skills and training for the second phase of the information revolution. The RDAs need to encourage the partners in each region in their quest to create transitional learning regions for the 21st century, but must be prepared to commit to being genuine learning RDAs, prepared to experiment and debate, and not afraid to take risks.

One way RDAs will be judged is through the added value that their interventions bring and their reactions to working through the range of 'wicked issues' which successive governments have found it so difficult to address.

References

Cabinet Office (2000), *Reaching Out: The Role of Central Government at Regional and Local Level*, Performance and Innovation Unit, HMSO, London.

Centre for Local Economic Strategies (CLES) (1997), 'RDAs: The First Step to Devolution?', *Local Work*, No. 2, December.

Centre for Local Economic Strategies (CLES) (1999), *Strategies for Success? A First Assessment of Regional Development Agencies' Draft Regional Economic Strategies*, Research Paper No. 1, CLES, Manchester.

Department of the Environment, Transport and the Regions (1997a), *Building Partnerships for Prosperity*, DETR, London.

Department of the Environment, Transport and the Regions (1997b), *Developing an Integrated Transport Policy*, DETR, London.

Department of the Environment, Transport and the Regions (1998a), *Community-Based Regeneration Initiatives: A Working Paper*, DETR, London.

Department of the Environment, Transport and the Regions (1998b), *RDA Guidance*, DETR, London.

Department of the Environment, Transport and the Regions (1998c), *Planning for the Communities of the Future*, DETR, London.

Department of the Environment, Transport and the Regions (1999a), *DETR Annual Report 1999*, DETR, London.

Department of the Environment, Transport and the Regions (1999b), *Guidance to RDAs on Regional Strategies*, DETR, London.

Department of the Environment, Transport and the Regions (1999c), *Supplementary Guidance to RDAs*, DETR, London.

Department of the Environment, Transport and the Regions (1999d), *The Future of Regional Planning Guidance*, DETR, London.

Department of the Environment, Transport and the Regions (1999e), *Towards an Urban Renaissance: The Report of the Urban Task Force*, Chaired by Lord Rodgers of Riverside, DETR, London.

Department of the Environment, Transport and the Regions (2000), *Response to Regional Strategies*, DETR, London.

Dungey, J. and Newman, I. (1999), *The New Regional Agenda*, A joint publication of the Local Government Information Unit and the South East Economic Development Strategy.

European Commission (1997), *Community Economic Development*, EC, Brussels.

European Commission (2000), *European Community Structural Funds, South Yorkshire. Single Programming Document for Objective 2000-2006*, European Commission's response to the plan submitted by the UK Government and the South Yorkshire Partnership. EC, Brussels.

ERBEDU (1999), *The State of the Region,* Report prepared for Yorkshire and the Humber Regional Development Agency, Leeds Business School, Leeds Metropolitan University, Leeds.

Government Office for Yorkshire and the Humber (1998), *RDA Integration Plan*, GOYH, Leeds.

Groom, B. (1999), *Financial Times*, March 31ˢᵗ, London.

Jukes, P. (ed) (1998), *21st Century Regions*, ERA, London.

Lloyd, P. et al (1996), *Social and Economic Exclusion through Regional Development: the Community Economic Development Priority in European Structural Funds Programmes in Britain*, EC, Brussels.

Mawson, J. (1997), 'New Labour and the English Regions: A Missed Opportunity', *Local Economy*, vol. 12, no. 3, pp. 194-202.

Roberts, P. (1999), *From Here to Eternity: Future Prospects for the RDAs and Regional Governance*, paper presented at the Annual Conference of the Regional Studies Association, London, November.

Robson, B. et al (2000*), RDAs and Local Regeneration,* Final Report to the Joseph Rowntree Foundation, draft, York.

SEEDA (1999), *Building a World Class Region: an Economic Strategy for the South East of England*, SEEDA, Guildford.

Shutt, J. (2000), 'Lessons from America in the 1990s', in P. Roberts and H. Sykes, *Urban Regeneration: A Handbook*, British Urban Regeneration Association, Sage Publications Ltd, London.

Yorkshire Forward (1999), *The Regional Economic Strategy for Yorkshire and the Humber 2000-2010; Advancing Together Towards a World Class Economy*, Yorkshire Forward, Leeds.

5 Regional Development Agencies: The Experience of Wales

PHILIP BOLAND AND JOHN LOVERING

Introduction

While RDAs are new in England, they are not so new elsewhere in the United Kingdom. Along with Scotland, Wales has had a regional development agency for almost a quarter of a century. In this chapter we discuss some aspects of the relationship between the Welsh Development Agency and economic development in Wales.

Anyone familiar with Wales will be aware that economic development in the final decades of the 20th century failed to restore the levels of relative prosperity which it enjoyed in earlier periods. Most economic indicators show it to be close to, or below, the least advantaged English regions, notably in terms of per capita income and R&D spending. In some aspects – such as the regional wages league, male employment rates, or many aspects of poverty – Wales is now worse off than it was when the WDA was created. Only if attention is narrowed onto certain indicators of manufacturing performance does Wales rise towards the higher end of regional rankings. Prima facie, therefore, it would seem that the Welsh Development Agency's contribution to the economic welfare of the people of Wales has been modest at best.

This observation would be uncontentious were it not for the fact that for many years there has been a sustained effort to suggest that Wales is in fact undergoing some kind of economic renaissance, and that the WDA has been the main instrument bringing this about. This notion has been espoused by successive secretaries of state since the 1970s, but in recent years it has been echoed by various actors and organisations which have made it their business to boost the image of Wales – such as the Institute of Welsh Affairs (part-funded by the WDA), certain academics and numerous journalists. In the late 1990s, the idea that Wales is on an upswing became virtually a new orthodoxy, fuelled by the success of some Welsh pop groups and film stars ('Cool Cymru'), the visible transformation of once-blighted areas such as Cardiff Bay, and perhaps above all by the creation of the first elected national body, the National Assembly for Wales. Symptomising the new mood among the more affluent groups, a society for expatriate Welsh in London was founded known as SWS – Successful Welsh and Sexy ('sws' also means 'kiss' in Welsh).

Whatever the validity of the claim that a new zeitgeist has transformed the cultural milieu, there is precious little evidence of a general economic improvement. Wales remains relatively short of jobs, and many of the existing jobs are poorly paid. Cardiff and the Vale of Glamorgan (and much of the rural border with England) enjoy incomes on a par with the most affluent English counties, but the much larger population of the Valleys is poorer than any but the least advantaged London borough. Wales entered the new century by applying for Objective 1 funding from Europe. While this primarily reflected the success of the Blair government in arguing for a greater UK share of European spending, the bid also meant that Welsh public authorities and even the WDA at last acknowledged the parlous state of much of the Welsh economy.

There is a striking contrast between the glossy image of Wales painted by years of marketing publicity, and the reality exposed by more robust indicators. In this chapter we do not attempt to present a comprehensive evaluation of the work of the Welsh Development Agency (such a study needs to be done, but has yet to be attempted). Our starting point is this gulf between the world as portrayed by the Agency, and the detectable reality. Of course, many of the schemes in which the WDA has been involved have been very useful within their remits, and the majority of WDA staff have worked hard to improve Welsh economic life. But the nagging contrast between image and reality suggests that, nevertheless, something has gone wrong. The conclusion we draw is that the case of Wales shows how the presence of a powerful regional development agency can seriously affect the ways in which decision makers – and even the electorate – perceive the regional economy and the policies which are required to improve it. The Welsh case also shows that this influence is not likely to be benign if the perceptions so engendered are geared to the imperatives arising from the realpolitik of WDA survival rather than to questions of regional economic welfare as an economist would understand them.

The vicissitudes of the WDA should be of interest to those concerned with the new RDAs in England, for these are all following the 'Welsh model' in some important and crucial respects. The Labour government's former Minister for the Regions, Richard Caborn, had stated explicitly that the Welsh Development Agency represented a 'good model for the English RDAs'

(Murphy and Caborn, 1996; Lovering, 1999a). The implication of this chapter is that there is a very real danger that the English regions may find themselves emulating the experience of Wales in ways that are neither sensible nor desirable.

The Context of Welsh Regional Development

The origins of the Welsh experience with a regional development organisation lie in local and extra-local responses to the impact of successive cycles of economic decline and growth since the 1930s. In the late 1930s, Wales, along with the North East, was the first part of the UK to experiment with industrial estate development intended to attract mobile firms. In the era of sustained economic buoyancy and income growth which got underway after the late 1940s, Wales was targeted by a number of 'regional policy measures' which had tangible effects (Humphrys, 1977; Morgan, 1982). In the context of high levels of employment and growth at home and expanding markets abroad, firms increased output and employment, and some were susceptible to incentives to relocate to Wales. Some of the most prominent foreign-owned companies in Wales today arrived in this period. At the same time, the public sector expanded and created new fields of 'quality' employment, with disproportionate impact in Wales, creating a new underpinning for Welsh standards of living. Throughout the 'Keynesian' era, incomes in Wales, as in the rest of the UK, grew and became less unequally distributed. Unemployment fell to historically unprecedented levels, social welfare provision expanded, and the quality of life for virtually all categories of society improved. This period often referred to as the 'Golden Age of Capitalism' is beyond the working experience of anyone under 40. It was followed from the mid-1970s by a long-term decline in rates of growth which eventually gave rise to a reversion to the economic ideas of the pre-Keynesian period, along with a more general resurgence of conservative ideas and attitudes. National economic management became premised on the idea that it is more important, and feasible, to maximise competition and control inflation than to seek to achieve what has traditionally been conceived as full employment. This did not involve the so-called rolling back of the state so much as its reorientation, changing the forms of support for preferred industries and activities, rather than simply abandoning such support. Academically, these changes were legitimised by the 'neo-classical revival' (a textbook simplification which does an injustice to the sophistication of proper neo-classical economics – see Krugman, 1996).

This policy shift was initially accompanied by a dramatic (and economically unnecessary) collapse in UK manufacturing employment and the demise of many companies. In the 1990s, this was followed by accelerating economic 'globalisation', based primarily on an agreement among major governments to allow almost untrammelled freedom for finance to flow across national (and of course regional) borders. Globalisation has been premised on governmental policies which target the maintenance of the high value and international freedom of movement of financial assets, rather than high levels of employment of reasonable quality (Shutt, 1998). The corollary of these within the nation has been the re-engineering of social and spatial policies to allow or even encourage a polarisation of economic life. The 'winners' in this new (but actually rather old) order – both companies and employees – are doing very well, but the 'losers' fare worse than during the 'Golden Age' (Byrne, 1999). Winners and losers alike also find their economic lives framed by a new pervasive sense of economic insecurity (Elliott and Atkinson, 1998).

In the mid-1990s, parties from the social-democratic tradition came to power in Britain, France and Germany. This has ushered in a new chapter, replacing the crude free-market ideologies of the 1980s with the softer discourse of the 'Third Way', indicating a supposedly new compromise between the interventionist and free-market ideological positions (Giddens, 1998). In practice, this represents not a break with the globalisation-oriented strategies which became the orthodoxy in the late 1980s and early 1990s, so much as a more consistent emphasis on them through the addition of a more 'developmental' aspect to industrial and labour-market strategies (Coates, 2000). This is most evident in the ubiquitous emphasis on innovation as a key goal of industrial policy at national and regional levels, and the construction of a new apparatus of social engineering to manage the effects of job shortages (Lovering, 1998). By the end of the 1990s, the rhetorical cornerstone of UK domestic economic strategy, including regional policies, had become the promotion of a so-called 'knowledge-based' economy (Cooke and Morgan, 1998). This was rationalised by the idea that advanced northern hemisphere countries will be able to compete successfully against countries with cheaper workforces only if they continually introduce new products and services and develop non-transferable expertise in innovation. Although the validity of this doctrine is extremely questionable, its advocates have risen to the ascendancy with the advent of 'Third Way' governments in the late 1990s (for a breezy journalistic summary of the new orthodoxy see Leadbeater, 1999; for the key 'how-to' text see Porter, 1990; for the political-economic foundations of the influence of these ideas see Balanya et al, 2000).

Each of these phases of economic policy and rhetoric left its mark on the Welsh Development Agency, the focus of economic strategy design and delivery in the Principality.

The Welsh Development Agency: From a 'Keynesian' Instrument of Redistribution to a Promoter of Globalisation

The gradual construction of a dedicated apparatus of economic governance for Wales was one of the unanticipated consequences of the era of active UK regional policy that endured from the 1940s to the 1970s (Morgan, 1982; Jones, 1997). In 1954, Cardiff was designated capital of Wales. A few years later the Council of Wales was established, followed in 1960 by the Welsh Grand Committee. Immediately after winning the landslide 1964 general election, the Labour Party headed by Harold Wilson created the post of Secretary of State for Wales, along with the Economic Planning Council for Wales and the Welsh Office (to which responsibility for implementing housing, local government and transport policy was delegated). In 1968, the Rural Wales Development Corporation was set up. In 1976, the next Labour government under James Callaghan (a definitive product of the Labour Party in South Wales) added to this list the Welsh Development Agency. The WDA was originally to be linked to the National Enterprise Board (NEB) in a national strategy for industrial regeneration, but in the event the NEB did not materialise as originally envisaged, and the WDA was left without a UK-wide strategic economic planning context. It began to develop its own ways to survive. The WDA was thus born at the tail end of the Keynesian era, reached puberty and learned how to look after itself in the era of Thatcherite free-marketism, and entered full adulthood in the age of globalisation and the 'Third Way' doctrine of salvation through innovation and the knowledge economy. The WDA is one of the largest and most experienced regional development agencies in the EU today. But it has changed chameleon-like through its history, and is evolving still.

In the 1970s, the work of the WDA, which was focused on factory and infrastructure building, was rationalised in terms of the Keynesian-Myrdalian conception that counter-balancing the uneven regional effects of national economic development through geographical resource transfers would be beneficial not only for the recipient regions, but also for the wider national economy (McCrone, 1969). Companies were encouraged to consider relocating in Wales because this would not only benefit Welsh job seekers, it would also help to reduce overheating in the English regions (to this extent the Agency reflected the lessons identified decades earlier by the 1940 Barlow Report into the inter-war regional problems of the UK). Relocations would typically involve an engineering company moving from an area such as the West Midlands to one of the development sites lying close to the A5, A55, or (from the late 1960s) the M4, or around Newtown (just inside the Welsh border). The main weakness of this policy was that it tended to deliver public resources to footloose firms, without securing a lasting improvement in the host area. Critics at the time were inclined to regard many of the firms so attracted as 'cowboys', and the WDA was sometimes dubbed by its Welsh critics the 'West Midlands Development Agency'.

In the 1980s, the emphasis shifted at first to site clearing, with the WDA finding a new role in removing the signs of de-industrialisation, and turning itself in effect into an estate agent (which helped to compensate for reduced central government funding). It is largely thanks to the WDA that the visible signs of the once-huge Welsh coal industry have been almost entirely eradicated – 600 pits have disappeared. In this respect South Wales is very different from, for example, the Ruhr coal belt. In the latter, many coal mines and steel factories have been converted to other uses, including business development units and social facilities, such as music venues or community arts centres. The removal of visible signs of the industries upon which the Welsh economy was founded and which shaped Welsh political and cultural life, was not only a major piece of restructuring of the built environment. It was also a remarkable cultural-political intervention.

The WDA Discovers a New Role Promoting Inward Investment

Since the mid-1980s, the most widely recognised activity of the Agency has been place marketing, mainly oriented to the promotion of foreign direct investment (FDI). During the Thatcher years this reorientation was attractive not only to the economic policymakers in Cardiff, but also to those in Whitehall. A Conservative Party political broadcast in the run-up to the 1987 general election featured a video-game-style journey along the M4, highlighting the glossy and glamorous new industries which had come into South Wales as a result of the arrival of multinational companies from the US, Germany and Japan. By seizing upon the economic fashions popular in Whitehall, the Agency found itself a new lease of life, and made the most of it. The resulting publicity persuaded numerous observers in the UK, and indeed beyond, that Wales has been remarkably successful in attracting inward investment, and moreover that this has turned the regional economy around (e.g. Alden, 1996; Price et al, 1993; Institute of Welsh Affairs (IWA), 1993).

In fact the achievements of the Agency in attracting inward investment have been generally exaggerated, and FDI has not had the transformative effect on the Welsh economy that many have claimed. These myths reflect the lavish public relations efforts of the WDA itself, decades of tendentious speeches by politicians of both Conservative and Labour persuasion, envious comments by business people, journalists and politicians in English regions – notably the South West – and superficial consultancy and academic analysis. But they do contain a small germ of truth. Throughout the 1980s and 1990s, Wales became in effect the leading site for the British government's experiment in economic 'globalisation', through the promotion of inward investment by multinational companies (Hill and Munday, 1994; Mainwaring, 1997; Lovering, 1998).

By the 1990s, the era in which the WDA functioned as a traditional development agency, redistributing resources from richer parts of the UK, was long past (except for subsidies to inward investors). The emphasis on inward investment began to reach ludicrous levels. The WDA drew adverse publicity when the BBC discovered that its staff had approached the manufacturers of Cornish Clotted Cream and the inward investment agency for North West England with offers to help them move to Wales. It was successful in luring other companies from English regions – such as the firm Fenner, which moved from its long-established location in Hull to Maerdy at UK taxpayers' expense. But these questionable adventures have consistently received much less attention than the Agency's successes in attracting overseas firms. These peaked with the arrival of the South Korean computer company Lucky Goldstar (LG), on a huge site just west of Newport in 1996. The LG case pitched Wales in a head-to-head battle with Scotland to offer more attractive inducements. The huge subsidy offered, publicly acknowledged as £247 million but privately said to be very much higher, was cranked up by well-known consultancies hired by the company to play off Wales against Scotland. The competition reached preposterous proportions with both Secretaries of State jetting out to Korea to promote the economic advantages of their location vis-à-vis their UK 'competitor'. Quite properly, William Waldegrave, then Conservative Minister for Industry, reacted by demanding greater Treasury control over competition between UK development agencies. His initiative was later consolidated following the Labour victory of 1997 and Gordon Brown's arrival at the Treasury.

The LG case became a turning point because it failed to deliver. Despite promises of huge subsidy in cash and kind, the ripping-up of existing environmental protection at the site (leading to the destruction of environmentally sensitive grasslands), the re-drafting of local development plans (Phelps and Tewdwr-Jones, 1998), and a welter of hype in the Welsh and UK media, the LG project failed to create a fraction of the jobs promised. In 1996, the WDA chief executive, Barry Hartop, together with Secretary of State William Hague, declared on BBC TV's six o'clock news that in all 'up to 26,000 jobs would be generated'. Five years later (by which time both Hartop and Hague had long since moved to jobs outside Wales), the total employment created was almost exactly one-tenth of this figure, with little likelihood of a major increase to come. The largest of the new factories had been mothballed, making it probably the most expensive and largest building in Europe to have been built to do little else than contain empty space.

The spectacular failure of the LG (now Hyundai) project marked the end of a chapter in the WDA story. Inward investment can no longer be portrayed as the 'magic bullet', which will cure Wales of its economic ills. At the same time, the arrival of devolution has raised the competitive stakes – other UK regions are now better organised to fight for inward investment (as other chapters in this book show). Welsh access to funds contributed by English taxpayers is less easy than in the past. Devolution has also officially transformed the policymaking context in Wales within which the WDA operates.

The Welsh Chameleon: Devolution and Another Makeover for the WDA

With these developments forthcoming, the Agency began to change its self-publicity. Attempts to attract new inward investment were downplayed and efforts to make the most of the investment that had already arrived were played up (Phelps et al, 1998). At the same time, New Labour set out its plans to expand the size and scope of the Agency (Welsh Office, 1998). In early 1999, these plans were implemented, turning what was already a large quango into an even larger one. The WDA added to its portfolio the work of the Land Authority for Wales, and the Development Board for Rural Wales. The new body was initially to have been named the 'Economic Powerhouse for Wales', but in a rare outbreak of humility wiser counsel prevailed.

Befitting its new official position as the sole public organiser of economic life in Wales, the Agency repositioned itself as more than merely a technical economic actor. Borrowing once again from influential academic and quasi-academic theories of economic development, the WDA once again redefined its mission. It now presents itself as the key instrument in a much-needed socio-cultural transformation of Wales geared to the imperatives of 'regional competitiveness' in a globalised world. To this end the new WDA claims to be beefing up its activities as regional 'animateur', and taking on more responsibility for the spread of entrepreneurship, even extending as far as the 'social economy'. The new emphasis on entrepreneurship in part reflects the popular belief that the Welsh stand out as lacking these skills but, like so much else in the field of economic development policy, it can be argued that this belief is based on a priori assumptions, rather than any rigorous comparative research. In the National Assembly for Wales' submission to the European Commission seeking Objective 1 funding, the new role of the WDA as overseer of economic development, with a wider socio-economic and even cultural role, was given central place (for a pertinent discussion of an English parallel see Jones and MacLeod, 1999).

The new era was christened with a new statement of WDA strategy produced by a new expert panel (WDA, 1999). The analysis revolves around the idea that its proper goal should be to promote the development in Wales of a 'knowledge economy'. The emphasis on inward investment is downplayed to give room for more policies to promote new businesses and assist existing industries, including for the first time parts of the food industry. Yet many observers believe that inward investment remains the 'jewel in the crown' (Morgan, 1998). The main change for the Agency consequent upon its expansion, and devolution, would therefore seem to be mainly at the level of the theoretical justification for its continued emphasis on globalisation and a wider conception of the realm of activities in which it should be able to intervene.

Much Ado About Rather Little: The Impact of Foreign Investment in Wales

At this point it is appropriate to look a little closer at the significance of inward investment in Wales. As noted earlier, many commentators have concluded that the influx of FDI has enabled Wales to transform itself, some seeing in this an evolution from a 'problem' to an 'economically powerful' region (Alden, 1996 p.155). Enthusiasts believe that Wales illustrates the regenerative properties of 'transplants' (a diseased body being revitalised by a graft from a healthier donor). But such views draw on rhetoric rather than research, generally failing to look beyond the headline figures produced by the public relations departments of the WDA or Welsh Office. Admittedly the figures are striking at first glance. According to the latest publicly available data, foreign-owned manufacturing plants in Wales accounted for some 75,500 jobs in 1998 (Digest of Welsh Statistics, 1999 p.180). Electronics companies accounted for a quarter of these, followed by automobile component firms. Employment in foreign-owned manufacturing companies rose by 13% during the 1980s, contrasting sharply with a 20% fall in the UK as a whole. FDI accounts for about a quarter of all employment in UK manufacturing, but in Wales it accounts for around a third (Hill and Munday, 1994).

Here as elsewhere the headlines can be a poor guide to the real story. The real contribution of FDI in Wales has been much less unique, and much less significant, than most observers have claimed. In the early 1990s, for example, the rise in jobs provided by FDI was greater in the North of England (Hudson, 1995). For all the attention lavished on new European, Japanese, Taiwanese and Korean arrivals, 45% of the jobs in foreign-owned manufacturing are in North American companies, many of which have been in Wales for decades. Three-quarters of employment is in plants employing more than 200 people and nearly half in firms employing over 500. Much has been made of the fact that little Wales with only 5% of the UK population has managed to attract 20% of all FDI coming into Britain. But the figures on which this ratio is based only take into account grant-aided inward investment, which falls some way short of the total (Gripaios, 1996). Wales' true share of the UK total of incoming investment is not known with any accuracy, but is likely to be much less impressive.

The prominence of FDI in Wales in image terms is out of proportion to its real economic significance. The increasing share of employment accounted for by foreign companies in the 1980s and 1990s was due more to the decline of employment in Welsh and UK-owned firms in Wales than to growth in the foreign-owned sector (Munday, 1995). And most of the recorded employment increase in the foreign-owned sector is not attributable to the creation of genuinely new jobs. Existing jobs have fallen into the FDI category as a result of acquisitions of firms already operating in Wales (as in Britain as a whole, acquisitions rather than new inward investment accounted for the major part of the increased number of jobs within the FDI sector in the 1990s) (Invest in Britain Bureau, 1995). The total increase in jobs in overseas-owned manufacturing plants in the last decade for which data are available (to the mid-1990s) was fewer than 22,000. Of these, just over 12,000 were due to new openings, just over 9,000 to expansions, and nearly 18,000 to acquisitions. In the meantime, 18,000 jobs were lost through divestment, closure or contraction.

One way to interpret the above is that, but for the acquisition of existing companies, the net increase in jobs would have been a mere 4,000. Over the same period, around 20 times as many jobs were created in the public sector (Lovering, 1999b), a fact entirely unnoticed by those who have preferred to focus on the private sector, inward investment and the Welsh 'manufacturing renaissance'. Strictly speaking therefore, the claim that FDI has made a major contribution to employment in Wales depends on the strong and entirely untested assumption that the jobs in the firms acquired would have been lost if those companies had not been taken over. In the absence of any proper research on this question, all that can be said with certainty is that FDI has not played a major role in creating jobs – but precisely how small remains to be calculated.

As for the longer-term impact of inward investment, it has been asserted that the development of industrial clusters around FDI plants in Wales has made an important contribution to indigenous business growth (Price et al, 1993; IWA, 1993; WDA, 1999). But again no systematic evidence has been produced to support this claim. Nor are there any solid data to confirm the success of attempts to encourage 'embedding' of inward investments. Strong opinions and policy prejudices have too often been formed on the basis of uncontextualised case studies or a priori theories (e.g. Huggins, 1997; Cooke, 1998). In sum, the 'static' impact of FDI has been modest and the claim that it is nevertheless having a major 'dynamic' impact via 'embedding' and the development of clusters is an expression of intentions or wishes rather than evidence. The detectable result of decades of inward investment in Wales has been the emergence of a set of influential companies in what are often effectively industrial enclaves (some of which include selected local suppliers) (Phelps, 1997; Phelps et al, 2000). The pockets of employment these have created are often important at the local level (they account for nearly 7,000 jobs in the Rhondda, Cynon and Taff valleys for example, almost as many around Wrexham, and nearly 7,500 around Bridgend). But they have not turned the foreign-owned manufacturing sector into a major source of new employment for Wales as a whole. Overall, less than 7% of Welsh employees work in foreign-owned manufacturing firms, and less than 2% work for one which arrived in the last decade.

Moreover, much of the employment in the FDI sector is low-pay and low-skill (Roberts, 1994). While some US and European companies pay above-average wage levels, Pacific-Asian companies have tended to pay below them (Hill and Munday, 1994). According to the personnel manager of one such plant – Panasonic – only 400 out of the 2,500 jobs it provided could be described as 'quality jobs' (Ipsen, 1997).

The idea that the Welsh economy has been turned around by WDA-induced FDI is not evidence-based. In sectors such as automobiles and electrical engineering, more jobs were created in the 15 years before 1980 (and before the dominant emphasis on FDI) than in the 15 years thereafter. FDI in Wales predominantly represents corporate responses to the availability of relatively low wages, low social and infrastructural costs, amenable industrial relations, subsidies, access to the EU market, and the advantages of a location where business is conducted in the English language. It is surely not entirely coincidental that the UK regions with the highest dependence on FDI (Wales, the North of England, Northern Ireland and Scotland) are also the regions with the lowest average wages, and the greatest ability to give grants. It could be argued that the prominence of foreign inward investment in Wales reflects the success of the WDA in selling Wales rather than developing it. The WDA's efforts to attract inward investment have had a bigger effect on the ownership of Welsh manufacturing than on the jobs it provides, and probably an even more exaggerated impact on perceptions.

Economic Governance in Wales: From an 'Unelected State' to an Elected Monolith

In governance terms, Wales was re-constructed in the 1980s as an 'unelected state', manifested in the presence of some 350 quangos (Morgan and Roberts, 1993). The dominant player in quangoland was, and continues to be, the WDA. Critics such as Morgan have concentrated on the inefficiencies and inequities which marred the WDA's public image in the early and mid-1990s. The appointment of staff was secretive, allegedly favouring 'jobs for the boys'. It was said that senior officials were appointed without being formally interviewed and with no references being sought. The media alleged that prostitutes had been paid for, to encourage potential inward investors. More certainly, there was a lack of effective strategic control of the Agency. A parliamentary inquiry into the WDA identified a 'lack of probity at the very top of the Agency' (cited in Morgan and Mungham, 2000, p.37). Critics saw the WDA in the mid-1990s as the apex of a wider problem in Wales – that the agencies populating quangoland were a law unto themselves.

However, evidence of petty corruption and inefficiency is not necessarily relevant to the question of the effectiveness or the strategic direction of the Agency. And while misdemeanours may have been not uncommon in the past, it is unlikely that they remain so now that the Agency has become more clearly accountable to public scrutiny and exposed to the 'modernising' mission of New Labour in Wales. The reasons why the WDA has been and continues to be associated with a rather monolithic top-down and industrially partisan approach to Welsh economic matters and a narrow intellectual formulation of the policy issues (albeit a formulation which has changed through the years) lie deeper – in the structural position of the Agency within the political economy of Wales and the UK. The main lesson of interest beyond Wales to be drawn from the history of the WDA is that the creation of a regional development agency – where not subject to an ongoing analytically searching scrutiny – is likely to elevate particular industrial (and thereby also social) interests above others. This is likely to be accompanied by intellectual distortions which obscure the reality of the regional economic problem, and thereby irrationally de-limit the range of policy options which are considered relevant to addressing it.

The above problems are inherent in the discourse of regional competitiveness – a concept which conceals more than it reveals since it strictly has no clear indisputable meaning (see Krugman, 1996; Lovering, 1995). In practice, therefore, to talk of regional competitiveness means to identify particular sectors and economic activities to be supported, while others are not. The real problems associated with the prominent role of the WDA – we would argue – will persist so long as the business of defining and implementing the discourse of economic development in Wales continues to be framed by the discourse of 'regional competitiveness' in the face of 'global economic pressures', and the formally responsible body (the National Assembly for Wales) fails to critically unpack these terms. Those who criticise the WDA for malpractice or inefficiency while at the same time insisting on the inescapability of the imperatives of globalisation-competitiveness sail close to self-contradiction. The WDA is the institutional expression in Wales of that ubiquitous but loaded couplet, and as such it is structurally prone to partisanship and undemocratic practice. The economic development committee of the elected Assembly, to which the Agency is notionally accountable, will be of little practical significance so long as the dominant ideas of what regional economic development entails remain unchallenged.

Indeed, devolution has if anything reinforced the doctrine of regional competitiveness and has thereby enhanced the hegemony of the WDA and the ideas associated with it. In debates within the economic development committee of the National Assembly, there has been little criticism of the Agency or its mission. Several individual Assembly members of various parties are highly critical of the Agency (some would even like to disband it) – and some of these critics are former WDA employees. Some have balked at the

Agency's proposals to lead the 'entrepreneurship' strategy under Objective 1. But the centrality of the Agency to Welsh economic development remains undented. In this context it is relevant to note two important Welsh specificities.

Firstly, the peculiarly fragmented nature of Welsh identity and the limited nature of the post-devolution system of economic governance helps to explain the inability of the Assembly to seriously get to grips with issues of regional economic development. Only a hopeless romantic could imagine that the Assembly represents the triumph of a new informed democracy in Wales. It must be remembered that only just over a quarter of the Welsh electorate actually voted for devolution (compared with three-quarters in Scotland (Mohan, 1999)). The devolution campaign in Wales – created late in the day in a top-down manner by the Labour Party, run by political affairs consultants, and focusing on media messages rather than popular engagement in strategic debate (Andrews, 1999; Woods, 2000) – conspicuously failed to stir hearts and minds (O'Leary, 1998). This was nowhere more strikingly so than in Cardiff – the one part of Wales which has unquestionably gained from devolution actually voted against it. Against this 'cultural' background, the inability of Assembly members to address fundamental economic questions is perhaps not surprising.

Secondly, it is not unimportant that the individual best equipped to tackle the WDA and give the new Assembly real leverage over it found himself sidelined soon after devolution took place. Ron Davies MP was the principal architect of the current form of devolution, and as an exceptionally experienced parliamentarian he dominated the Assembly's economic development committee's dealings with the WDA. But he placed himself beyond the political pale in the Labour Party when newspapers exposed his alleged sexual proclivities and he failed to turn widespread public sympathy in Wales to advantage. His much-publicised, ill-fated stroll on Clapham Common led him to be marginalised in the Labour Party, and the position of First Secretary of the new Assembly fell instead to Tony Blair's preferred candidate, Alun Michael. This aroused opposition in Wales, where Rhodri Morgan enjoyed a better media image and wider popular support. This unedifying story is relevant here because neither Michael nor Morgan identified himself with a distinct economic strategic agenda, and neither reached Davies's level of either economic competence or combativeness. Long before he assumed the leadership role on 15 February 2000, Rhodri Morgan had abandoned his formerly critical position towards the WDA.

That the National Assembly has been unable to engage with the fundamentals of the Welsh economy and think its way to new policy conclusions was vividly illustrated by the application for Objective 1 funding, the first major economic issue to be tackled following devolution. At the Berlin Euro Summit in March 1999, West Wales and the Valleys was allocated Objective 1 status, precipitating an application for over £2 billion in (matched) economic regeneration funding. The anticipated pot of money was viewed as something of a 'honeypot' to be divvied out among the big players. But the Objective 1 'debate' in Wales focused narrowly on the question of matched funding and the apparent reluctance of the London government to make any firm promises. Conspicuously lacking was any attempt in the Assembly or Wales more widely to engender a thorough – and public – debate over the economic and social strategies which should shape the uses made of any forthcoming funds. The priorities set out in the funding application were remarkably similar to those developed and implemented elsewhere, notably Merseyside, where such policies have not made any serious inroads on key economic indicators (Boland, 1999a; 1999b; 1999c; 2000). Replicating policies which have not impacted as intended elsewhere would not seem to be a promising starting point for Wales. But those policies dovetailed with the evolving agenda associated with the newly expanded WDA, with the endorsement of the Labour majority (and some members from other parties) in the National Assembly.

Taking the long-term view, if success is measured in terms of creating jobs and incomes for the people of Wales – its formal client group – the WDA has never been particularly successful, although it did do rather well in the 1970s (Herbert, 1995; Humphrys, 1977). But if success is measured in terms of the ability to adapt to a changing policy environment and build a supportive network of decision-makers, the Agency has been very successful indeed. And in terms of its impact on the dominant ideas about the Welsh economy and what to do about it, it has been enormously influential, both within Wales and beyond. Whatever the merits of its many worthy initiatives at the micro level, its influence on strategic thinking in Wales has not been entirely positive. The institutional momentum built up behind the WDA, and the wider analytical – one might perhaps more accurately say ideological – context within which regional economic development issues are constructed in Wales are such that devolution has had remarkably little influence, to date at least.

Regional Competitiveness, RDAs and Governance: The Wider Issues

The Keynesian-Myrdalian notion that regional policy should be about correcting employment imbalances within the various parts of the UK within an over-arching commitment to maximise the number of jobs available (McCrone, 1969) is now seen as archaic. In its place the idea has grown that regional measures should be one component in a wider strategy for reforming business and job-seeker behaviour geared to markets on the global level (Scott, 1999; Cooke and Morgan, 1999; for critiques see Lovering, 1999a; Keating, 1997; Jones and MacLeod, 1999). Regional economic development is now seen as properly taking its place alongside other measures intended to encourage the globalisation of business and a conducive restructuring of social and cultural life. As the UK government's 1998 White Paper on competitiveness put it, the regional dimension is an important element in 'the development of strategic long-term visions for competitiveness, especially through the development of clusters, networks and other partnerships' (DTI, 1998, p. 42).

This 'global' idea is readily accessible from the web sites of business gurus such as Michael Porter or consultancies such as McKinsey. It is easily tailored to local situations, and in Cardiff a small industry of consultancy has emerged specialising in extrapolations of this kind (e.g. WDA, 1999; Jones and Osmond, 1999; Cooke, 2000). But it is one thing to cut and trim a global intellectual product to fit local circumstances, and quite another to think originally and creatively about how to maximise economic welfare in a region or small country like Wales. The story of the WDA shows time and again how much easier it is to do the former than the latter. The latter is of course precisely what an elected democratic assembly might – and should – do, but the National Assembly for Wales is not at present geared to develop that capacity.

The tangible economic benefits generated by the Welsh Development Agency are hard to identify (it is significant that not one serious academic study has even attempted to do so). But its institutional impact has grown ever more hegemonic, and it continues to dominate thinking about the Welsh economy, even though it has no record of precision or originality on this score. As many critics have noted over the years, the Agency is actually misnamed. It has never had responsibility for developing the entire economy of Wales and all those who gain their living from it. It has always been an organisation catering in various ways and with uneven degrees of success for various sub-sections of the business sector, and for most of the period this has primarily meant a small group of very large internationally oriented firms. Phelps (1997) suggests that the Agency's years of private negotiations with potential inward investors have engendered a secretive exclusivist culture. Some optimists suggest that devolution means this is now likely to be challenged. According to Morgan (2000), for example, the WDA has now to make the transition 'from the semi-secret world of administrative devolution to the more demanding world of democratic devolution. It may be the most powerful economic quango in Wales, but the WDA has found the early days of the Assembly to be profoundly unnerving'. However, it is hard to find any evidence that this change is happening, and it is not enough simply to demand that those concerned 'try harder'; the pressures inherent in prevailing models of regional development tend to work in a different direction. So there is little reason to expect that the transformation the Agency is currently undergoing will be any more profound or relevant to real economic needs than previous reinventions. There is no necessary connection between devolution and democratisation in economic governance.

Indeed, devolution may result in a move in the opposite direction, and it is at least arguable that this is what is currently happening in Wales. It is highly significant, for example, that the Assembly has not developed any new indicators based on theories of economic welfare by which to assess the value of the WDA's work – in particular, it has not added any meaningful employment indicators. Insofar as such indicators are on the agenda in Cardiff at all, this is an 'unintended' consequence of the application for European Structural Funds.

Conclusions

Clearly the political economy of Wales promises some interesting times ahead. How the relationship between the Assembly and the WDA develops will be key not only to the delivery of Objective 1, but also to the wider evolution of economic governance in Wales. But there is no automatic mechanism inherent in devolution which will ensure the subordination of the WDA to a well-thought-out, democratically developed economic strategy (within which the Agency might for example be allocated a clearer but more modest role as the specialist in inward investment). The obstacles are of more enduring structural significance than the quirks or inadequacies of individuals or political factions.

Not that the influence of such structural factors is hard-wired of course. In the form of the National Assembly, Wales now has a forum through which new ideas and interest *might* in principle be brought to bear to challenge the received assumptions which structure the priorities and institutional missions concerning regional economic development. But to date the Assembly has lacked both the institutional resources and a sufficiently influential political constituency to articulate interests and ideas which differ from the orthodoxy – an orthodoxy not confined to Cardiff or even London, but shared with elites in London, Washington, and Brussels. The advent of devolution, in the context of the hegemony of the dogma of globalisation-regional competitiveness, does not mean that the WDA's glory days are over.

The Welsh Development Agency is a fascinating creature, whose significance extends well beyond economic development technicalities into the economic, institutional and political realms. The Welsh case shows how the institutionalisation of prevailing discourses of regional economic development will tend to generate a highly partisan construction of the key problems and the feasible policy set (for discussion of this point see Lovering, 1995, 1999a, 1999b; Jones and MacLeod, 1999). The construction of competing RDAs in England, in the absence of over-arching, well-informed and democratic accountable bodies (Mohan 1999), suggests that some Welsh lessons might usefully be studied in England.

References

Alden, J. (1996), 'The Transfer from a Problem to a Powerful Region: The Experience of Wales', in J. Alden, and P. Boland (eds), *Regional Development Strategies. A European Perspective,* Jessica Kingsley, London, 129-58.

Andrews, L. (1999), *Wales Says Yes,* Seren, Bridgend.

Balanya, B. et al (2000), *Europe Inc. Regional and Global Restructuring and the Rise of Corporate Power,* Pluto Books, London.

Boland, P. (1999a), 'Wales and Objective 1 Status: Some Lessons From Merseyside', *Welsh Economic Review,* vol. 11, pp. 36-40.

Boland, P. (1999b), 'Merseyside's Objective 1 Programme, 1994-1999: Implications for the Next Programming Period', *Regional Studies,* vol. 33, pp. 788-92.

Boland, P. (1999c), 'Contested Multi-Level Governance: Merseyside and the European Structural Funds', *European Planning Studies,* vol. 7, pp. 647-64.

Boland, P. (2000), 'Urban Governance and Economic Development: A Critique of Merseyside's Objective 1 Experience', *European Urban and Regional Studies,* vol. 7, pp. 211-22.

Byrne, D. (1999), *Social Exclusion,* Open University Press, Buckingham.

Coates, D (2000), *Models of Capitalism: Growth and Stagnation in the Modern Era,* Polity Press, Cambridge.

Cooke, P. (1998), 'Global clustering and Regional Innovation: Systemic Integration in Wales', in H-J. Braczyk et al (eds), *Regional Innovation Systems,* UCL Press, London, pp.245-262.

Cooke, P. (2000), *Nowhere to Run, Nowhere to Hide – Regional Economic Development in Wales,* Centre for Advanced Studies, Cardiff University, Cardiff, mimeo.

Cooke, P. and Morgan, K. (1998), *The Associational Economy. Firms, Regions and Innovation,* Oxford University Press, Oxford.

Department of Trade and Industry (DTI) (1998), *Our Competitive Future: The Knowledge Driven Economy,* Cm 4176, HMSO, London.

Digest of Welsh Statistics (1999).

Elliott, L. and Atkinson, D. (1998), *The Age of Insecurity,* Verso Books, London.

Giddens, A. (1998), *The Third Way: The Renewal of Social Democracy,* Polity, Cambridge.

Gripaios, P. (1996), *Wales: An Outsider View,* Plymouth Business School, Plymouth, mimeo.

Herbert, D. (ed) (1995), *Wales since the War,* University of Wales Press, Cardiff.

Hill, S. and Munday, M. (1994), *The Regional Distribution of Foreign Manufacturing Investment in the UK,* Macmillan, London.

Hudson, R. (1995), 'The Role of Foreign Inward Investment', in L. Evans et al (eds), *The North Region Economy,* Mansell, Aldershot.

Huggins, R. (1997), 'Competitiveness and the Global Region: The Role of Networking', in J. Simmie (ed), *Innovation, Networks and Learning Regions?,* Jessica Kingsley/Regional Studies Association, London.

Humphrys, G. (1977), 'Industrial Wales' in D. Thomas (ed), *Wales: A New Study,* David and Charles, London.

Invest in Britain Bureau (IIB) (1995), *Annual Report,* IIB, London.

Institute of Welsh Affairs (IWA) (1993), *Wales 2010,* IWA, Cardiff.

Ipsen, E. (1997), 'In Wales: Doubts on Foreign Investment', *International Herald Tribune,* 29 January.

Jones, B. (1997), 'Wales: A Developing Political Economy' in M. Keating and J. Loughlin (eds), *The Political Economy of Regionalism,* Frank Cass, London, pp. 388-405.

Jones, G. and Osmond, J. (1999), *Building a Knowledge-driven Welsh Economy,* Institute of Welsh Affairs, Cardiff.

Jones, M. and MacLeod, G (1999), 'Towards a Regional Renaissance? Reconfiguring and Rescaling England's Economic Governance,' *Transactions of the Institute of British Geographers,* vol. 24, pp. 295-313.

Keating, M. (1997), 'The Political Economy of Regionalism,' in M. Keating and J.Loughlin (eds), *The Political Economy of Regionalism,* Frank Cass, London.

Krugman, P. (1996), *Pop Internationalism,* MIT Press, London.

Leadbeater, C. (1999), *Living on Thin Air,* Viking Books, London.

Lovering, J. (1995), 'Creating Discourses Rather than Jobs: The Crisis in the Cities and the Transition Fantasies of Intellectuals and Policymakers', in P. Healey et al (eds), *Managing Cities,* Routledge, London.

Lovering, J. (1998), *Constructing The Welsh Economy: Changing Perspectives On Regional Economic Development,* The O'Donnell Lecture 1998, published by Swansea University, Swansea.

Lovering, J. (1999a), 'Theory Led by Policy: The Inadequacies of the New Regionalism Illustrated from the Case of Wales', *International Journal of Urban and Regional Research,* vol. 23, pp. 379-95.

Lovering, J. (1999b), 'Celebrating Globalisation and Misreading the Welsh Economy: "The New Regionalism" in Wales', *Contemporary Wales,* vol. 11, pp.12-60.

Mainwaring, L. (1997), 'Catching Up and Falling Behind: South East Asia and Wales', *Contemporary Wales,* vol. 8, pp.9-28.

McCrone, G. (1969), *Regional Policy in Britain,* George Allen and Unwin, London.

Mohan, J. (ed) (1999), *The United Kingdom? Economic, Social and Political Geographies,* Arnold, London.

Morgan, K. (1982), *Wales 1880-1980: Rebirth of a Nation,* University of Wales Press, Cardiff.

Morgan, K. (1998), 'Regional Renewal. The Development Agency as Animateur', in H. Halkier, et al (eds), *Regional Development Agencies in Europe,* Jessica Kingsley, London, pp. 229-52.

Morgan, K. (2000), 'Development Dilemmas of Democratic Devolution', *Town and Country Planning,* in press.

Morgan, K. and Mungham, G. (2000), *Redesigning Democracy: The Making of the Welsh Assembly,* Seren, Bridgend.

Morgan, K. and Roberts, E. (1993), *The Democratic Deficit: A Guide to Quangoland,* Department of City and Regional Planning, University of Wales, Cardiff.

Murphy, P. and Caborn, R. (1996), 'Regional Government – An Economic Imperative' in *The State and the Nations: the Politics of Devolution,* Institute for Public Policy Research, London.

Munday, M. (1995), 'The Regional Consequences of the Japanese Second Wave: A Case Study', *Local Economy,* vol. 10, pp. 4-20.

O'Leary, P. (1998), 'Of Devolution, Maps and Divided Mentalities', *Planet,* 127, pp. 7-12.

Phelps, N. (1997), *Multinationals and European Integration: Trade, Investment and Regional Development,* Jessica Kingsley/Regional Studies Association, London.

Phelps, N. and Tewdwr-Jones, M. (1998), 'Institutional Capacity-building in a Strategic Policy Vacuum: The Case of the Korean company LG in South Wales' *Environment and Planning C, Government and Policy,* vol. 16, pp. 735-55.

Phelps, N. et al (1998), 'Tying the firm to the Region or Tying the Region to the Firm? Early Observations on the Case of LG in South Wales', *European Urban and Regional Studies,* vol. 5, pp. 119-38.

Phelps, N. et al (2000), 'Region, Governance and FDI: The Case of Wales' in N. Hood and S. Young (eds), *The Globalization of Multinational Enterprise Activity and Economic Development,* Macmillan, London.

Porter, M. (1990), *The Competitive Advantage of Nations*, MacMillan, London.

Price, A. et al (1993), *The Welsh Renaissance: Inward Investment and Innovation,* RIR Report No. 14, Cardiff University, Cardiff.

Roberts, A. (1994), 'The Causes and Consequences of Inward Investment: The Welsh Experience', *Contemporary Wales,* vol. 6, pp. 73-86.

Scott, A. (1999), 'Regional Motors of the Global Economy', in W. Halal and K. Taylor (eds), *Twenty-First Century Economics,* Macmillan, New York.

Shutt, H. (1998), *The Trouble with Capitalism: An Enquiry into the Causes of Global Economic Failure,* Zed Books, London.

WDA (1999), *Towards an Economic Analysis of Wales,* Welsh Development Agency, Cardiff (available on web site: www.wda.co.uk).

Welsh Office (1998), *Pathway to Prosperity: An Economic Strategy for Wales,* Welsh Office, Cardiff.

Woods, M. (2000), 'Local Branch Activity and Organisation in the Yes for Wales Campaign 1997,' *Contemporary Wales,* vol. 12, pp. 54-76.

PART II
BUSINESS CHANGE AND REGIONAL DEVELOPMENT IN THE WEST MIDLANDS

Preface to Part II:
An Overview of the West Midlands Economy

BARBARA SMITH AND CHRIS COLLINGE

Any overview of the West Midlands regional economy has to recognise the momentous changes that have taken place in the last 50 years (see bibliography in the appendix for sources on this). It is difficult now to recall the seemingly prosperous, expanding regional economy of the 1950s and 1960s with unemployment regularly below 1%, around half the national average. The acute shortage of labour drew in those seeking work from depressed parts of the UK and the Republic of Ireland and from overseas. Even the then expanding coal mines recruited from such areas. The economic planning that took place, in support of physical planning, was concerned to attract jobs and firms to the new towns and overspill reception areas where the expanding population was to be housed, given the lack of new housing, housing land and shortage of labour in Birmingham and the Black Country.

There were temporary halts to the growth of manufacturing, especially the car industry, as government imposed stop-go policies, restricting hire purchase and boosting purchase tax, to cope with balance of payments problems, for example in 1956 and 1962. Pressure was such that regional policy pushed growing or innovating firms, including what became Rover, Peugeot and Vauxhall, to open plants in development areas and, in special cases, in overspill areas.

Manufacturing was king and provided 1.2 million jobs – 56.6% of total regional employment – at the start of the 1960s, compared with 38.4% in Great Britain as a whole. Coal mining still provided 55,000 jobs, and metal manufacturing, including automotive, 40.5% of regional employment (compared with 19.5% for Great Britain), with 100,000 more jobs than all services added together.

But the tide was turning. Employment, overall and in manufacturing, peaked in 1966, as it did in Great Britain as a whole. The gradual ending of protection exposed the competitive weaknesses in the national and regional economies which, for the latter, specifically included inadequate investment, overmanning, poor industrial relations, high relative pay, and weak skills and training. There was also an unsympathetic regional policy, which restricted productivity and adaptation to change. The manufacturing bias, which had been the region's strength, became a liability as markets were lost to lower-cost, more productive and often more innovative competitors in Europe, the US, Japan and the Far East.

Unemployment rose steadily from the mid-1960s to 3.0% in 1971 and, after the 'dash for growth' in 1974, to 5.9% in 1976. Manufacturing employment fell to barely 1 million by 1975, to comprise 46.2% of total employment, with numbers down 200,000 to 86.2% of what they had been in 1965.

These trends have continued alongside the significant expansion of services and improvements in manufacturing productivity. Relative pay levels have fallen and industrial relations have improved, in the face of anti-trade union legislation and severe unemployment. Trends in the West Midlands have often led the national economy, with relatively higher unemployment and more severe decline of manufacturing output and employment, but rarely with the equivalent rapid growth in service jobs. In particular, the years 1981 to 1983 saw unemployment in the region reach 15.3% (1983), or 354,000 people. This figure was two or three percentage points above the Great Britain average, which saw close to 12% of all people being unemployed, with the rate remaining in double figures until 1987. During these years, mining, manufacturing and some services were severely hit: 291,000 jobs were lost in manufacturing between 1980 and 1995. The loss since then has been only 30,000, but also 20,000 in mining. Service growth, although adding 300,000 jobs between 1980 and 1995, has been limited, since regional services are often tied to manufacturing. After falling to 6% in the boom of 1990, double-digit unemployment rates returned in 1992 and 1993 before the recovery following the effective devaluation of sterling on departure from the European Monetary System. By 1990, the manufacturing share of employment was down to 27% (compared to 18.8% in the UK), far exceeded by the 62.3% represented by services. In 2000, the respective proportions are currently 21.9% and 69.7% in the region with total employment at the same level as 1990. It might be said that the industrial heartland has become a largely service economy, but that would be misleading and over-simplistic.

This is because the proud tradition of the West Midlands as the industrial heartland of Britain, with its particular focus on automotive and related engineering activities, survives and has been strengthened by diversification into the 'new' economy and other activities; for example, a clothing industry has developed. Indeed, while the region has been at the centre of the dramatic changes wrought in the automotive and related engineering industries since the 1980s, and has suffered much of the pain associated with industrial restructuring and globalisation, it emerged during the 1990s with much of its manufacturing base intact and in position. Evidence for the strength and confidence of this base can be seen in the series of large investments undertaken by global automotive companies in the late 1990s, including Ford/Jaguar, Peugeot-Citroen and BMW/Rover as well as LDV (Booth et al, 2000). National car production in 1999 reached 1.8 million vehicles, a figure not seen since the early 1970s; this represents good orders for component and steel suppliers, even if some orders have been lost to EU competitors.

The region is being challenged again, however, at the opening of the 21ˢᵗ century by the over-valued pound against the Euro, which has affected its main markets, and by events in the vehicle industry (see Bentley, chapter 6). In the first few months of 2000, the picture has been less buoyant, since the depreciated Euro has continued to hit exports and boost imports from the EU. Determined cost cutting and innovation by firms in the region have gone some way to combating this situation but cries of woe and threats of (and actual) disinvestment and redundancies have been mounting. This national problem has particularly affected the vehicle industry and its component and material suppliers, boosted by the possibility of legislation on car pricing and slack demand. On top of this came BMW's decision to shut or sell the Rover plant at Longbridge because of the losses being made there (see Bentley, chapter 6).

Manufacturing companies provide a large reservoir of production skills and experience (and custom) which is attractive to high-tech industries, including for example software and telecommunications companies (see Collinge and Srbljanin, chapter 9). Some of the latter have spun off from local firms or entrepreneurs; others are the result of foreign direct investment. Since the 1980s, the West Midlands has also become the most successful region for attracting inward investment into the UK, which in 1999-2000 created 4,923 jobs and safeguarded 12,807 (*Birmingham Post*, 20 May 2000).

Gross Domestic Product

An overview of this sort cannot ignore the current economic difficulties that are being experienced in economies both locally and world-wide. The UK has been experiencing a manufacturing recession brought on by high interest rates, the pound's over-valuing in relation to the Euro and, until recently, weak consumer confidence; this recession is being felt with particular force in West Midlands manufacturing. In place of expected growth in output, regional manufacturing GDP fell in 1998 and 1999, and it is likely that this fall will persist into 2000 as recovery is postponed (Table 1). This downturn in manufacturing will also impact on certain parts of the service sector, such as transport and communications, and hotels and catering, the latter linked to business tourism, which is important in the region. Business services, though similarly linked, gain activity from ongoing urgent business restructuring (see Dahlstrom, chapter 8). The confidence mentioned above is now associated with considerable nervousness.

Table 1 Recent and forecast annual GDP growth rates*

Manufacturing GDP

	1997	1998	1999	2000	2001
West Midlands	0.7	-1.9	-0.9	3.6	2.6
United Kingdom	1.0	0.1	-0.5	3.7	2.6

Total GDP

	1997	1998	1999	2000	2001
West Midlands	3.6	1.7	1.7	2.8	2.5
United Kingdom	3.4	2.5	1.8	3.2	2.7

*   per cent per annum growth based on Cambridge Econometrics' forecast made in December 1999.

Overall West Midlands GDP across all sectors combined is estimated to have experienced growth of 1.7% in both 1998 and 1999, with higher figures forecast for 2000 and 2001; these percentages are all below the national figures (Table 1). The region is currently experiencing job losses in manufacturing (Rover, Alstom, Dunlop, carpets, clothing, pottery) to add to those of recent years, but there are also job gains such as at Marconi in Coventry, quite apart from gains in business and related services (where the problem is much more one of recruitment). The hope is that the downturn will be short-lived, though this needs interest rate reductions, a fall in the exchange rate of the pound and a more buoyant world economy (and, perhaps, entry into the Euro). Nevertheless, the optimistic growth rates of Cambridge Econometrics' recent forecast shown in Table 1 seem to require modification for both the region and the UK.

Industrial Structure

These regional growth rates reflect the industrial structure and its restructuring. For many decades, there has been a shift across Britain (and other industrial nations) of production and employment away from manufacturing towards service activities, such as business and finance, hotels and catering and other services (e.g. leisure). This trend is shared by the West Midlands. So, although manufacturing represented 38.5% of regional GDP in 1971 (as distinct from employment), this figure had fallen to 27.5% by 1999, with a commensurate rise in the figure for service activities. However, the West Midlands remains the region in the UK with the highest proportion of its employment in manufacturing, at 22.3%. If we look at the region's share of UK manufacturing output, then the West Midlands produced 13.3% of UK manufacturing GDP in 1971, and still produced 11.3% of it in 1999, as against 8.3% of total UK GDP (estimates based on Cambridge Econometrics December 1999 figures). So, considering the structure of the regional economy in more detail, certain sectors are over-represented, with a larger share of the UK's production for that sector than would be expected from the region's share of UK output across all sectors (at 8.3% of UK GDP in 1999). These sectors are as defined in the Standard Industrial Classification as adapted by Cambridge Econometrics:

- motor vehicles and components, which constituted 31.5% of UK motor vehicle GDP in 1999;
- non-metallic mineral products (such as ceramics), which constituted 23.1% of the UK GDP for the sector;
  basic metals and metal products, at 21.3%;
- mechanical engineering, at 17.3%;
- rubber and plastics, at 17.0%;
- other manufacturing, at 10.6%.

A crucial factor affecting the region's future was BMW's commitment to the Rover plant at Longbridge and to the region more generally. This, as noted above, has changed dramatically. First, BMW announced that it was to source more of its components from overseas, to avoid the over-valued pound – a move also proposed by other companies. Over Christmas 1999, Longbridge (in common with Ford's Dagenham plant, but which is to close) had a prolonged shutdown to allow a reduction in stocks. In addition, as part of a new investment plan, since aborted, the workforce voted to support new working practices. The final act in this drama was BMW's sale of Longbridge and Land Rover in

May 2000 and the consequent break in production at Longbridge as production of the 75 and new Mini were switched between the Cowley and Longbridge plants.

On the other hand, however, the region is benefiting from the success of Peugeot, Jaguar (now part of Ford), LDV and Land Rover, all of which have been investing in new models and capacity. The region's component suppliers have also benefited from the expansion of Toyota and Honda, which have plants in adjoining areas. But demands for cost cutting, for greater responsibility for design to be passed down the supply chain, for internet-based supply chain links and the need to match prices with continental and other suppliers are generating future uncertainties throughout the supply chain (see Bentley, chapter 6).

Other manufacturing sectors, in contrast, are under-represented in the region, in the sense that they produce a below-average share of the UK GDP in that sector (8.3% in 1999). Such sectors include:

- chemicals and man-made fibres, at 3.9% of UK chemical GDP;
- other transport equipment, at 5.6%;
- food, drink and tobacco, at 6.1%;
- textiles, clothing and leather, also at 6.1%;
- electronic, electrical and instrument engineering, at 6.9%.

Among service sectors, only distribution, at 8.7% of UK output in that sector, is above the 8.3% average. All other service sectors, despite often representing a rapidly growing part of the West Midlands economy, still have a below-average proportion of the national output for their sectors. This implies that they each have some room to grow in the future as needed, if manufacturing continues to 'save' labour. These service sectors include:

- education and health, at 8.1% of UK GDP in this sector;
- transport and communications, at 7.2%;
- other business services, at 6.9%;
- hotels and catering, also at 6.9%;
- public administration and defence, at 6.4%;
- banking and finance, at 6.2%;
- insurance, at 5.2%.

If we consider GDP growth rates, however, services as a whole in the region are estimated to have grown faster than the same activities in the UK in 1999; this rate is expected to be higher in 2000, but below the rate of growth for the UK (see Table 2).

Table 2 Recent and forecast annual GDP growth rates in services*

	1999	2000	2001	1995-2000	2000-2005
West Midlands	3.1	3.5	3.0	3.9	3.1
United Kingdom	2.6	3.8	3.2	3.7	3.1

* per cent per annum growth based on Cambridge Econometrics' forecast made in December 1999.

During the period 1995 to 2000, the following manufacturing and service sectors are expected to have grown most strongly in the region:

- other transport equipment, at an average of 8.2% growth in GDP per annum;
- other business services, at 7.7% p.a.;
- transport and communications, also at 7.7% p.a.;
- retailing, at 3.9% p.a.;
- electronic, electrical and instrument engineering, at 3.4% p.a.;
- other services, at 3.1% p.a.;
- insurance, at 2.5% p.a.;
- banking and finance, at 2.4% p.a.;
- motor vehicles, at 2.3% p.a.

All these growth rates are at or above the overall growth rate for 1995 to 2000 shown in Table 3. However, all except electronic, electrical and instrument engineering, vehicles and banking and finance show lower growth in the years 2000 to 2005.

These growth rates for 1995 to 2000 have to be seen in comparison with the expected overall growth rates in the region and the UK. The period 2000 to 2005 is included in Table 3 as an indication of what the immediate future was thought to hold at the end of 1999.

On the other hand, many sectors are expected to have declined in output terms in the period 1995 to 2000, with GDP growth substantially below the West Midlands' average; some sectors show output actually declining (negative GDP 'growth'), for example:

- coal mining, at an average 'growth' rate of GDP of -9.9% p.a.;
- textiles, clothing and leather, at -5.2% p.a.;
- food, drink and tobacco, at -2.7% p.a.;
- other manufacturing, at -2.3% p.a.;
- basic metals and metal products, at -0.6% p.a.;
- agriculture, at -0.4% p.a.;
- public administration and defence, at -0.2% p.a.;
- paper, printing and publishing, at -0.1% p.a.;
- mechanical engineering, at 0.3% p.a.;
- construction, at 0.4% p.a.

Table 3 Total annual GDP growth*

	1995-2000	2000-2005
West Midlands	2.3	2.6
United Kingdom	2.7	2.6

*   Average per cent per annum growth based on Cambridge Econometrics's forecast made in December 1999.

A number of other sectors exhibit rates at or just above the manufacturing growth rate of 0.6% p.a. over the period 1995 to 2000, but below 1.0% p.a. These are:

- electricity, gas and water, at 0.6% p.a.;
- rubber and plastics, at 0.6% p.a.;
- hotels and catering, at 0.7% p.a.;
- non-metallic mineral products, at 0.9% p.a.

The forecast picture is much brighter for 2000 to 2005, though coal and textiles, clothing and leather continue with negative 'growth' and are joined by what is a minute oil and natural gas sector. Non-metal mineral products and electricity, gas and water are still expected to grow, but by considerably less than 1% p.a.

The region's industrial structure and growth record in the past, present and forecast for the future, are therefore diverse across sectors and companies, in GDP terms. There are also local specialisations so that change hits particular parts of the region more severely. Decline has particularly affected the agricultural and mining areas, the pottery and steel industries of North

Staffordshire and the carpet industry in Kidderminster. On the other hand, much of the growth in business services, business tourism and shopping has occurred in the regional centre, Birmingham, where a succession of major regeneration projects have included the National Exhibition Centre, the International Convention Centre and adjacent Brindleyplace and the Mailbox. Alongside this, development is now turning to the east side of the city, with Millennium Point, a new Bull Ring shopping centre and the Digbeth area. Telford, floundering as a new town in the 1960s and 1970s, has since become a dynamic centre for inward and other investment in call centres, plastics and high-tech industries, alongside earlier metal industry survivors. However, the broad character of developments can be summarised as a manufacturing sector broadly maintained, but with other business services and transport and communications pushing forward the service share of the economy and a reasonable overall growth rate in GDP. At a more disaggregated level, growth can be found in niche areas and in particular firms where output or profits have been and are expanding. In employment terms, growth is essentially modest, as discussed below.

Investment

GDP growth and positive change represent capital investment in buildings, plant, design and, often, innovation. However, under-investment has long been recognised as a problem over many years in Britain and, specifically, in the West Midlands and Birmingham. The West Midlands' share of national investment has rarely reached the region's share of the UK's overall or manufacturing GDP, thus building up cumulatively a serious deficit. However, in recent years, the region's share has just exceeded this level (see Table 4) notably in manufacturing, largely because of vehicle industry upgrading. The level of overall investment in the West Midlands in 2000 is expected to be 218% of that in 1980 (UK 202%), and in manufacturing investment 165% (UK 124%). However, actual manufacturing investment was lower in 1999 than in 1998 because of trading conditions in both the West Midlands and the UK, though estimated to be slightly up on 1999 in 2000. This investment has benefited and will benefit manufacturing productivity, relative to the UK as a whole.

Investment in the region has been boosted by inward investment, which includes takeovers and extensions. BMW's investment at Rover and Hams Hall, for example, counts as inward investment.

Table 4 West Midlands' share of UK fixed investment*

	1980	1990	1995	1998	1999	2000	Share of UK GDP in 1999
All fixed investment	7.8	7.5	8.3	8.5	8.4	8.4	8.3%
Manufacturing fixed investment	9.8	9.6	11.8	12.9	13.0	13.0	11.3%

* based on Cambridge Econometrics' December 1999 data.

As regards inward investment, the West Midlands has not suffered to the same extent as other regions from over-capacity and depression in the world semi-conductor market. While enquiries from South East Asia have fallen, the West Midlands has benefited from increased interest on the part of companies from North America, an area to which much of the promotional effort has now been redirected. Major inward investments include the creation of 1,000 jobs by Oracle, the US software company, in its new software development unit in Solihull, and the decision of Cap Gemini, the computer service company, to increase employment in Aston, Gravelly Hill and Redditch.

So far, as noted above, the West Midlands tops the list of regions for foreign direct investment in the UK. This has been occurring across a wide range of industries, including property recently. However, North American and Japanese manufacturing companies are now being attracted by the low-cost environment offered in East European countries such as the Czech Republic and Hungary, and it is from this quarter that competition for investment (and for automotive components) is expected to come.

Employment

It was only in the last quarter of 1998 that the impact on employment of the current recession in manufacturing became apparent in particular places, though the regional unemployment total continued to fall. Labour's New Deal is moving young workers out of unemployment into jobs and/or training (or out of the unemployment count), but higher manufacturing unemployment can certainly not be ruled out from recent events. However, those losing their jobs in closures and redundancies seem to be finding other work, as total unemployment in the region has continued to fall since 1993. The claimant count in April 2000 (*Birmingham Post*, 18 May 2000), seasonally adjusted, was 107,900 – down 2,200 on the previous month, giving a rate of 4.2%. This rate is just above the national rate of 3.9% – the lowest figure since 1980. The International Labour Office's unemployment rate, which includes non-claimants, stands at 160,000, down 24,000, representing 6.1% of the labour force. Vacancies are up, reflecting a considerable labour shortage in many industries, notably of skilled labour. Nevertheless, there remain pockets of severe unemployment; for example, in parts of inner Birmingham the rates are still, in May 2000, over 15%.

On the other hand, the total numbers in employment continue to rise, feeding money into the regional economy. Although the bulk of the additional jobs are part-time and temporary, jobs such as these have brought many additional women into the labour force. This rise in employment is recent and modest, raising the total by about 100,000 over the figures in the 1960s and 1970s. This reflects, as elsewhere, the outcome of population change, falling male activity rates and rising female ones, with the latter trend expected to continue and to add another 100,000 by 2005. About 80% of those of working age are in employment in the West Midlands, a similar percentage to the UK figure, with 27.7% in part-time jobs. Some 46.3% are women workers.

Earnings

While average earnings increase year on year, those in the West Midlands remain below the UK average. Average manufacturing earnings in the region were 95% of those in the UK in 1995, but have now fallen to only 92%, with no improvement envisaged. In services, average earnings are in a better relative position at 95% of the UK average. In 2000, manufacturing earnings are expected to reach just over £22,200 a year compared to £15,100 in services. This puts a different light on the switch in regional employment from manufacturing to services when both the earnings differential and the increase in part-time working are considered. Low pay remains a significant problem, relieved only to a degree by the introduction of the minimum wage, which is not considered to have caused job losses.

The Policy Environment

The fortunes of the region are likely to be affected by various changes in the policy environment. In July 1998, the government announced a major review of assisted area status, which determines where regional selective assistance and other industrial aid are applied across the country. This review was part of a Europe-wide reassessment, which has resulted in a reduction in UK areas eligible for assistance. Since 1984, Birmingham and other parts of the region have benefited from regional assistance. Many firms have obtained grants, including Jaguar for the Castle Bromwich plant and LDV for the expansion of its activities. At present, transitional relief for 2000 to 2006 is available to the old EU Objective 2 areas, which were eligible for Structural Funds. These areas included Herefordshire, Shropshire and Staffordshire Moorlands, and Birmingham, the Black Country and Coventry, though from March 2000, Birmingham limited to intermediate area status (a 50% cut in assistance). Loss of this assistance is considered likely to be harmful to Birmingham's ability to attract investment. The agricultural west of the region will probably keep its assistance, but at a lower level.

The UK government launched its Competitiveness White Paper in 1998 (DTI, 1998). This White Paper stressed the stimulation of entrepreneurship and innovation, and further deregulatory initiatives. These priorities have been taken up enthusiastically in the West Midlands, for example, by the Government Office of the West Midlands (GOWM) in its *Working to Win. A Framework for Competitiveness in the West Midlands* (GOWM, 1998) and in the *Regional Innovation Strategy* (AWM,1999). In the last year, the organisational structure has changed significantly with the arrival of Advantage West Midlands (AWM), the Regional Development Agency, (incorporating the West Midlands Development Agency), and West Midlands Chamber of chosen regional leaders (see Part I).

Under the regeneration and competitiveness headings, considerable sums of money are coming into the region from both the private sector (e.g. the Birmingham Alliance in the Eastside development) and the public sector (lottery and millennium funds, European Regional Development Fund (ERDF) and European Social Fund (ESF), and UK government assistance). The latter includes the £129 million in regional selective assistance (RSA) for the Task Force set up following BMW's sale of Rover.

The Future

Three critical challenges remain to be met: the upskilling of the labour force; the improved availability of industrial land, both green and brown field; and much more sustained and generous capital investment in infrastructure (especially transport) and in industrial and business assets. These challenges demand sympathetic policymaking and positive action on all sides. The exceptional examples of the present need to become the general rule for progress to be assured. However, the powers of AWM are limited to stimulation, advice and co-ordination and may not prove effective in making this happen with the needed speed and decisiveness.

References

AWM (1999), *West Midlands Regional Innovation Strategy and Action Plan*, Advantage West Midlands, Birmingham.

Birmingham Post, 18 May 2000.

Birmingham Post, 20 May 2000.

Booth et al. (2000), *The West Midlands,* in Cambridge Econometrics (2000), *Regional Economic Prospects. Analysis and Forecasts to the Year 2010 for the Regions of the UK*, February.

Cambridge Econometrics (2000), *Regional Economic Prospects. Analysis and Forecasts to the Year 2010 for the Regions of the UK,* February.

Department of Trade and Industry (1998), *Our Competitive Future: The Knowledge Driven Economy,* HMSO, London.

GOWM (1998), *Working to Win. A framework for Competitiveness in the West Midlands.* Government Office for the West Midlands, Birmingham.

6 The Automotive Industry: Change and Challenge for the RDAs

GILL BENTLEY

Introduction

Events that took place in the auto industry in the West Midlands during March to May 2000 serve as a reminder that while in the 'intelligent region' (Cooke and Morgan, 1991) economic development agencies may devise and design strategies to secure regional competitive advantage, what might appear to be 'historical disturbances' occur. The reference is of course to the announcement in March 2000 by BMW of its intention to sell off Rover, in the first instance to Alchemy Partners, a venture capital company. The Rover plant at Longbridge was eventually sold for £10, to the perhaps appropriately named Phoenix Consortium, headed by John Towers, a former chief executive of Rover. Land Rover was sold to Ford for rather more. This is a story, however, which begins earlier, when in 1995, Rover was sold to BMW and when the die was already cast by wider changes taking place in the industry. Indeed, such developments must be seen in the context of the restructuring of the automotive industry in Europe and worldwide. More pertinently, they act as a reminder that there is a need to base policy on a proper understanding of business change.

This chapter therefore takes the opportunity to review the changes taking place in the automotive industry and the challenges that these changes pose to a regional development agency, such as in this case Advantage West Midlands. The RDA's objectives for regional economic development and its intentions for developing the industry are examined. Similarly to all the RDAs, AWM has taken its cue for its industrial strategy from the government's White Paper, *Our Competitive Future: The Knowledge Driven Economy* (DTI, 1998), basing its approach to economic development on the idea of developing clusters. While it is possible to point to a number of case examples of how clusters have been developed, it is by no means an uncontested approach and, moreover, the notion of clusters is questioned. What is more, however, is that changes taking place in the automotive industry mean that it is doubtful that the industry could be the focus of the development of a local productive system. As recent research has shown, geography matters, and with firms in the supply chain becoming global operators, as the original equipment manufacturers (OEMs) alter their sourcing strategy, this makes the cluster approach problematical (Sadler, 1999).

This chapter therefore looks at how production reorganisations impact on the geography of production. There are several views on the path of development that the automotive industry is taking. These leave little room for a national, still less a UK regional perspective. In principle, the changes in the industry are a reflection of a tension between globalising and localising forces, where the internationalisation of production and technological change come into conflict with national goals which identify car makers as the flagships of national economic progress (Lagendijk, 1997). This implies the need for appropriate national/regional institutions to secure development. A further issue therefore is the extent to which the RDAs have the powers and resources to be able to achieve their objectives for sustainable regional economic growth, and it is a dilemma where the locality demonstrates some dependency on a particular industry.

These arguments are illustrated in the chapter's overview of the automotive industry in the West Midlands. The region has the highest proportion of UK employment in the automotive industry in both vehicle and component production. This makes the region somewhat dependent on the retention of firms in the industry. As the case of BMW/Rover shows, in the events recounted here, the news of BMW's intention to sell off Rover threw the region into a frenzy in the effort to retain productive capacity and jobs. In the circumstances, therefore, this chapter is partly the history of the attempt to save Rover. What it serves to show is that vested interests in the global economy can thwart plans for regional development. The West Midlands region nearly lost productive capacity in both its OEMs and firms in the supply chain in the car industry, amounting to 24,000 jobs (Rover Task Force, 2000). The loss of Longbridge would have resulted in a different future for the region, and leads to the question 'to what extent can national or regional interests prevail?' It is suggested that there are very real limits to the scope for RDAs to secure a sustainable regional economy.

The chapter looks first at the regional economic strategy, and the significance of the automotive industry to the West Midlands region, before it moves on to look at the changes taking place in the auto industry, which it illustrates by looking at the events in the BMW/Rover case example.

Clusters, Competitiveness and Regional Development

Creating Advantage, the regional strategy for the West Midlands, was published in October 1999 (Advantage West Midlands, 1999). One of its twin objectives is to 'create wealth through enterprise', under which it aims to 'develop a dynamic and diverse business base'. As part of the programme to achieve this, the RES identified a number of new and existing sectors that AWM wanted to support in order to transform the West Midlands economy. One of these was the automotive industry. A Business Growth Task Group was to be charged with the task of proposing a strategy for the development of the sector. This included the scope to use traditional tools of economic development but, taking the cue from the government White Paper, *Our Competitive Future: The Knowledge Driven Economy* (DTI, 1998), it also included the intention to foster and sustain the development of clusters.

The cluster approach is based on the notion that regional competitive advantage can be achieved by developing production clusters in which the path of development is determined by the firms in the clusters and by economic development agencies. Cluster theory has become something of a shibboleth in economic development, superseding other theories on how to justify approaches to regional economic development policy. McCrone (1999), however, argues that it is another example of 'old wine in new bottles'. According to Porter's by now well-known theory of competitive advantage,

> A cluster is a geographically proximate group of interconnected companies, associated institutions in a particular field...The geographical scope of a cluster can range from a single city to...a network of countries. Clusters...include end product or service companies; suppliers...financial institutions; and firms in related industries...Government agencies...can be considered part of it. (Porter, 1998)

This is an all-encompassing definition. The inclusion by Porter of the role for government is a new development and absent from earlier work (Porter, 1990). However, from a regulation theory perspective, institutions and institutional thickness are aspects of the mode of regulation of the system of accumulation, in the regime of accumulation (Amin, 1994; Amin and Thrift, 1999). A simpler definition of a cluster would include the idea that firms are geographically proximate, in a subcontracting relationship with each other but, most importantly, would have a shared vision about the development of the industry or sector in which they operate. An alternative term is a local productive system (Saublens, 1999).

The desire to sustain a local productive system is however fraught with difficulties. Changes taking place in the automotive industry challenge such a view of the industry and of how regional economies can be developed. Changes in the organisation of production suggest that a new spatial division of labour is emerging, which would threaten the development of clusters. This argument will be explored later in the chapter. It is clear, however, why AWM chose the automotive industry for attention. The significance of the automotive industry to the economy of the West Midlands is shown in the following section.

The Automotive Industry in the West Midlands

There is no doubt that the West Midlands is the automotive region of the UK. The number of jobs and the inter-relationships between the firms in the industry in the region strongly suggest the presence of a local productive system.

Jobs in the Automotive Industry in the West Midlands

As Table 6.1 shows, just over 225,100 people in Great Britain worked in the automotive industries in 1997 (1% of the nation's jobs). This includes jobs in motor vehicle production (Standard Industrial Classification (SIC) 341), bodies (SIC 342) and in the parts and accessories sector (SIC 343). As the table also shows, 34% of these jobs were to be found in the West Midlands. Figure 6.1 shows that the West Midlands accounts for 40% of national employment in vehicle production and 33% of employment in parts and accessories. No other region in Great Britain hosts as many jobs in automotive production as the West Midlands. The regional specialisation is confirmed by the location quotient of 3.62.

There are other automotive producing locations in Great Britain, as shown in Table 6.1. The other significant concentrations of employment in the automotive sector are Merseyside and the North West (Ford and GM Vauxhall), the North East (Nissan) and Wales (Bosch, component producers). Other important locations are London, Dagenham in Essex (Ford), Yorkshire and the Humber (Toyota in Derby), the South East (Honda and BMW/Rover at Swindon) and the Eastern region (GM Vauxhall at Luton).

The structure of employment in the regions is quite different (Table 6.2). Wales is a centre for the production of automotive components, whereas Merseyside has a high proportion of employment in vehicle production. As far as the West Midlands is concerned, the table shows that while a low proportion

Table 6.1 Regional distribution of employment in the automotive industries in Great Britain and location quotient (LQ), 1997 (SIC 34)

Region	No of jobs (000s)	% of Great Britain jobs	Total GB jobs (000s)	As % of jobs in each region	LQ
South East	17.9	8.0	3,202.3	0.56	0.57
Eastern	19.1	8.5	2,059.0	0.93	0.94
London	11.8	5.2	3,476.2	0.34	0.34
South West	13.2	5.9	1,888.2	0.70	0.71
West Midlands	76.1	33.8	2,135.7	3.56	3.62
East Midlands	14.7	6.5	1,654.9	0.89	0.90
Yorks & Humber	15.7	7.0	1,947.4	0.81	0.82
Merseyside	5.2	2.3	443.5	1.17	1.19
North West	20.8	9.2	2,155.3	0.97	0.98
North East	11.5	5.1	904.3	1.27	1.29
Wales	14.7	6.5	987.4	1.49	1.51
Scotland	4.4	2.0	1,991.8	0.22	0.22
Great Britain	225.1	100.0	22,846.0	0.99	na

Source: Annual Employment Survey data from 1997, Office of National Statistics, © Crown Copyright 2000.

of its employment is in automotive bodies, it has roughly an equal proportion of jobs in vehicle production, and in components. Approximately 38,000 people (50%) were working in vehicle production and 33,000 (44%) in the parts and accessories sector in 1997.

Employment in the industry is also significant to the West Midlands. As Table 6.1 shows, 76,000 people were working in the automotive industry in the West Midlands in 1997. This was 3.6% of the region's jobs (See Table 6.1 and Figure 6.2). This is not as many jobs as found in the business services sector (see the similar chart for business services, as discussed by Dahlstrom in chapter 8). The number of jobs in the auto industry will have fallen since 1997, because of the redundancies made at BMW/Rover.

However, the figures understate the number of jobs in the auto industry as a whole. For every job in the automotive industry, there are at least five more in firms further down the supply chain in other industries which are dependent on the motor industry. Tilson, for example, discusses the role of the rubber and plastics industries in supplying parts and developing new materials

Table 6.2   Employment in motor vehicles, bodies and parts and accessories by region (SICs 341, 342 and 343), 1997, percentage

Region	Motor vehicles %	Bodies %	Parts %	All jobs %
South East	48.0	5.0	46.9	100
Eastern	56.5	11.5	31.9	100
London	55.9	26.3	17.8	100
South West	26.5	10.6	62.9	100
West Midlands	50.1	6.3	43.6	100
East Midlands	23.1	21.1	55.8	100
Yorkshire & the Humber	7.0	39.5	53.5	100
Merseyside	90.4	1.9	7.7	100
North West	49.0	17.3	33.7	100
North East	46.1	9.6	44.3	100
Wales	10.9	8.2	81.0	100
Scotland	18.2	47.7	34.1	100
Great Britain	42.1	13.2	44.7	100

Source: Annual Employment Survey data from 1997, Office of National Statistics, © Crown Copyright 2000.

for the automotive industry, in chapter 7. The business services sector also provides services to the automotive industry.

Famous Firms

The West Midlands is host to a number of major automotive assemblers: Jaguar (owned by Ford); Peugeot (owned by PSA Peugeot Citroen); and Rover and Land Rover. Land Rover is now owned by Ford, while Rover, owned by BMW until May 2000, is now owned by the Phoenix Consortium, with BMW retaining some parts of the production facilities in the UK. The BMW/Rover story is discussed in more detail below. The region is also home to a number of other lesser known vehicle producers, including Alvis, Carbodies (London taxis), Dennis Eagle (dumper trucks), LDV (vans), Massey Fergusson (Agco Tractors) and the Morgan Motor Company (hand-built sports cars) (Tilson, 1997).

Figure 6.1 Regional distribution of employment in vehicle (SIC 341) and parts and accessories (SIC 343) production, 1997 (percentage)

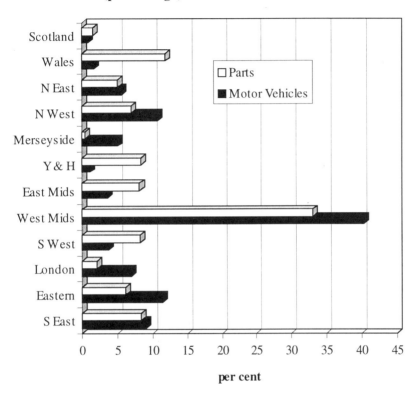

per cent

Source: Annual Employment Survey data from 1997, Office of National Statistics, © Crown Copyright 2000.

Also found in the region are component producers in each of the main component groups: the driveline; chassis and underbody; engine components; body panels; interior trim; electrical components and design and engineering. Tilson (1997) estimates that there are around 2,000 component producers in the West Midlands. Among the firms based in the West Midlands which are in the first tier of the supply chain are: Valeo (suspension systems); Johnson Controls (seating); Mayflower Vehicle Systems (car bodies); Rockwell (body/chassis systems and brakes); UTA-UTC (interior trim; steering wheels); LucasVarity (lighting); Magnetti Marelli (lighting and electronics); Quinton Hazell (part of the Dana Automotive Aftermarket Group); GKN Plc (drive shafts, universal joints, and other products); VDO Instruments (electronics);

and SP Tyres UK (tyres). Internationally known, many are multinationals and are American or Japanese owned. Firms in the second tier include Sarginsons Precision Components (light alloy foundry which manufactures aluminium castings) and Premier Stampings (produces a range of die forgings).

Figure 6.2 Share of employment in the automotive industries by region and compared to the Great Britain average, 1997

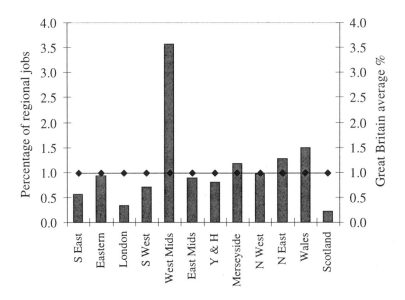

Source: Annual Employment Survey data from 1997, Office of National Statistics, © Crown Copyright 2000.

Local Production and Local Purchasing

Tilson (1997) emphasises the diversity of automotive component production in the West Midlands. As she points out, the region's traditional metals processing and engineering strengths enable it to supply products to the vehicle manufacturers along the supply chain, from the smallest screw to specialist processing equipment, as well as products made from rubber, plastics, glass and textiles.

A study by Wolverhampton Business School (1996) revealed similar diversity in the industry and, in addition, that many of the firms in the region are small firms employing less than 250 workers. Another study, by Lees and Smith (1993), of Walsall in the West Midlands confirmed this pattern and found that many firms were family owned. The study also suggested that firms in the locality were dependent on UK assemblers. This was confirmed by Tilson (1997); all the firms questioned in her study sold at least 70% of their products locally.

The pattern of local sales and purchasing, together with the number of jobs, indicates the presence of a local productive system, or cluster of firms in the region. It is a cluster which is under threat from developments in the automotive industry.

Understanding Business Change: Developments in the Automotive Industry

The automotive industry has been undergoing a complex series of changes. Figure 6.3 shows the levels in the supply chain, with the OEMs at the top of the chain and the first tier and lower tier suppliers below. It illustrates the pressures on firms in the industry, including the general conditions for production (Tilson, 1999). Drivers to change include general demand conditions, government policy and the regulatory environment. Government policy embraces economic policy and regional/industrial policy. As discussed below, in the case of BMW/ Rover, the RDA's lack of power of determination of regional development assistance was a factor in the outcome of the events.

The general conditions of production for the automotive industry in the UK at the end of the 1990s were marked by considerable turmoil in the foreign exchange market. Rising prices in the UK, which were the result of the high value of the pound on the foreign exchange market, affected exports from the UK. The Asian financial crisis was a prelude to a fall off in the demand for imported cars in that market (Bentley, 1998). At the same time, devaluation in the Asian economies resulted in price cuts to sustain domestic output, which made imports to the UK cheaper. It also led to the cancellation of a number of investments by Asian companies in projects in the UK, including those in the automotive sector.

Fundamentally, however, firms need to remain competitive in what is a crowded world market. Capacity exceeds demand. Overproduction in the European market for example is estimated to be running at about 7 million cars, or 42% of demand. Worldwide, demand is estimated to be at 58.1 million units. With global capacity thought to be 79.2 million units, overproduction stands at 21 million units, or 36% more than demand, and 73% of capacity utilisation (Pemberton, 2000). The responses to this situation, by firms in the

Figure 6.3   The supply chain and supply chain pressures

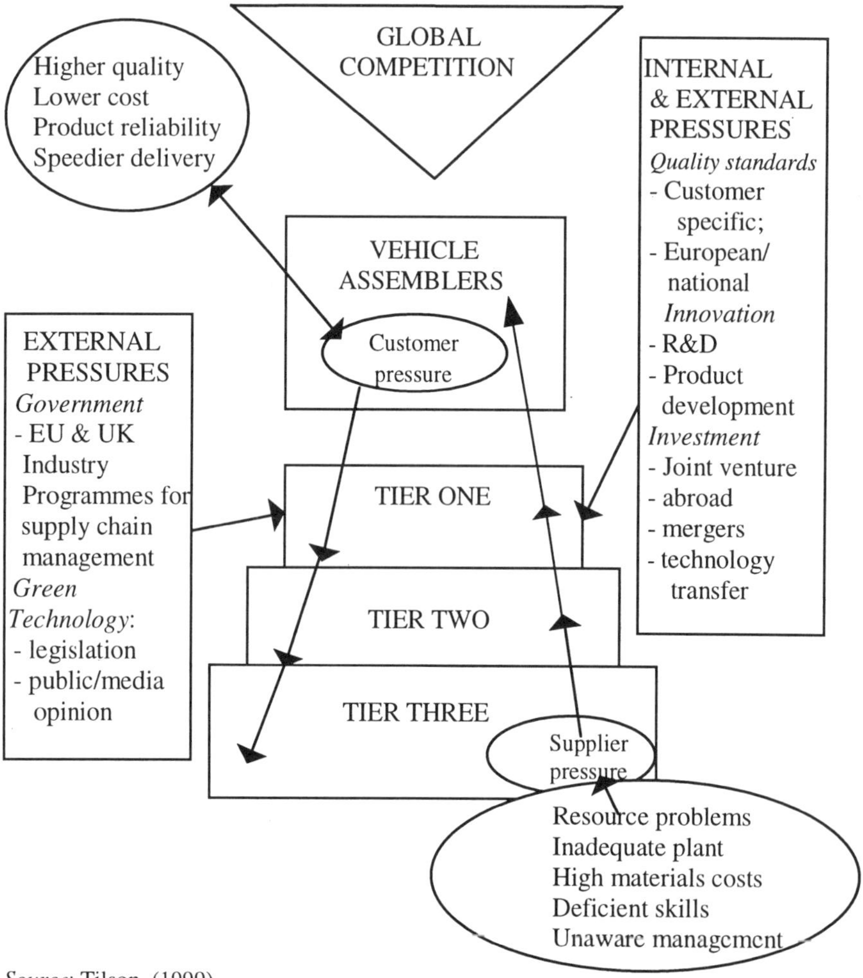

Higher quality
Lower cost
Product reliability
Speedier delivery

GLOBAL
COMPETITION

INTERNAL
& EXTERNAL
PRESSURES
Quality standards
- Customer
  specific;
- European/
  national
Innovation
- R&D
- Product
  development
Investment
- Joint venture
- abroad
- mergers
- technology
  transfer

VEHICLE
ASSEMBLERS

Customer
pressure

EXTERNAL
PRESSURES
Government
- EU & UK
Industry
Programmes for
supply chain
management
*Green
Technology*:
- legislation
- public/media
  opinion

TIER ONE

TIER TWO

TIER THREE

Supplier
pressure

Resource problems
Inadequate plant
High materials costs
Deficient skills
Unaware management

Source: Tilson (1999).

industry have been various, including merger and acquisition activity, production reorganisations and a changing spatial division of labour in the changing system of production.

Systems of Production in the Automotive Industry

According to regulation theory, developments such as those taking place in the automotive industry can be characterised as systems (or regimes) of accumulation. Regimes comprise the system of accumulation (or production) and the mode of regulation. The latter concerns the macro-level structure of consumption and encompasses general demand conditions for production, including government policy. The system of accumulation refers to micro-level social relations of production (Wells and Rawlinson, 1994). Figure 6.4 maps out the elements of the different systems of production in the automotive industry. It refers to what is produced, how it is produced and with what production technology and labour process. It also refers to supply chain relationships and the spatial organisation of production.

It is generally accepted that the industry has been moving from the classic Fordist system of production to a post-Fordist system (Law, 1991; Wells and Rawlinson, 1994). The move towards lean production, or flexible specialisation, characteristic of post-Fordism, is well documented in the literature (Womack et al, 1990; Wells and Rawlinson, 1994; Lagendijk, 1997). The process entails changes which are both internal and external to the firm (Figure 6.5 illustrates the strategic responses that automotive firms adopt to overcome the problems they face). The changes within the firm encompass change in the organisation of production (towards automation, teamworking, flexibility) and changes in its external linkages (strategic alliances and supply chain management linkages), as well as changes in products and markets. The changes in the organisation of production and in external linkages impact on the geography of production. In particular, the 'just-in-time' (JIT) system of the delivery of components altered the spatial organisation of production. A key characteristic of the post-Fordist system therefore is the 'geography of proximity' fostered by the need for spatial proximity of OEMs and supplier firms (Lagendijk, 1997). This has facilitated the development of production clusters. Local centres of production are often focused on 'national champions' (Lagendijk, 1997).

As we enter the 21st century, however, we can see some evidence that the industry is moving into a new phase, what Lamming (1993) calls 'post-Japanisation'. Lagendijk (1997) describes this as a 'post-national' phase of development. In this phase, technological change is having an impact on the structure of the components industry and supply chain relationships. These production reorganisations are, in turn, changing the spatial organisation of production. The changes threaten the development of local productive systems. The chapter looks next at production reorganisations, before turning to look at the changing geography of production.

Production Reorganisations

Technological developments in the automotive industry include changes in both product and process. Driver airbags and ABS (anti-lock breaking

Figure 6.4 Production systems in the automotive industry

A CHANGING SYSTEM OF PRODUCTION		
FORDISM	POST-FORDISM	POST-JAPANISATION
Products and markets		
Mass	Small batch	Mass /Batch
Standardised	Customised	Bounded choice
Quantity	Quality	Quality
Mass market	Niche market	Mass/Niche
Production technology		
Tools	CNC tools	CNC tools
Automation	Automation	Automation
Labour process		
Repetitive tasks	Multiple changing	Repetitive tasks?
Semi & unskilled	Skilled labour	Unskilled labour?
Authoritarian	Teamworking	Subcontractors
Firm structure		
Multinationals	Trans-nationals	Hollow
Component producers		
OEMs	SMEs	Trans-nationals
Operating principle		
Economies of scale	Economies of scale	Scale & scope
Supply chain management & supplier relationships		
Just-in-case	Just-in-time	At supplier cost
Integrated plants	Disintegration	Devolution
AND A CHANGING GEOGRAPHY OF PRODUCTION		
Decentralisation	Centralisation	Dispersal
Globalisation	'Glocalisation'	Regionalisation
Internationalisation		Europeanisation

system) have been introduced into cars. Electronic systems such as global positioning systems are a newer development. However, a more major change is in the way in which cars are produced. As Scheele (2000) suggests, the driving force for this is the attempt by the OEMs to further squeeze out the costs of production. This is being achieved by further reductions in stockholding and also by reducing the time it takes to produce a car.

Many OEMs are moving towards adopting a 'platform strategy'. This enables carmakers to use a basic engineering structure as the basis for the assembly of a number of different models. This development has allowed greater standardisation and rationalisation. The approach has been paralleled by the trend towards modularisation, or modular assembly. This involves the supply of complete systems and modules, rather than individual components (Cahners Business Information, 2000). Modules are delivered to the assembly

Figure 6.5 Competitive strategies in the automotive industry

1. PRODUCT/MARKET STRATEGIES
   - Ford and GM have attempted to develop a 'world car'
   - Daimler-Benz, Jaguar have specialised production on a narrower spatial base
   - search for new markets in Central and Eastern Europe
   - joint ventures with overseas players to seek market growth and access technology

2. TECHNOLOGICAL CHANGES
   - the increasing use of electronics in cars
   - development of futuristic cockpit electronics systems to replace conventional dashboards
   - greater use of global positioning systems
   - engineering to shorten production times
   - fuel efficiency; cars that do 70 mpg
   - emission reduction via new fuels
   - green production (low solvent paints)

3. CHANGES IN PRODUCTION PROCESS/TECHNOLOGY
   - metal cutting lasers which produce so concentrated a pulse that no finishing is required
   - new materials ceramics
   - growing use of plastic components in engine manifolds and fuel systems
   - development of the lighter car
   - development of a 'platform strategy'; a basic engineering structure serves production of a number of different models
   - introduction of modular design; this produces savings for car makers
   - supply of complete systems rather than individual components

4. REORGANISATION OF SUPPLIER RELATIONS
   - globalisation of supply relations (e.g. BMW)
   - closer relations to achieve quality, price standards and delivery
   - consolidation of suppliers through merger and acquisition;
   - development of world-class suppliers
   - rationalisation of the number of first tier suppliers by the assemblers; extending to the third and subsequent tiers

5. CHANGES IN LABOUR PROCESS
   - introduction of 'Japanese' working methods

6. SPATIAL REORGANISATIONS
   - moves to low cost locations with access to core regions
   - US and Japanese car-part makers and suppliers locate nearer to assemblers, to provide a better service
   - globalisation of component producers leading to dispersal of component producers

site and are slotted into the vehicle. These developments are impacting on supplier firms and are leading to a change in the assembler-supplier relationship.

The main impact of modularisation is that component producers are able to integrate several systems. Modularisation is therefore leading to increasing specialisation within firms in the supply chain, and integration. Assemblers have in any case wanted to deal with fewer suppliers, to simplify the supply chain relationship. They have been demanding prompt delivery at low prices, but with no sacrifice in quality. Component producers have had little choice but to respond by becoming 'world-class' suppliers. This has resulted in a pattern of merger and acquisition among component producers, including the closure and relocation of production plants, similar to that taking place in the OEMs (Anderson Consulting, 1999). A report by PriceWaterhouseCooper suggests that the number of component producers in the UK has fallen from 13,000 to 8,000 in the 10 years to 2000. It is predicted that the demand for standard components could reduce the number of first tier suppliers from 800 to just 30 (*Financial Times*, 16 May 2000). Commentators forecast a knock-on effect on firms lower down the supply chain. A key issue for policy makers however is whether these firms are able to make the change to become world class suppliers.

New supply chain relationships and management systems are emerging. Increasingly, modularisation involves the devolution of responsibility to the module suppliers. This is quite different from the integrated production of Fordism, where components were held 'just-in-case', and the vertical disintegration of post-Fordist production, which saw the operation of the JIT system. Devolution not only shifts responsibility for the stock of inputs to the supplier, but also the development of modules. From the point of view of the OEMs, this represents a new form of supply chain relationship, a transformation from the JIT system to what might be termed 'at supplier cost' (see Figure 6.4).

A further impact of the shift to modularisation is that it is leading to changes in the intra-firm division of labour within the OEMs. Some commentators have argued that a modular system of production will mean that module suppliers will be subcontracted to work in the assembly plant to build cars. Ford has already gone down this road and is outsourcing parts of the final assembly process to suppliers at its new £800 million Ford Amazon plant in North East Brazil (*Financial Times*, 9 August 1999). Other commentators have suggested that automotive producers will hand over the organisation of production to subcontractors, withdrawing from all aspects of final assembly (*Financial Times*, 4 August 1999). This would even include the management of the production process. Such 'hollowing out' of the firm would leave the OEM, or major shareholder, only owning the marque.

These changes are impacting on the geography of production. While the geography of Fordism is characterised as one of decentralisation, and post-Fordism by a geography of proximity, the spatial organisation of the post-Japanisation phase is one of decentralisation and dispersal.

Spatial Organisation of Production

As Bloomfield (1991) suggests, the geography of Fordism is characterised by decentralisation. An internationalising industry resulted in the location of integrated production plants in different parts of the world (usually, in low labour cost countries); this was dispersal aided by low transportation costs. The geography of post-Fordism is different. The concentration of OEM production facilities in several locations, and the necessity of the close proximity of supply chain firms, resulted in centralisation. The geography of post-Fordism is characterised by the development of local production complexes (Storper, 1992). A geography of proximity emerged as the pattern of development (Lagendijk, 1997). This pattern applies to 'national champions'. Large firms benefit from local sourcing of components, when just-in-time delivery and shared problem solving are necessary (Doel, 1997).

Bordenave and Lung (1996) map out the spatial concentrations of the automotive industry in Europe, and identify concentrations in Germany and the UK. The spatial concentration of production also applies to Japanese transplants in the UK. Nissan, Toyota and Honda, sought a high local content and adopted local sourcing strategies to secure local embeddedness, establishing a supply chain to achieve just-in-time delivery of components. This pattern of local sourcing by the Japanese transplants is also a strategy of 'glocalisation', or 'global localisation', an internationalising strategy where the inter-firm division of labour is set within the international division of labour (Solvell, 1988). For Van Tulder and Ruigrok (1993), glocalisation represents a global strategy to produce vehicles for local markets. Production is dispersed internationally but concentrated within a region and geared to production for local markets and local taste. It is co-ordinated centrally. Ford, with its move to develop a 'world car', is arguably adopting a strategy of globalisation, where the intra-firm division of labour is organised globally, and production is for a global market (Parry-Jones, 1995).

The new phase of development, in which there is consolidation of component producers and the sourcing of components by auto assemblers on a worldwide scale, is changing the geography of proximity. Sadler (1999) considers whether the internationalisation of automotive component production is leading to the hollowing out of the automotive industry in Europe and whether Europe is simply becoming an auto assembly centre. While there is some evidence of a shift in production and employment away from Europe to the rest of the world, Sadler finds that auto component producers are dispersing production and employment from their domestic market area to other locations within Europe. This includes component producers based in the UK.

Sadler (1999) also finds that the auto assemblers are decentralising production away from the European core area; Bordenave and Lung (1996) find that this decentralisation is favouring the new markets of Central and Eastern Europe. This leads Sadler (1999) to argue that what is happening is a trend towards the 'Europeanisation' of the industry. Firms are orienting sourcing and sales on a European basis rather than on individual national markets. Bordenave and Lung (1996) concur with this argument. Looking at the impact of production reorganisations on the spatial configuration of activities in Europe, they consider that there are four possible directions the industry could take by 2005 (Figure 6.6). This classification is based on the activities of the automotive assemblers (whether they will decentralise to peripheral locations or concentrate in the European core), and the relative location of suppliers (whether they will polarise or disperse).

Figure 6.6   Possible spatial configurations of the automotive industry in 2005

Location tendency of component producers

Location tendency of auto assemblers	Polarisation	Dispersal
Concentration	Unipolar Agglomeration	Unipolar Dispersed
Decentralised	Multipolar Agglomeration	Continental Integration

Source: Bordenave and Lung, (1996).

The multipolar configuration refers to the development of local production complexes. Bordenave and Lung (1996) consider that on the basis of trends observed in the mid to late 1990s, the industry is moving away from this development path towards integration at the continental scale; i.e. a dispersed multipolar spatial configuration. Lagendijk (1997) considers that there is a 'merging filiere' in Europe, brought about by the internationalisation of component producers. Pointing to automotive component producers such as

Bosch and ITT, Lagendijk found that these companies are dispersing production throughout Europe, to serve several national markets. Ford Europe, GM Europe and Volkswagen-Audi are decentralising production throughout Europe. In other words, there is a trend away from the agglomeration or clustering of component suppliers around OEMs. This suggests that the strategy of both auto assemblers and component suppliers is to produce and sell within Europe, for a European market, and to internationalise production on the European scale, to *regionalise* production. Local production complexes, centred on national champions, and domestic markets will therefore be difficult to sustain.

It is in the light of these changes, that the case of BMW/Rover can be better understood. The importance of national champions, such as BMW/ Rover, is that they are 'flagships of national economic progress', 'a symbol of industrial strength' (Lehman, 1992). In this context, it is clear why there was a fight over the possible closure of BMW/Rover. It is also clear why national and regional governments feel the need to take action, especially to deal with possible closure, and the impacts of closure. The chapter now turns to the issues posed by the case of BMW/Rover.

The BMW/Rover Story

The events surrounding the sale of BMW/Rover represent a roller coaster of a story and are arguably a microcosm of what is happening in the auto industry (see Figure 6.7 which shows key dates in the diary of events). They include a strategic alliance; growing capital concentration; the internationalisation of production; consolidation; supply chain clustering; the restructuring of the supply chain; the challenge of becoming world-class suppliers; the need to defend market share; and the role of government in the process. In this case, this included the role of the European Union in funding for economic development. Further issues were the background economic conditions for production, and the threat of closure. The threat of closure was made several times from the point that it was clear that BMW/Rover was in trouble, until the sale to the Phoenix Consortium in May 2000.

Strategic Alliance and Takeover

The Rover Group has several plants in the UK, including Cowley, Oxford and the body-pressing facility at Swindon. Other sites include the main site at Longbridge, Birmingham; Land Rover at Solihull near Birmingham; the design and engineering centre at the Motor Heritage Centre, Gaydon, Oxfordshire, and a new engine plant, due to be finished in 2001, at Hams Hall, Birmingham.

Rover was bought by BMW in 1994 for £800 million. Prior to this it had entered a strategic alliance with Honda. Beneficial to Rover, the alliance enabled technology transfer into Rover which, it can be argued, was part of the process of restructuring in which Rover was attempting to come to terms with new competitive pressures. The company had already begun to rationalise its supply chain; by careful placing of contracts, the company saved considerable sums in purchasing components. At the same time, the alliance brought changes in working practices to the firm.

The alliance with Honda ended at the subsequent sale of Rover to BMW. The sale offered bigger rewards to Rover, in the form of capital investment. However, as part of the process of capital concentration, this saw yet another UK-owned auto firm pass into foreign ownership and control. While this took the level of capital concentration among OEMs in the UK to such a level that it is impossible to speak of the UK car industry (only the car industry in Britain), it illustrates the Europeanisation of the industry. At the same time, the acquisition of Rover by BMW exemplifies an internationalising strategy. It enabled BMW to increase its market share and extend its product market. BMW also wanted the 'jewel in the crown', Land Rover, which would give it a new product market.

From the point of view of Rover and, in particular, the Longbridge plant, the takeover promised new investment and the opportunity to modernise and upgrade the plant. BMW invested some £3 billion in Rover over the period 1994 to 2000 (House of Commons, 2000). Most of this was put into the Land Rover plant in Solihull in the West Midlands, and at Cowley, to build the Rover 75, and in the plant at Swindon. Some £500 million was spent on Longbridge, mainly on product development, in bringing the new 'mini' to market. Overall, however, BMW planned to invest around £1.7 billion in Longbridge, to modernise the factory to build the new mini, as well as a new car to replace the Rover 200 and 400.

Changes in Working Practices

In late 1998, it became clear that all was not well. Sales were falling and losses were mounting, at the rate of £400 to £500 million a year. The company had made job cuts of about 1,500 in July of that year and had sought productivity deals. This was not enough and, at the same time that the new Rover 75 was being launched at the Birmingham Motor Show, Bernd Pischestreider, BMW's

Figure 6.7   BMW/Rover: key dates in the diary of events

Oct 1998	BMW threatens to close Longbridge; investment frozen unless workers agree to new working practices and redundancies. Seeks government assistance.
Nov 1998	BMW and the unions agree a deal to lift closure threat at Longbridge; £300 million investment in Land Rover.
Dec 1998	Dr Hasselkus, Chair of Rover, replaced by Professor Samann; Bernd Pischestreider, Chair of BMW, replaced by Professor Joachim Milberg.
Mar 1999	BMW threatens to pull out of Longbridge, unless it gets government grant; DTI agrees grant of £150 million in RSA and other local grants for BMW/Rover. Porsche objects.
June 1999	Aid package signed between BMW and DTI.
Aug 1999	Mario Monti appointed European Commissioner for Competition Policy.
Dec 1999	European Commission says it will be six months before a decision will be made on whether grant of RSA breaks competition rules.
Mar 2000	BMW announces it is to sell Rover to Alchemy Partners, and Land Rover to Ford.
Apr 2000	Negotiations with Phoenix Consortium begin.
May 2000	Rover (Longbridge) sold to Phoenix Consortium.
June 2000	Land Rover sold to Ford for £1.8 billion.

Chair, announced that BMW would close Longbridge unless workers accepted fresh productivity deals (*Daily Telegraph*, 21 October 1998). BMW was also seeking redundancies and, it was evident, a government grant to support its investment. This was refused. Peter Mandelson, then Secretary of State for Trade and Industry, said that Rover had to solve its own problems and should not look to government for assistance (*Birmingham Evening Mail*, 21 October 1998). It was said that closure would result in 14,000 jobs being lost in the plant, with an estimated three times as many in the firms in the supply chain.

Frenzied negotiations with the unions followed, and workers were given six weeks to come to agreement. BMW was reported as seeking productivity gains of 30%, to match those on its German production lines, and a 20% reduction in staffing costs. Proposals included 'flexi-hours' working where extra hours are stored rather than paid as overtime. A deal was struck at the end of November 1998 and Longbridge was saved (*Birmingham Post*, 27 November 1998). The deal involved the loss of 2,500 jobs, which was to be achieved through voluntary redundancies (*The Times*, 28 November 1998). Other changes included voluntary Saturday working, but the working week was cut from 37 to 35 hours, in exchange for the adoption of the flexible working practices. Workers backed the deal at a union meeting in early December. However, uncertainties about the sustainability of Longbridge continued to simmer.

November 1998 also saw the announcement of a £300 million investment in the Solihull-based Land Rover plant. Despite its relative success, fears were expressed about Land Rover's future too. It was thought that production of Land Rovers would be switched to the US (*Birmingham Evening Mail*, 23 November 1998). At the same time, BMW/Land Rover took the step of also internationalising production, by investing £89 million in a facility in Brazil, to manufacture the Freelander for this newly growing market.

It was clear that a boardroom battle was going on in BMW. Sales fell to the lowest ever figure of 11,200 cars a month, giving Rover only 4.6% of the UK market. In 1998, sales were around 20,500 cars a month. The falling sales called into question Bernd Pischestreider's strategy of keeping Rover and BMW operations separate. Others had argued that operations should be more integrated (*Birmingham Post*, 5 February 1999). Pischestreider was subsequently replaced by Professor Joachim Milberg, whose plans for Rover were somewhat different. Meanwhile, Dr Walter Hasselkus, Group Chair for Rover, was also replaced in December 1998, by Professor Werner Samann (*Birmingham Post*, 17 December 1998). Samann at this time warned that unless the company made a profit by 1999, there would be further redundancies. He also said that Rover was going to source more parts from abroad. The high value of the pound was making imports cheaper.

The Switch to European Suppliers

In March 1999, BMW announced again that it would pull out of Rover and would not invest in Longbridge, unless certain conditions were met. BMW sought further redundancies, changes in working practices, new supplier relationships and a government grant. It should be remembered that the German company had already improved productivity at Rover. It went on to obtain trade union and workers' agreement to 'German style' working practices, and redundancies. Some 3,500 workers were to leave Longbridge over this period up to early 1999, taking the 14,000 workforce at Longbridge down to 9,500.

BMW also wanted a government grant. The announcement was made by Professor Milberg, at the Geneva Motor Show, in March 1999. BMW would build the new Rover at Longbridge, but it wanted support from the British Government. When it looked like the £200 million it wanted was not forthcoming, it was reported that BMW would move production to Hungary. 'Pay Up or We Pull out' was the headline in the *Birmingham Evening Mail* (5 March 1999). BMW was initially offered £118 million, but in negotiations the offer was raised to £150 million, with £129 million in regional selective assistance and the rest coming from the Birmingham Economic Development Partnership.

Agreement was reached between BMW and Stephen Byers, the new Secretary of State for Trade and Industry. In view of later events, it is with some irony that the announcement was made on the 1st April 1999. BMW said that Longbridge would be rebuilt, in a £1.7 billion investment, to produce the new mini and the R30, the car which was to replace the Rover 200 and 400 (*Birmingham Evening Mail*, 1 April 1999). The government saw it as saving 50-60,000 jobs in the region, in both Rover and the firms in the supply chain. The deal, however, was not signed until June 1999 (*Birmingham Post*, 23 June 1999). It was reported that the DTI and BMW were 'confident that the grant would not breech EU competition laws'. It had been approved in principle by the Technical Committee for Competition of the European Commission. Porsche, however, objected, seeing it as unfair competition and said that it would complain to the European Commission (BBC Radio 4, 10 March 1999).

BMW had already started rationalising its supply chain, as might have been expected. As noted above, the development of world-class suppliers has led OEMs to source on a global basis. As far as BMW was concerned, it had its suppliers in continental Europe and it was cheaper for it to source on a European-wide basis rather than from within the West Midlands. The high value of the pound on the foreign exchange market was making components produced in Europe cheaper. Announcements appeared in the local press that a number of firms had lost their contracts to supply Rover. BMW was reported as seeking a 20% cut in prices from its remaining suppliers, as might be expected, without sacrificing quality. Firms lower down in the supply chain were warned that they too would have to become world class (KPMG, nd).

Crisis: Sale or Closure?

While the government had agreed in mid-1999 to grant BMW regional selective assistance, by December 1999 the European Commission still had not approved the grant arrangements. A new commissioner for competition policy had been appointed in August 1999, which arguably was a factor in the delay (House of Commons, 2000). Stephen Byers, the Secretary of State for Trade and Industry, indicated that it might take the Commission until June 2000 to reach a decision (*Birmingham Post*, 10 December 1999). It was clear that BMW could not wait. In March 2000, BMW announced that it was going to sell Rover. Longbridge was to be sold to Alchemy Partners, a venture capital company (*Birmingham Evening Mail*, 16 March 2000). It was to 're-badge' Rover as MG cars, and announced that 5,000 jobs were to go in the Longbridge plant. This came as a considerable shock to Rover workers and people in the West Midlands. Of concern was the impact on the supply chain, and on firms, shops and people in the city of Birmingham at large.

Lengthy negotiations took place between Alchemy and BMW, but the deal fell through. It appeared that Longbridge would close after all. A campaign was waged by people in Birmingham, to keep Rover open, including a march through the city and a rally. Various delegations went to BMW's headquarters in Munich. A Task Force was set up by the RDA to look into the consequences and options (Rover Task Force, 2000). In April 2000, the Phoenix Consortium, headed by John Towers, a former managing director of Rover, and other local businesspeople, stepped into the breech. During the negotiations throughout April, it again appeared that these too would fall through. Finance was an issue. In May 2000, however, Longbridge was sold to Phoenix, for £10, with BMW making funds available to the company to run Longbridge (*The Guardian*, 10 May 2000). Land Rover was sold to Ford, for £1.8 billion. BMW did not sell the Cowley plant and was to use it to build the new mini there, rather than at Longbridge, as it had originally planned. BMW also retained the powertrain assembly section at Longbridge.

BMW had finally divested itself of a company that was making a loss; Longbridge was saved. Factors in the BMW decision to sell and the impact of possible closure posed a number of challenges to government, and not least to a regional development agency.

Change and Challenge: Concluding Remarks

It is clear that the automotive industry has been undergoing profound changes. New developments in a post-Japanisation phase include the trend towards outsourcing of modules, made possible by technological developments in production engineering, for example, the use of the platform strategy to build cars. A key driving force, however, is the need to squeeze costs out of the supply chain, which the OEMs are achieving by pushing costs and responsibility for sub-assembly onto the component producers. This is impacting on component producers, which have to become world class. The response is consolidation, through merger and acquisition, to achieve economies of scale and scope. A changing geography is suggested, with the supply firms dispersing, but with the assemblers also decentralising, in a display of Fordist behaviour, seeking low labour-cost locations. Lagendijk (1997) argues that a 'merging filiere' can be identified. The Europeanisation of production and consumption, however, holds out little hope for 'national/regional' clusters of production, such as that in the West Midlands. It challenges the RDAs to secure sustainable regional development, particularly where policy is based on cluster theory, and especially where an OEM in the region, at the heart of a cluster, may threaten to cease trading completely.

The automotive industry is a major employer in the West Midlands, not only in the assembler firms (of which the most famous are Jaguar, Peugeot and BMW/Rover), but also in firms in the tiers of the supply chain. It is estimated that 76,000 people worked in the industry in 1997. This does not include the number of people employed in firms lower down the supply chain. It is important, from the point of view of jobs and production capability, that the industry is sustained. At the same time, it needs to be recognised that the auto market is overcrowded. There is excess supply over demand. This forces the firms in the industry to adopt competitive strategies. Closure must follow the emergence of any unprofitable operation.

The BMW/Rover story illustrates such an outcome and also some of the developments taking place in the industry. It poses challenges to the RDA in terms of the strategic options available for dealing with the situation. The first challenge came from the decision of BMW to switch to sourcing components from continental suppliers. If this change can be said to represent the hollowing out of the industry, the closure of the plant most certainly would have resulted in the potential collapse of the supply chain and would have threatened further the development of the automotive production cluster in the region. BMW's earlier warning that it would relocate production in Hungary, while a typically

Fordist characteristic, also posed this threat. However, the threat to move production also came as a result of the government's decision not to award regional selective assistance to BMW, although it can be argued that the threat to move was just an excuse to enable BMW to be awarded RSA. In any case, the issue of RSA poses further contradictions for the RDA and in general raises questions about the role of government in securing favourable conditions for production.

Regional development funds are in principle available for regional development. The scale of RSA funding expected by BMW, however, puts administration of this *regional* development fund in the hands of *central* government. The RDAs have no control over RSA; they only have the function of advising ministers about applications to the fund. The situation is compounded because central government in turn is constrained by EU competition policy. The award of such assistance is seen as being potentially anti-competitive in the single European market. The delay by the European Commission in giving a decision over RSA, however, was also a factor in BMW's decision to sell (House of Commons, 2000). In addition, BMW's decision was fuelled by what it saw as the exchange rate policy of the UK and the failure to join European Monetary Union (EMU). This had resulted in high prices and had affected exports of Rover cars.

However, at least the sale to the Phoenix Group presented the opportunity to re-establish Rover as a 'national champion' and sustain the supply chain, averting in the short to medium term the hollowing out of the industry in the Midlands. However, if the RDA is to have a catalytic role in securing the development of the industry, then at the very least, companies have to be prepared to collaborate and co-operate, as the cluster approach would suggest. As noted above, however, the announcement by BMW to sell Rover caught everyone by surprise, including the UK Secretary of State for Trade and Industry, who was needlessly exposed to some criticism (*Birmingham Post*, 4 April 2000). What this contemporary industrial story demonstrates is that the RDA has little power to save key firms in the region from closure. If it cannot do this, then the strategic option left open might be to assist firms in the supply chain to find other customers for their goods.

References

Advantage West Midlands (1999), *Creating Advantage: The West Midlands Economic Strategy*, Advantage West Midlands, Birmingham.

Amin, A. (ed) (1994), *Post Fordism: A Reader*, Blackwell, Oxford.

Amin, A. and Thrift, N. (1999), 'Living in the Global' in A, Amin and N. Thrift (eds), *Globalization, Institutions, and Regional Development in Europe* Oxford University Press, Oxford.

Anderson Consulting (1999), *Mergers and Acquisitions in the Automotive Components: The New Deal Terrain*. Anderson Consulting.

Annual Employment Survey, (1997).

Bentley, G. (1998) *Industry Developments in the Automotive Components Sector in the West Midlands*, 1998 Sector Update for the West Midlands Development Agency, Centre for Urban and Regional Studies, the University of Birmingham, Birmingham.

Birmingham Evening Mail, 21 October 1998, 'You're on Your Own'.

Birmingham Evening Mail, 23 November 1998, 'Now Land Rover Plant at Risk'.

Birmingham Evening Mail, 5 March 1999, 'Pay Up or We Pull Out'.

Birmingham Evening Mail, 1 April 1999, '21st Century Longbridge'.

Birmingham Evening Mail, 16 March 2000, 'Longbridge Stays – But Loses Mini'.

Birmingham Post, 27 November 1998, 'Longbridge Saved'.

Birmingham Post, 17 December 1998, 'Lack of Used Car Nous Cost Rover Chairman His Job'.

Birmingham Post, 5 February 1999, 'Munich Prepares Longbridge D-Day'.

Birmingham Post, 23 June 1999, '£150m Aid Buys off Fears for Longbridge'.

Birmingham Post, 10 December 1999, 'BMW Backs Longbridge to Secure Aid Package'.

Birmingham Post, 4 April 2000, 'So Who Said What and When'.

Bloomfield, G.T. (1991), 'The World Automotive Industry in Transition' in C. M. Law (ed), *Restructuring the Global Automobile Industry. National and Regional Impacts*, Routledge, London and New York.

Bordenave, G. and Lung, Y. (1996), 'New Spatial Configurations in the European Automotive Industry', *European Urban and Regional Studies*, vol. 3, no. 4, pp. 305-21.

Cahners Business Information (2000), *The Auto Industry: Fast Track to Modular Assembly* (http://www.manufacturing.net/sponsor/mmh/special/index.htm as at 20 May 2000).

Cooke, P. and Morgan, K. (1991), *The Intelligent Region: Industrial and Institutional Innovation in Emilia Romagna*, Regional Industrial Research Report 7, University of Wales, Cardiff.

Daily Telegraph, 21 October 1998, 'Rover threat to Close Longbridge'.

Department of Trade and Industry (1998), *Our Competitive Future: The Knowledge Driven Economy*, HMSO, London.

Doel, C. (1997), *The Supply Chain in Regional Development*, paper prepared for a LEPU seminar on improving competitiveness through supply chains and networks, Local Economic Policy Unit, South Bank University, London.

Financial Times, 4 August 1999, 'Ford to Farm out Jobs in Final Assembly: Carmaker's Chief Executive Sees Move as the Model for Future Manufacturing'.

Financial Times, 9 August 1999, 'Ford's Full Service'.

Financial Times, 16 May 2000, 'Carmaker Consolidation to Continue'.

The Guardian, 10 May 2000, 'He Liked Rover So Much He Bought It. For £10'.

House of Commons (2000), *BMW, Rover and Longbridge*, Select Committee on Trade and Industry Eighth Report, HMSO, London (www.parliament.the-stationery-office.co.uk as at 13 April 2000).

KPMG (nd), *West Midlands Automotive Supply Chain Development Study*, Birmingham and Solihull TEC and West Midlands Development Agency, Birmingham.

Lagendijk, A. (1997), 'Towards an Integrated Automotive Industry in Europe: A 'Merging Filiere' Perspective', *European Urban and Regional Studies*, vol. 4, no. 1, pp. 5-18.

Lamming, R. (1993) *Beyond Partnership: Strategies for Innovation and Lean Supply,* Prentice Hall, London.

Law C. M. (1991), 'Motor Vehicle Manufacturing: The Representative Industry' in C. M. Law (ed), *Restructuring the Global Automobile Industry. National and Regional Impacts*, Routledge, London and New York.

Lees, J. and Smith, P. (1993), 'A Sectoral Analysis of the Walsall Economy', *Journal of Industrial Affairs*, vol. 2, pp. 6-15.

Lehman, J-P. (1992) 'France, Japan, Europe and Industrial Competition: The Automotive Case', *International Affairs*, vol. 68, no. 1, pp. 37-53.

McCrone, G. (1999), 'Industrial Clusters: A New Idea or An Old One?', *Scottish Affairs*, no. 29, Autumn, pp. 73-83.

Parry-Jones, R. (1995), 'Globalisation of the automotive industry as exemplified by Ford 2000' in D. Stirley and K. Read (eds), *Fifty Years of Excellence*, Atlalink and MIRA, The Motor Industry Research Association, London.

Pemberton, M. (2000), 'The Car Industry – the Next 20 Years', *World Automotive Manufacturing*, vol. 23, March, pp. 15-7.

Porter, M. (1990), *The Competitive Advantage of Nations*, MacMillan, London.

Porter, M. (1998), *The Role of Clusters in Economic Development*, by Ron Martin, paper presented to Cambridge Econometrics Annual Conference, July 1999, University of Cambridge, Cambridge.

Rover Task Force (2000), *Interim Report to the Secretary of State for Trade and Industry*, Advantage West Midlands, Birmingham.

Sadler, D. (1999), 'Internationalization and Specialization in the European Automotive Components Sector: Implications for the Hollowing Out Thesis', *Regional Studies*, vol. 33, no. 2, pp. 109-120.

Saublens, C. (1999), *Clusters, Industrial Districts, Local Productive Systems*, Euro-Report Nr 6, European Association of Development Agencies, Brussels.

Scheele, N. (2000) *Globalisation: A Metalforming Industry Response*. Presentation given to a conference at the National Metalforming Centre, West Bromwich, 15 May 2000.

Solvell, O. (1988), 'Is the Global Automobile Industry Really Global?' in N. Hood and J-E. Vahlne (eds), *Strategies in Global Competition,* Croom Helm, London.

Storper, M. (1992), 'The Resurgence of Regional Economies, Ten Years Later the Region As a Nexus of Untraded Interdependencies', *European Urban and Regional Studies*, vol. 2, no. 3, pp. 191-221.

Tilson, B. (1997), *The Drive for Change in the Automotive Components Sector and Implications for Suppliers in the West Midlands Region*, for the West Midlands Development Agency, Centre for Urban and Regional Studies, the University of Birmingham, Birmingham.

Tilson, B. (1999), 'A Tidal Wave for Change. The Case of the Automotive Supply Chain in the West Midlands', *Local Economy*, vol. 13, no. 4, pp. 295-309.

The Times, 28 November 1999, 'BMW Deal Lifts Closure Threat at Longbridge'.

Van Tulder, R. and Ruigrok, W. (1993), 'Regionalisation, Globalisation or Glocalisation: The Case of the World Car Industry' in M. Humbert (ed), *The Impact of Globalisation on Europe's Firms and Industries*, Pinter Publishers, London.

Wells, P. and Rawlinson, M. (1994), *The New European Automobile Industry*, St Martin's Press, New York.

Womack, J. P., Jones, D. T. and Roos, D. (1990), *The Machine that Changed the World*, Rawson Associates, New York.

Wolverhampton Business School (1996), *A Study of Automotive Component Suppliers in Telford*, for the Telford Development Agency, Wolverhampton Business School, Wolverhampton.

7 Towards an Innovation-Rich Regional System for Product and Process Development in Rubber and Plastics

BARBARA TILSON

SECTION I: BUSINESS ISSUES, PRACTICES AND PROSPECTS

Introduction: The International Context of Competition and Change

The business environment for manufacturing industry is undergoing constant redefinition through intense international competition and continual technological change. The pressures are as acute for West Midlands industry as they are for international players, and therefore this discussion of rubber and plastics processing has wider implications for the stimulus and support of business growth, competitiveness and innovation. The processing of rubber and plastics (polymers) constitutes a key component of the national economy, and it is also significant in the industrial mix of the West Midlands region where a great diversity of mouldings, extrusions, composites, laminates and sheets are supplied to customers such as the automotive, construction, food and drink, electronics and engineering sectors. Consolidation and restructuring among these industries are influencing changes to customer-supplier relationships. UK processors are increasingly pitched against strong overseas contenders and they encounter pressure in both their domestic and export markets through the competitive costs and quality of overseas rivals. Larger processors are refocusing their activities onto either high-growth or core production areas. Prices of raw materials fluctuate, and both over-capacity and shortages prove problematic in terms of pricing and supply. Advances in information technology and communications are revolutionising production and commerce, and contribute to closer links between processors, their industry customers and retailers. Environmental compliance exerts ever more stringent and costly demands,

151

while producer responsibility obligations, affecting the manufacture and use of packaging, foreshadow take-back schemes proposed for other production sectors, such as vehicles and electronic consumer goods, emphasising material and component recyclability and waste minimisation.

Fierce price competition is forcing greater emphasis on innovation, including through sharing product and process development. Certain innovatory activities are likely to be outsourced, notably design engineering or styling, software solutions or technological research. To achieve a competitive edge, manufacturers must not only achieve high rates of productivity and efficiency, but are also increasingly offering value added and differentiation through the unmatched calibre or uniqueness of their products or services. Packaging manufacturers are tending to focus on high value added product niches, such as speciality food packs, while they yield their markets for high-volume, low-margin standard products to thrusting competitors such as China. Makers of general consumer goods are similarly affected.

Vehicles suppliers are highly vulnerable as they are beset by growing international competition and pressure to perform at world class levels in order to retain supply contracts. The prospect of new fuel and propulsion technologies poses both a threat and an opportunity, and suppliers have been described as 'standing on top of a wave looking into a gulf'.[1]

In discussing the challenges and opportunities for achieving a more innovative dynamic in the West Midlands, this chapter examines factors underlying the attainment of an innovation-rich regional system which has the resources and dynamism to catalyse and facilitate innovation in manufacturing industry. Attention is focused on two contrasting sectors of polymer processing – the automotive and packaging industries – giving a whole-sector perspective, through addressing environmental issues; materials, product and process development; skills and training; and technological collaboration. The chapter is structured in two parts. Section I looks at business issues, trends and prospects, while Section II discusses the components of innovation richness.

Within an extensive research context, the discussion makes reference to a 1997 survey of 16 companies across the West Midlands region ('the West Midlands study') conducted by the writer as part of an economic review by the University of Birmingham.[2] The majority of surveyed firms employed 100 - 249 people, with an annual turnover of £10 - £24.9 million. One third (five) were independent, most (nine) being subsidiaries of UK firms, and two were European-owned. The largest employer produced polymer resins, one was in the tyres business, and the remainder were processors. Though supplying to many sectors (up to five was standard), most had one or more key customers, predominantly automotive, building, food and drink, domestic appliances, electronics/IT/telecoms, packaging, furniture, boat-building, and local authorities. Over half (nine companies) supplied to the automotive industry, and one quarter (four) produced packaging. Nearly a third (five) manufactured components for electrical, electronic and communications customers, and another third supplied to the building industry.

Sector Characteristics and Performance

The processing of rubber and plastics constitutes a major employment activity nationally and for the West Midlands region. Across the UK, some 6,825 enterprises producing polymer goods provide jobs for 235,700 people, representing 5.6% of the UK's total manufacturing employment (1995 figures). The level rose slowly during the 1990s from the low point of the decade in 1992. Although the average regional employment of 9.1% in rubber and plastics processing is far surpassed by the South East (20.2%), it is also exceeded by the West Midlands (16.2%), confirming its economic significance. Job numbers in the plastics industry have increased at the expense of those in rubber processing. Between 1993 and 1995, employment in plastic processing in the West Midlands rose by 1,000 (4.4%) to reach 23,500 jobs. In contrast, rubber processing jobs contracted by 7.5% though the West Midlands retained the highest regional employment, fielding 14,700 jobs in 1995 (Figure 7.1). The decrease reflects the effects of a switch to improved plastic materials from rubber, glass and metals in production sectors like automotive, engineering and packaging (Office for National Statistics, 1998a). At the same time, competition and market changes have forced western tyre producers like Goodyear, Michelin and Pirelli (all with West Midlands plants) to downsize as they rationalise.

Many of the UK's world class players have West Midlands links, including British Polythene Industries, Rexam, Linpac, McKechnie and Hepworth, and there are also prominent inward investors from Europe, the US and the Far East, notably those supplying to vehicles assemblers. Despite the presence of these standard bearers, the importance of rubber and plastics processing to the regional and national economies makes it vital to secure overall improvement in the sector's international performance.

By some indicators, an improvement is discernible in the performance of the rubber and plastics processing sector. From 1990 to 1995, national output of rubber and plastic products increased by 29% to reach £17.1 million on the back of expanding demand.

Figure 7.1 Regional employment in rubber and plastic products, 1995

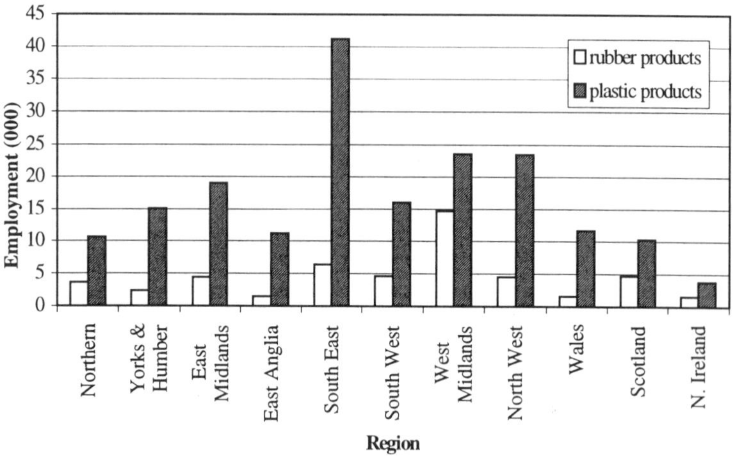

Source: Office for National Statistics (1998a).

Gross value added (GVA) at factor cost reached £6.2 million in 1995 for plastic and rubber product manufacture, comprising 4.8% of the UK manufacturing total. Per head of population GVA rose from £21,300 to £26,500 from 1990 to 1995. This figure disguises a disquieting trend, however. Whereas productivity indices for 1992 to 1997 show improvements up to 1994, productivity decreased during the following two years, while France and Germany improved their relative positions (Figure 7.2).

The UK (at 3.18 million tonnes) is the fourth largest consumer of plastic materials in Europe, roughly equal to France, but well behind Italy and Germany. Total European Union consumption was 25.27 million tonnes (1996 figures) (Figure 7.3).

Manufacturers of polymer products tend to serve UK markets, and a negative trade balance exists (-£522 million at 1996 figures) (Office for National Statistics, 1998a). UK demand is greatest for thermoplastics such as rigid and film polyethylene, polypropylene and PVC (Association of Plastics Manufacturers in Europe, 1999). Polymer materials and goods are supplied to many sectors, but key markets – many of which figure in the West Midlands region's industrial mix – are containers for food and drink, components for the motor industry, casings and innards for electrical and electronic appliances such as computers and televisions, building products such as pipes and windows, and toys and housewares. Thermosetting plastics such as aminoresins, phenolics, polyurethanes and epoxides are used in a variety of applications such as

Figure 7.2 National productivity comparisons, 1992 to 1997

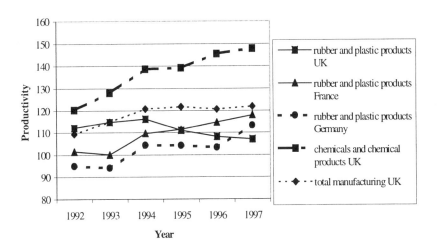

Note: the base is 1990 = 100. Whole year data are shown from 1992 to 1996, and second quarter data for 1997.

Source: Office for National Statistics (1998a).

automotive and electrical parts, coatings and adhesives.

A significant UK producer of thermosetting resins, BIP, is located at Oldbury in the Black Country. The UK has particular strengths in packaging (focused in the West Midlands on the urban conurbation and the more rural areas of the region in Herefordshire and Worcestershire),[3] in co-extrusion techniques for producing multi-layered products (such as vehicle fuel tanks) and in injection moulding for sectors such as vehicles and engineering which are also important to the economic health of the West Midlands.

Over-capacity in certain activities, such as plastics compounding, and high prices of raw materials mean that processors operate on tight profit margins. Saturation in western markets has forced companies to tap growth opportunity in economies such as Russia, the former Yugoslavia, India and South East Asia, though at the close of the millennium the strength of sterling hampered their competitiveness. Nearly one-fifth of the firms in the West Midlands study planned market diversification. In export markets, though, UK firms are pitted against often entrenched indigenous players and overseas national policies which may prohibit wholly overseas-owned plants. Tactics include acquiring subsidiaries and establishing new plants abroad, and forming marketing and

Figure 7.3 Consumption of plastic materials in major European Union countries, 1996

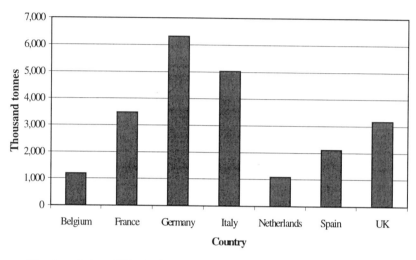

Source: The Association of Plastics Manufacturers in Europe (1999).

distribution agreements or joint ventures with the foreign partner (Andersen Consulting, 1999).

The Supply of Rubber and Plastic Components to the Vehicles Industry

The production of rubber and plastic vehicle components is significant in the West Midlands, with particularly strong clusters in Telford and the West Midlands county. Both plastics and synthetic rubber are also used in tyre manufacture, and Staffordshire is a production stronghold in the region (Tilson, 1998a; 1998b). Immense challenges are faced by suppliers to vehicles manufacturers. Despite the turnaround achieved by UK producers of parts and accessories in performing increasingly competitively in 1996-97 after selling goods below cost in 1995 (Office for National Statistics, 1998b), purchasing changes by some automotive assemblers, notably Rover, will not favour local suppliers unless they demonstrate world class calibre and competitiveness. The DTI Chemicals and Biotechnology Directorate had also warned in the 1997 Sector Challenge: 'Many UK companies have been content with low value added products and processes. UK component suppliers have not improved their performance sufficiently to meet customers' growing demand for suppliers who can assume responsibility for development of entire sub-systems' (DTI, 1998c).

Assemblers ratchet up suppliers' performance by demanding that they achieve recognised quality standards such as QS 9000 and ISO 9000-2 and by requiring pricing decreases. The West Midlands study confirmed that the producers of vehicles increasingly look to their suppliers to take a share of the burden of innovation in products, components, processes, systems or services. Processors must comply with their customers' expectations for higher quality at reduced cost. They must attain more reliable, speedy and synchronised delivery of complete systems and participate in the product and process development of new vehicle models.[4] This might entail developing the technical competence to supply systems, rather than individual components or sub-assemblies, and to install those systems directly onto the customer's production platform, or to offer a full design-to-installation capability.

Skills and Competencies for an Era of Business Complexity and Change

Technological advances and the increasing complexity of production processes exert pressure for higher level expertise in design, production, electronics and materials. Firms now need a far broader skills matrix, but are unlikely to possess the required range and level of competencies in-house to tackle the whole spectrum of innovatory requirements, not least because new technology is increasingly complex and its development is also likely to occur outside their main production activity. For vehicles suppliers, for example, technological change occurs in information technology and communications, in new power methods, and in relation to unfamiliar materials or processes. This factor, added to the high costs of innovation, makes collaboration more likely through firms establishing joint ventures or strategic alliances to share the costs of research and technology development, or by company acquisition to access new technologies and markets through technology and knowledge transfer.[5]

External initiatives devised to help polymer processors and other, suppliers include a project on Supply Chain Technology for SMEs complementing the DTI and Engineering and Physical Sciences Research Council's (EPSRC) Innovative Manufacturing Initiative's Cogent product design programme focused on the automotive industry. The DTI's four-year Partnership in Plastics programme supports exports, the supply chain, training, benchmarking and technology transfer (DTI, 1998b). In the West Midlands, supplier improvement initiatives include Accelerate, the Society of Motor Manufacturers and Traders/ Industry Forum and the Vigilance mentoring schemes for automotive and engineering firms.

Across the polymer industries, skill deficiencies pose a continuing UK problem, with the labour force in Wales and the East and West Midlands more likely to hold no relevant qualifications than those living elsewhere (British Polymer Training Association, 1997). The West Midlands study demonstrated unfulfilled demand for skills in toolmaking and technical support for injection and extrusion processes; competencies like CAD/CAM and other specialist engineering disciplines such as design, chemical and maintenance, as well as project management; and for sales personnel with technical knowledge. Similar skill needs were raised by the writer's parallel surveys of automotive components supply and electrical and electronic engineering.[6] Raising skill levels is vital, too, because firms renowned as technology leaders, with strong competencies and a record of product innovation, can attract the best scientists and engineers and elicit higher performance and commitment from their employees more easily (Mueller, 1993). Therefore, as processing companies' reputations heighten, they should attract a higher calibre of personnel. Training is a primary means of improving employees' skills and enabling workforce flexibility via multi-skilling. Improving their workforces can also help firms to achieve sustained productivity (Jones and Tang, 1998; *Financial Times*, 14 May 1996), while organisational learning progresses their competitive advantage.[7] It is not surprising, therefore, that the West Midlands study indicated that training was the top priority for which firms needed external support: the TECs and commercial providers were major sources.

Wells (1992) pointed to the importance of developing local training and technology networks such as those found in Baden-Württemberg for the automotive industry. The West Midlands moved further in this direction in the 1990s: for example, automotive plastics moulder, F W Woolley, established an in-house training centre in Birmingham open to external use; Rover opened its training centre to its suppliers; and the Engineering Employers Federation purchased a training centre to serve its members (Tilson, 1998b). Birmingham and Solihull TEC and industry partners such as Rover, Jaguar, Peugeot and LDV obtained funding from the region's Skills Development Fund to purchase advanced equipment for further education (FE) colleges to update the skills of automotive engineers and teach students modern factory methods (Advantage West Midlands, 1999a). Polymer processors could benefit, to sustain their expertise at the cutting edge of technological change.

Both the West Midlands study and Europe-wide research have indicated that processors also need better marketing skills and market intelligence, including exports assistance (Bosworth et al, 1996). In recognition of how SMEs can help each other, the European trans-regional Sesames project to support innovation and technology transfer in automotive suppliers in four German and Italian regions includes the objective to 'combine their efforts in gathering and diffusing economic intelligence, in terms of technology, market, regulations and competition in the automotive cluster'.[8]

Challenging the Status Quo: Environmental and Performance Issues

Materials Advances

Engineering thermoplastics and composites are strategic technologies for the 21st century. Innovation in industry sectors such as construction, vehicles, audio-visual appliances and computers cannot proceed without advances in materials and production technology. To spur on research and commercial applications, both the European Commission's research and technology actions (e.g. the Framework Programme, Brite-Euram and Eureka) and the UK's Technology Foresight Programme have targeted materials innovation. The Foresight Materials Panel's vision of the future (1995) encompassed weight-saving and higher temperature materials, biomaterials, materials modelling, high-temperature superconductors, sensors and devices, and environmentally friendly processing technologies. Phase 3 of the Programme (from 1998) prioritises business involvement and cross-sectoral initiatives linking materials to strategic applications like aerospace and electronics (Office of Science and Technology, 1995; 1997).

Market demand is growing for lightweight high-performance components in plastics and composites to replace metals, for example in aerospace parts, despite the technical difficulties in separating multi-materials composites for recycling. Design, production and joining techniques for plastics and dissimilar materials are crucial processes. Advanced materials and components are constantly being developed for the burgeoning electronics and communications industries, including specialist plastic components and micro-fasteners for computers, and for optic fibres in which the UK is among the world leaders: a prime innovator, Marconi Communications, is West Midlands-based.

Much of the innovation in synthetic rubber compounds with greater longevity, flexibility and recyclability is by the large, consolidated, speciality chemicals producers overseas such as Enichem, Exxon, Dow and Du Pont though, as the West Midlands study showed, rubber processors provide value added through developing compounds in-house to customer specification as well as manufacturing the components from those compounds. International tyre producers compete to introduce new compounds, product designs and construction techniques. Medical and surgical advances are also a major impetus to materials improvements. But rubber's uses are eroded by improved thermoplastics and plastic-rubber compounds such as thermoplastic elastomers offering the processability of thermoplastics with the performance properties of synthetic rubber and cost advantages in automotive, film and sheet, medical and construction applications. The UK general rubber goods industry's declining international importance prompted the British Rubber Manufacturers Association to obtain 1997 Sector Challenge funding for firms to benchmark Japanese automotive practices (Tilson, 1998a; 1999b; 1999c; DTI, 1996; DTI and British Plastics Federation, 1996).

Waste and Recycling

Legislation (both existing and forthcoming) on pollution control, waste recovery, recycling and disposal,[9] combined with increased public awareness and media coverage about the despoilation of the natural environment and the diminution of irreplaceable resources, drives the demand for and manufacture of smaller, lighter, longer-lasting products produced with minimum waste and without harmful emissions, in materials which can be recycled or re-used. Environmental regulatory demands impose added costs as well as organisational and production changes on businesses. There is a danger that their R&D investment will be focused on responding to these requirements. Restricting the scope of research and innovative activity to satisfy environmental regulations can stifle product and process innovation, as experience warns from the US, when the Nixon administration imposed burdensome environmental and health regulations at the time of the 1973 oil crisis. In the chemical industry – which develops most of its new technologies itself - the best technical personnel were tied up with projects to satisfy these regulations at the expense of R&D in new products and processes. This adversely affected chemical companies' productivity when demand decreased and plant lay under-utilised (Chakrabati, 1990). Clearly, it is important that the UK does not mirror this experience, because manufacturers of vehicles, electrical appliances, consumer electronics and packaging rely on constant materials and process advances. This necessitates high levels of focused investment. The conundrum is to introduce safer, less polluting and more energy-efficient operations and also to develop products and processes with these environmental features.

Environmental Drivers and Innovation in the Packaging Industry

Packaging is the largest single application for plastics, consuming one-third (32%) of output worldwide and over two-fifths (44%) of the UK total (British Plastics Federation, 1999a; 1999b). Some nations like China and Taiwan, with which UK processors compete, have no additional cost burden from environmental regulations and are more competitive in low-priced goods like plastic bags in markets such as Europe. This has spurred UK manufacturers to achieve differentiation through higher value added products such as more complex film packaging. Driving change in the packaging industry is the UK's *Producer Responsibility Obligations (Packaging Waste)* regulations of 1997 which followed a 1994 European Commission directive setting out targets. Under the initial UK regulations, all sections of the supply chain from materials supplier to producer and seller were obligated unless output was under £5 million and they handled less than 50 tonnes of packaging per year. From 2000, businesses with a turnover as low as £2 million must prove they recover and recycle their obligated quota (DTI, 1998a; Valpak, 1999).

In a 1998 consultation paper entitled *Less Waste, More Value* the UK government raised the prospect of economic measures to encourage the greater use of recycled materials in new products and to increase recycling (DETR, 1998). Innovation in the design, construction and materials development of containers, film wrap and bottles can help to conserve raw materials and increase recyclability, though trace contaminants in the secondary material make using plastics recyclate to manufacture food and drink packs problematic. Techniques which consume less materials include thin-walling and container re-use. A significant example of materials substitution on the supermarket shelf was the replacement of the glass milk bottle by Plysu's plastic carton (Key Note, 1997; *Financial Times*, 12 February 1998). For multi-trip transit packaging plastics have partly replaced wood and metals, giving enhanced longevity and easy handling at comparable cost.

The Association of Plastics Manufacturers in Europe (1999) estimated that 1.5 million tonnes of plastic packaging is recycled annually in Europe, with material recycling from domestic waste at 10.1%. Three methods for plastics recycling comprise (1) mechanical recycling to reprocess production waste; (2) feedstock recycling, involving reduction to the basic chemicals; and (3) incineration with or without energy recovery. As an alternative to German feedstock technology, BP and partners from the Netherlands, France, Italy and Belgium piloted a plant in Grangemouth, Scotland.

In anticipation of the packaging waste regulations, the UK's Producer

Responsibility Group, led by BP, Marks & Spencer and Scottish & Newcastle, was appointed in 1993. In 1995, 100 packaging, food and retail companies formed Valpak (Tilson, 1998a; Valpak, 1999). The concept of producer responsibility implies the safe post-use disposal of products, the development of technologies to identify and separate different materials, and the 'designing in' of product and component recyclability. But the UK has a catch-up role to play on European recycling leaders like Germany, whose Duales System Deutschland (DSD) collection/bring scheme was established in 1992 by 600 companies to meet recycling targets, and includes the DKR plastics subsidiary. Initial problems with 'waste mountains' occurred due to the inadequacy of the recycling infrastructure in coping with the volume of material collected by the enthusiastically 'green-conscious' public. In 1998, the DKR received 634,000 tonnes of plastics for recycling, employed 3,000 people in recycling jobs in 20 'preparation' plants, and had seven feedstock and 77 mechanical recycling plants in operation (Deutsche Gesellschaft für Kunstoff-Recycling, 1999).

One solution to the problem of waste plastics is using degradable plastics such as biopol, tone, bioceta and mater-bi. However, the UK's tradition of landfill and incineration of waste plastics, combined with a conservative approach to using degradables, their inappropriateness for engineering applications, the issue of the material robustness of film wrap used to package food, and the need for sunlight to enable decomposition, has limited their use. Biodegradable plastics like biopol and even edible plastics based on yeast have potential for packaging, and future EC legislation is certain to stimulate further interest (British Plastics Federation, 1996; Tilson, 1998a).

Recent innovations include the completely biodegradable plastic bag that Solvay (based in Brussels) has developed based on a polyester material, polycaprolactone, but whose strength in the presence of moisture makes it suitable for food packaging (*Financial Times*, 3 June 1999). A US joint venture, Cargill-Dow, was also formed by Dow Chemical and Cargill agriproducts to produce a biodegradable plastic based on polylactic acid. Cargill-Dow has established a UK alliance with Autobar, a major European packaging supplier, to produce easily disposable margarine and ice-cream tubs (*Financial Times*, 27 January 1998). In 1998, Du Pont described its purchase of a supplier of soy proteins, Protein Technologies, as 'strategic' for the 21st century (*Financial Times*, 29 January 1998). These moves indicate that there is potential in biodegradables for processors to exploit and this poses questions about the need which West Midlands firms may have for external support for sourcing collaborators, technology transfer opportunities and product and market intelligence.

Environmental and Safety Issues in the Automotive and Engineering Industries

Weight-saving plastics are a key priority in autos to offset the increasing weight and volume of on-board electronics and safety features and to aid fuel economy (Maxwell, 1994). The Association of Plastics Manufacturers in Europe (1999) estimated that 100 kg of plastics has replaced 200-300 kg of conventional materials in the typical car, resulting in a 750 litre saving in fuel consumption over a lifespan of 150,000 km. This equates to 12 million tonnes of oil saved and a reduction of around 30 million tonnes of CO_2 emissions across Europe each year. Plastics research concerns structures and materials, hybrid and electric vehicles, advanced electronics and telematics.[10] Rubber component innovation involves safety devices like airbags and improved barrier components, and ways to enable drivers to continue once tyres have deflated. Major manufacturers like Michelin are introducing run-flats or, like Goodyear, are improving tyre structure.[11] Rubber has been partly superseded by plastics such as PVC which can be more easily recycled and by thermoplastic elastomers.[12]

The encroachment of plastics on the traditional domain of steel car bodies and the prospect of higher performance engineering thermoplastics and composite mouldings replacing forgings, castings and pressings in interiors and even for under-bonnet applications has alarmed the steel industry. Projects such as the ultra-light steel automotive body (ULSAB) project have successfully enabled the steel industry to fight back. In the early 1990s the all-plastic car seemed feasible,[13] but this now seems less likely because of the development of improved steels and manufacturing technology, the use of light metals like aluminium and magnesium, and the greater competitiveness of carbon fibre composites.

Environmental concerns have stimulated research into renewable, non-polluting and disposable replacements for petrochemical-based plastics. Organic materials under investigation include jute, hemp, sisal, flax and cotton, as well as soya and cashew nut oil, either employed as stand-alone, blended with mainstream plastics, or used to reinforce plastics and resins. Mounting pressure for product recyclability is driving this research interest in plant fibres, for example in flax and linseed blended with polypropylene for car interior panels; jute in cars produced by General Motors at its Gujarat plant and as a substitute for synthetic fabrics; and hemp fibres replacing glass fibre composites in Daimler-Chrysler's head-rests (*Financial Times*, 7 November 1996). Cuban researchers have developed an epoxy adhesive from sugar instead of oil which acts like a metal filler and is strong enough to be used in ships.[14] A forthcoming European Commission directive will force assemblers (reluctantly) to take back their used vehicles for recycling from 2006. To this end, Toyota and Volkswagen formed a strategic alliance in 1998 to develop vehicle recycling technology. Ford has researched into technologies both to identify individual plastics and to recycle batteries, and also acquired its first US car recycling plant in 1999.[15]

Of the effects of the environmental directive, an economic commentator (*Financial Times*, 16 September 1999) declared: 'At best, it will lead to significant cost cutting and restructuring. At worst it could bankrupt those companies that fail to adapt to the requirements'. Bankruptcy is considered more likely through the higher costs of R&D, distribution and purchasing. A period of 'extreme turbulence' is predicted, raising questions about how to help polymer processors and other suppliers. To compound their uncertainty, processors must contend with new fuel and propulsion technologies, whether electric power, hybrid gas-petrol, fuel cells, or even solar power. Until now, innovation has consisted of ongoing incremental changes in the styling of vehicles and their construction, but radical departures from the current mechanics of powering vehicles will affect processors in *all* materials.

SECTION II: TOWARDS GREATER INNOVATION IN RUBBER AND PLASTICS PROCESSING

Developing New Materials, Products and Processes

The Office for National Statistics (1999) defines research and development as 'creative work undertaken on a systematic basis in order to increase the stock of knowledge...to devise new applications'. But the question arises of what meaning this generic term has for different companies. The West Midlands study indicated that firms tended to describe what they did as R&D even if the evidence was not identifiable for a 'first-to-market' or 'fast-follower' strategy, according to the four technology innovation postures established by Zahra et al (1994).[16] Firms' innovatory effort tended to be described as R&D if it concerned features which, though not new to the market, were *new to them*, such as their adoption of a different plant organisational system, changed processes, a creative approach to their service provision, or individualising their product or activity to tailor it to customer needs.

Compelling and far-reaching changes drive innovation in polymer processing. The West Midlands study revealed that change was foreseen by all 16 companies interviewed (Table 7.1). Companies gave a clear message that they needed help with product development, process equipment, and new machinery and materials-related technologies. As the pace of change quickens and business becomes more complex, firms must constantly access advanced technologies, rejuvenate their production activities as their technology matures to avoid obsolescence, and diversify through product, service or market. They must co-ordinate the tangible and intangible assets – such as skilled labour, reputation, brand image, technological expertise, efficient working practices, trade contacts and machinery – which comprise their distinctiveness (Mueller, 1993).

Whereas innovation leaders have valuable 'brand equity' in their markets (Dyer et al, 1999, p.15), the comparatively small size of polymer processing companies (69 % with annual turnover <£1 million) makes them unlikely to possess the resources to attain competitive advantage. Ownership status is also significant. Prime manufacturers in both polymer materials and markets like automotive, aerospace and consumer electronics mainly have their headquarters overseas where leading-edge R&D is pursued by assemblers and major first tier suppliers.

In 1990, Amendola noted (p. 497): 'In plastic components production, an independent and innovation-prone industry has not actually appeared yet'. This was still evident as the century ended. The backward vertical integration which is characteristic of the automotive industry contrasts with increasingly decentralised innovation in electronic components and occurs because automotive assemblers possess 'only limited opportunities for external borrowing of innovative capacity... (and) need to internalise know-how on process technology and on specific synthetic materials design criteria'. Decentralisation is clearly more conducive to diffusing innovation and requires that strong ancillary functions are available, including design, cost analysis, performance simulation, prototype production and testing.

Getting products quickly into the marketplace is vital to ensure competitiveness. Delays can occur through risk aversion, poor interdepartmental communication, inadequate teamwork, bureaucratic snarls, poor strategic thinking, an inability to define the product concept and design quickly or to access and process information speedily from external sources (Mansfield, 1988).

Important insights into the successful facilitation of materials R&D and commercialisation are yielded by studies of the Japanese government's support

Table 7.1 New and emerging technologies likely to affect processors

1.	SUBSTITUTION/MATERIALS CHANGES Thermoplastics replacing composites. Substitute materials for injection moulding. Improved composites. Increasing use of metallocenes. Increasing use of linear low density polyethylene (LLDPE) for thinner film. New materials formulations by petrochemicals companies.
2.	FORMING TECHNIQUES AND OTHER PROCESS CHANGES Changes to plastics processes. Extrusion technology enabling higher proportion of recycled materials to be used. Alternative bag-making technology becoming predominant. Decoration of product: changes to printing techniques. Process, simulation and control. Manufacture/assembly in one operation. Lower styrene emission resin technology. Recycling processes. Change from product to systems supply.
3.	PRODUCT CHANGES/END-USE Failsafe tamper evidence on closures. Recycled products. Substitution of hardwood in construction/horticultural/other applications.
4.	OTHER CHANGES European/UK legislation/regulation e.g. on environment/packaging/recycling. Move away from PVC to thermoplastic elastomers (TPEs) due to bottle leakage directive. Increasing regulation re glass-reinforced plastic (polyester composite). Change in cable industry: changeover to low smoke fuel + use of ethylene propylene diene monomer. Withdrawal of customers to Far East. Market diversification. Materials price rises, e.g. PVC, artificially ratcheted because of excess supply forecast. Change in the automotive industry. Collapse of the £. Federal state of Europe. Effects of IT changes. Competition from other industries. Change of government (from Major to Blair).

Cases: 16. Firms could identify more than one point.

Source: Survey of 16 plastics and rubber processing companies, Tilson (1997, 1998a).

for innovative firms. The Ministry of International Trade and Industry (MITI) initiated a series of research programmes in the 1980s and 1990s on advanced materials, including new polymers for high-tech, high-growth applications such as automobiles, electronics and communications (Wakasugi, 1992; Lastres, 1994). There was increasing integration of research, design, production and the applications for materials; multidisciplinary teamwork; a larger variety of tailor-made materials of high purity; higher value added; better compliance with environmental regulation; and multi-materials plant and flexible production systems, as compared to dedicated plant and equipment in conventional materials production. Information-intensive and external and internal information flows were in place via computerised intra- and inter-firm links. There was intense collaboration at national and international levels, and very high R&D investment in basic research and specific market applications. Networks of research, production and applications of advanced materials were important and included the participation of small and large-sized firms.[17]

Lastres (1994) asserted that an important plank of Japanese competitive strategy was 'the capacity to meet customers' requirements, and the provision of services associated with the products sold in the international markets' (Lastres, 1994, p. 120). Business process re-engineering was also required 'to adapt to the new organisational forms required by the production and commercialisation of advanced materials', and to access detailed information about materials applications. Acquisition played a major role in the latter objective 'in the downstream verticalisation of the consumers of advanced materials and upstream verticalisation of the materials producers' (Lastres, 1994, p. 124). Central to MITI's R&D policy was the promotion of industrial collaboration between multiple companies on basic research, applied R&D and standards. The resolution of intellectual property and high costs were important issues.

In Wakasugi's (1992) view, major facets of Japanese strategy on technology transfer were:

- the purchase of overseas technologies, feeding off the west's focus on basic research rather than devoting available research resources in this direction, and instead focusing R&D on developing applications;
- the integration of the R&D division into the overall corporate structure (unlike in the west, where R&D operated as an independent unit), with a very close relationship between R&D, production and marketing;
- a unified corporate goal;
- the assignment of talented engineers to production, rather than to R&D;

- internal knowledge transfer between divisions, including via the mobility of R&D staff around different divisions. This enhanced their broad technical knowledge and expertise whereas, in the west, research staff tended to work in isolated, static units;
- the preferential tax treatment on R&D spend enjoyed by Japanese firms.

Albach et al (1996) contrasted the promotion of innovation by the Japanese and US governments in promising fields such as materials and process technology through tax rebates, allowances to industry for R&D and a purposeful governmental purchasing policy, with the obstruction to research in some European countries through rigid laws and regulations.

The European Commission's guidelines for promoting innovation provide invaluable pointers for targeted action and support which seem highly apposite for polymer processors. The guidelines include (1) new forms of financing (e.g. venture capital) to encourage start-ups; (2) spin-outs/spin-offs; (3) specialised business services; (4) technology transfer; (5) interactions between firms and higher education/research institutes; (6) [measures to] encourage small firms to carry out research and technological development (RTD) for the first time; (7) enhanced networking and industrial co-operation; and (8) developing human capabilities (Landabaso, 1999). Lastres (1994, p. 190) strikes a chord in arguing that the main objective of government policy for science and technology should be to concentrate on:

> Rapidly diffusing new technologies, so that local industries procure and utilise the new technology earlier than international competitors; enhancing the rate at which information flows through the system, so that the general awareness of technological opportunity is raised and visions are blended; increase the *connectivity* of the different constituent parts of the scientific and technological system to accelerate the learning process. (my italics)

Appreciating that systems and processes for new product development can be dysfunctional within individual companies and their supply chains suggests a role for external mentoring, facilitation, training and *un*learning. The UK government and, in the regions, the regional development agencies, have an important role in stimulating and redirecting technology investment and fostering R&D. It is also important to ensure the strength of scientific research conducted at university and corporate levels in order to maintain the continued flow of knowledge to feed innovation, and to ensure that this research reaches successful commercialisation (West Midlands First, 1999; Advantage West Midlands, 1999b).[18]

In Conclusion: Towards Collaboration For Innovation

To survive in the changing business environment, processors must collaborate in order to innovate. In the information and communications industries, the diffusion of advanced technologies has made trans-organisational strategic alliances for product development and technology transfer more workable, by 'bringing together knowledge from a range of disciplinary and geographically disparate sources' (Millar et al, 1997, p. 399). Other sectors do not exhibit the same dynamic orientation, and this interaction will need to be nurtured and facilitated. The West Midlands study indicated that product development in rubber and plastics processing – as for other sectors – increasingly necessitates technology transfer from other disciplines. Some firms sought – or planned to acquire - overseas partners as a means to access not only closed markets but also new technologies. A range of external linkages reflected the need to outsource some innovative activities, such as design engineering and R&D, so as to tap sources of knowledge and expertise. Product diversification, however, is a risky and difficult business which firms may prefer to tackle through company acquisition rather than through initiating their own programmes for product development (Wilhelmsson and Mcqueen, 1999). This has two important implications (1) it makes it more likely that innovative firms which have developed new products will be targets for acquisition, and (2) it places a greater emphasis on the need for collaborative linkages in order to help to overcome the problems inherent in product diversification.

Vertical and horizontal alliances enable firms to pool their strengths by working together innovatively in a holistic intra-supply chain relationship to cut costs and increase product and delivery quality. The West Midlands study of polymer processors, and the writer's parallel study of automotive suppliers,[19] revealed that the existence of customer-supplier linkages for innovation influences the extent to which processors engage in R&D activity. This is shaped by (1) supply chain position; (2) the distinctiveness and lack of duplication of suppliers' expertise; (3) their innovation 'role' in the supply chain; and (4) intra-supply chain innovation, including the assembler's diversification and new product development activities. Whether a company operates as a 'performance' or 'cost-price' (branch) plant is also key to the extent of innovative activity pursued. Performance plants are at the leading edge of change, and typically have heightened autonomy and innovative capacity. They operate in specialised markets, placing emphasis on product quality and qualified personnel. In contrast, branch plants operate within a framework of centralised control, focusing on specific tasks conducted by lower waged personnel (Amin et al, 1994, pp. 111-112; Pike, 1998).

In a successful collaboration, firms can share the risk of technological development and access novel technologies to develop innovative products.[20] But collaboration can have its disadvantages, as research also shows that collective action risks blunting initiative and inhibiting competition (Marshall, 1920; Keeble and Wilkinson, 1999). Dyer et al (1999, p. 21) advise that companies can be assisted to build high-performing new product development teams through training in team building and team support for senior and functional managers.

An obstacle to obtaining supply chain synergies for innovation in product and process development through inter-firm linkages occurs for polymer processors through the history of backward vertical integration for R&D in the chemical industry. This contrasts with the decentralisation in the electronics and communications industry, which helps to make that sector so dynamic. As Chakrabati (1990) observed, the chemical industry is primarily the source of its own new technologies. It follows that there is a limited practice of user-producer contact to develop polymer materials. Given that materials user-producer collaboration stimulates the successful creation of innovative products and processes, their limited contact is clearly an innovation inhibitor (Habermeier, 1990, p. 271; Dyer et al, 1999, p. 21). The question is how to ensure that polymer processors can be involved in collaboration for innovation. Galvanising partnerships under the aegis of Accelerate, European programmes or other means, provides a crucial service.

It also seems that the solution lies substantially in processors taking their own initiative to attain an assertively innovative posture. The West Midlands study indicated that automotive suppliers processing metals or polymers who have a history of proactive involvement in product and process innovation are likely to retain that innovative role if they are subsequently taken over, even by an overseas inward investor.[21] Therefore, helping companies to attain and to sustain an innovative orientation will reap continued rewards for the regional economy, whatever companies' ownership status, and will help to attract high-calibre overseas innovators (DTI, 1998c). This is confirmed by a study of the European automotive industry which noted that 'to attract inward investments a technologically vital local supplier base' is important as 'a strong attractor to the location of new transplants' (Cahill and Ducatel, 1997, p. 20).

Miller (1994, p. 28) confirmed evidence from the West Midlands study for the importance of regional firms attaining innovative leadership, in concluding that assemblers' decisions to disperse R&D include 'the need to interact with suppliers in pockets of innovation or industrial districts', and 'access to engineering or design talents available in specific areas through alliances, linkages and presence'. Dunning (1994) also argued that it is more likely that what he terms 'know-*why*' (i.e. basic materials or product research) as opposed to 'know-*how*' research (i.e. adapting products, materials or processes for local markets) will be conducted by an overseas multinational enterprise if there is a cluster of similar R&D activities and/or there is access to university or co-operative research institutions.

Processing companies are not merely passive recipients of technology and knowledge expertise. Those which become innovation-rich have a technology-initiating and capacity-enhancing role to bring to the product and process development activities of companies at the ends of their supply chains, whether these are chemicals/polymer materials manufacturers or assemblers such as automotive producers. Japanese supplier-customer technical co-operation is an exemplar of close, extended collaboration for product design and production problem-solving. Utterback and Suárez (1993, p. 4) pointed out that suppliers may be more willing to play a creative role if the customer displays loyalty and co-operation towards them, when the bond may become so close as to throw into question 'our very concept of a firm and its boundaries'. This has important implications for initiatives like Accelerate, which are encouraging automotive supply chain partnerships to work towards attaining greater competitiveness, in enabling partners to understand their relative stances. Any initiative must also overcome the reticence which small firms, unlike large ones, are known to exhibit towards linking up with competitors, preferring to collaborate with their customers (Barker et al, 1996, pp. 479-480).

The apparent speed with which Japanese firms can innovate is explained by the way in which they access information from external sources (Mansfield, 1988). Clearly, their success illustrates that it is important for processors, and for industry more generally, to *speedily* access, circulate, assimilate and act upon knowledge capital in order to maximise the potential. This highlights the need for support for partnership sourcing and the role of external public and private sector agencies, not only in acting as information sources and partnership brokers, but also in overseeing the introduction and effective operation of the organisational structures which facilitate the success of knowledge and technology transfer activities and the transfer of *experience*.

Häusler et al (1994, p. 47) advocated an 'interactive' or 'circular' model of innovation incorporating 'notions such as *feedback* between scientific research, technical development and production, the *simultaneousness* of research and development activity, the *interactive* nature of innovation processes and the *interdependence* between various actors in industrial R&D'

(my italics). Coherent and mutually reinforcing socio-economic systems have evolved in the Sophia-Antipolis district of Nice and Baden-Württemberg through a very dense infrastructure to support local firms, including local government, chambers of commerce, regional banks and service centres (Cooke and Morgan, 1998; Longhi, 1999).

Research into innovation in advanced materials and products in Japanese companies confirmed that in Japan, too, participation in networks involving other companies, suppliers and customers, and industrial and academic associations is an essential means of developing knowledge through discussing experiences, obtaining feedback, obtaining information and learning about others' products and needs. It is especially useful for a newcomer to a specific field of activity (Lastres, 1994, p. 125). As Rycroft et al (1999, p. 13) observed: 'complex networks *coevolve* with their technologies'. Informal communication channels are also recognised as a valuable involuntary method of disseminating information, as the transfer of information between companies, typically relating to incremental organisational or process innovations, can occur through leakage via employees' out-of-work contact. 'Know-how' is particularly open to involuntary transfer (Schrader, 1991; Mueller, 1993). The benefits that networking can have in diffusing knowledge and best practice emphasise the advantages of bringing firms together in ways that allow opportunities for informal communication to occur.

This chapter has flagged up a range of pertinent issues which should be addressed in order to maximise the innovative potential in rubber and plastics processing – prominently, the need for greater inter-firm collaboration on R&D and for interactive networks which include support agencies and public sector bodies. A targeted approach to enticing inward investors in high-prospect activities could help the West Midlands region to develop a higher international profile for novel processes and joining techniques, the production and processing of biodegradable plastics, and advanced thermoplastics and composites for aerospace, automotive, medical and electronic applications. If the West Midlands innovation system is to achieve the kind of richness which stimulates and sustains a highly charged innovative culture, then it would also be desirable for linkages to the materials suppliers (i.e. the chemicals companies) to be more strongly forged. Cross-regional and cross-national alliances would need to be established, though this could be balanced by the encouragement of inward investment of overseas polymer materials producers. Strengthening the indigenous polymer materials and products research in the region is vital to help provide a stronger and more diverse source of knowledge and technology transfer close at hand to facilitate the development of new products. With a strong support and service infrastructure in place, in prospect is an interactive regional system in which every facet is constantly refreshed, adapted and strengthened, ensuring a self-perpetuating and increasingly innovation-rich culture.

Notes

1   *Financial Times,* 16 September 1999, quoting A. Blair-Smith, automotive research chief, Commerzbank, Frankfurt.

2   Tilson (1998a). The writer also conducted parallel sector reviews of automotive components supply for Tilson (1998b) and electrical/electronic engineering, published by the Centre for Urban and Regional Studies.

3   Tilson (1998a) incorporating data from Tilson (1997).

4   Many writers have discussed these issues, including Mair (1992); Wells (1992); Lamming (1993); Tilson (1998b; 1999a); KPMG (1998); and *Birmingham Post,* 9 October 1999.

5   See also Lamming (1993); Howells (1999).

6   See note 2. The survey findings fed into the sector reports.

7   See Ross (1993), on training in West Midlands engineering SMEs; Olian and Durham (1998).

8   *Innovation*, 2, August 1999, p.8. The regions are Baden-Württemberg, Weser-Ems (Germany), Puglia and Piemonte (Italy).

9   Existing, forthcoming and proposed European Commission directives and UK regulations include the Environmental Protection Act 1990; Integrated Pollution Prevention and Control Directive; Energy Tax; Landfill Tax 1996; *Making Waste Work* – 1996 White Paper; Control of Substances Hazardous to Health Regulations 1988; The Producer Responsibility Obligations (Packaging Waste) regulations 1997; End of Life Vehicles (post-use take-back, due to come into effect in 2006); Emissions standards affecting vehicle producers; Waste from Electrical and Electronic Equipment (post-use take-back, in preparation 1999); the management of the waste stream for used tyres; directive to encourage the composting of biodegradable waste.

10 *Foresight Link*, January 1998.

11 *Automotive Engineer*, October 1997.

12 *British Plastics and Rubber*, October 1997.

13 See, for example, Amendola (1990).

14 BBC1 Tomorrow's World, 17 February 1999.

15 *Materials World*, July 1998; *Automotive Engineering International,* June 1998.

16 See Zahra et al (1994). First-to-market and fast follower technology strategies underpin radical change, the former at the leading edge of innovation, while imitator and late entrant strategies involve incremental change.

17 Lastres (1994, p.79), extracted from Table 4.2.

18 See also Chakrabati (1990); Tilson (1999b; 1999c).

19 The survey of firms conducted in 1996/7 for Tilson (1998b).

20 For a fuller discussion of this topic see Barker et al (1996); Mowery (1989); Häusler et al (1994).

21 An evaluation of product and process development roles is based on the interview surveys of polymer processing and automotive components supply undertaken for the West Midlands study.

References

Advantage West Midlands (1999a), *Grant Help Forge New Partnership Between Automotive Industry and Colleges*, Advantage West Midlands (AWM), Birmingham, press release 5 August, AWM web site: www.wmda.co.uk/rda, accessed 3 October 1999.

Advantage West Midlands (1999b), *Creating Advantage: West Midlands Economic Strategy*, AWM, Birmingham.

Albach, H. et al (1996), *Innovation in the European Chemical Industry*, European Commission, European Innovation Monitoring System (EIMS) publication no. 38, Brussels.

Amendola, G. (1990), 'The Diffusion of Synthetic Materials in the Automobile Industry: Towards a Major Breakthrough', *Research Policy*, vol. 19, pp. 485-500.

Amin, A. et al (1994), 'Regional incentives and the quality of mobile investment in less favoured regions of the EC,' *Progress in Planning*, vol. 41, no. 1, pp. 111-12.

Andersen Consulting (1999), *The evolving role of executive leadership,* Andersen Consulting, London.

Association of Plastics Manufacturers in Europe (APME) (1999), *Key facts – Europe*, APME web site: www.apme.org/htm/europe, accessed 8 September 1999.

Barker, K, Dale, A. and Georghiou, L. (1996), 'Management of Collaboration in EUREKA Projects: Experiences of UK Participants', *Technology Analysis and Strategic Management,* vol. 8, no. 4, pp. 467-482.

Birmingham Post, 9 October 1999, 'Jobs Threat as BMW Puts Pinch on Parts Firms'.

Bosworth, D. et al (1996), *Technology Transfer, Information Flows and Collaboration: An Analysis of the C.I.S.,* European Commission, European Innovation Monitoring System (EIMS), publication no. 36, Brussels.

British Plastics Federation (BPF) (1996), *Statistics Handbook, 1996 Edition*, BPF, London.

British Plastics Federation (1999a), *The International Status Report*, BPF, London.

British Plastics Federation (1999b), *The UK/West European Plastics Market – The Industry's Story*, BPF, London.

British Polymer Training Association (BPTA) (undated, ?1997), *UK Polymer Processing Industry: Labour Market Assessment 1996/7*, BPTA, Telford.

Cahill, E. and Ducatel, K. (1997), *Advanced Technology and the Competitiveness of European Industry*, Institute for Prospective Technological Studies, European Commission report EUR 17732 EN, Seville.

Chakrabati, A. K. (1990), 'Innovation And Productivity: An Analysis of the Chemical, Textiles And Machine Tool Industries in the US', *Research Policy*, vol. 19, pp. 257-69.

Cooke, P and Morgan, K. (1998), *The Associational Economy: Firms, Regions And Innovation*, Oxford University Press.

Department of the Environment, Transport and the Regions (DETR) (1998), *Less waste. More value. Consultation Paper on the Waste Strategy for England and Wales*, DETR, London.

Department of Trade and Industry (DTI) (undated, 1996), *An Analysis of Synthetic Rubber Production and General Rubber Goods Processors in the UK*, DTI, London.

Department of Trade and Industry (1998a), *Packaging (Essential Requirements) Regulations*, DTI, London.

Department of Trade and Industry (1998b), *Partnership in Plastics*, DTI web site dti.gov.uk, accessed 26 November 1999.

Department of Trade and Industry (1998c), *Sector Challenge Winners 1997*, DTI web site dti.gov.uk, accessed 26 November 1999.

Department of Trade and Industry and British Plastics Federation (1996), *Plastics Processing in the UK*, DTI, London.

Deutsche Gesellschaft für Kunstoff-Recycling mbh (DKR), *Facts and Figures*, DKR web site: dkr.de/955, accessed 19 October 1999.

Dunning, J. (1994), 'Multinational Enterprises and the Globalization of Innovatory Capacity', *Research Policy*, vol. 23, pp. 67-88.

Dyer, B. et al (1999), 'What First-to-Market Companies Do Differently', *Research-Technology Management*, vol. 42, no. 2, pp. 15-21.

Financial Times, 14 May 1996, 'America's Recipe for Industrial Extinction'.

Financial Times, 7 November 1996, 'A Crop of Ideas for Extracting Fibres'.

Financial Times, 27 January 1998, 'Cargill-Dow Eye European plant'.

Financial Times, 29 January 1998, 'Du Pont Hurt by Charges'.

Financial Times, 12 February 1998, 'Plastic to Win More of Drinks Container Market'.

Financial Times, 16 September 1999, 'Wind of Change Starts to Blow'.

Financial Times, 3 June 1999, '"Green" bag'.

Habermeier, C. F. (1990), 'Product Use and Product Improvement', *Research Policy*, vol. 19, pp. 271-83.

Häusler, J. et al (1994), 'Contingencies of Innovative Networks: a Case Study of Successful Interfirm R&D Collaboration,' *Research Policy*, vol. 23, pp. 47-66.

Howells, J. (1999), 'Research and Technology Outsourcing', *Technology Analysis and Strategic Management*, vol. 11, no. 1, pp. 17-29.

Jones, O. and Tang, N. (1998), 'Mature Firms in the UK Mid-corporate Sector: Innovation Strategies and Employment Prospects', in R. Delbridge and J. Lowe, (eds), *Manufacturing in Transition*, Routledge, London and New York, pp. 112-29.

Keeble, D. and Wilkinson, F. (1999), 'Collective Learning and Knowledge Development in the Evolution of Regional Clusters of High Technology SMEs in Europe', *Regional Studies*, vol. 33, no. 4, pp. 295-303.

Key Note (1997), *Plastics Processing*, Key Note, Harmondsworth, Middlesex.

KPMG (1998), *West Midlands Automotive Supply Chain Development Study*, Birmingham and Solihull TEC and West Midlands Development Agency, Birmingham.

Lamming, R. (1993), *Beyond Partnership: Strategies for Innovation and Lean Supply,* Prentice Hall, Hemel Hempstead.

Landabasso, M. (1999), *Promoting regional innovation systems in Europe: the RIS experience*, European Commission DG XVI A2 Regional Policy and Cohesion, Brussels, presentation to the launch of the Regional Innovation Strategy for the West Midlands, Coventry Techno-centre.

Lastres, H. (1994), *The Advanced Materials Revolution and the Japanese System of Innovation,* The Macmillan Press, London.

Longhi, C. (1999), 'Networks, collective Learning and Technology Development in Innovative High Technology Regions: The Case of Sophia-Antipolis', *Regional Studies*, vol. 33, no. 4, pp. 333-42.

Mair, A. (1992), 'Ford of Britain in the 1990s: Corporate Strategy in Europe and the Future of the Ford Localities', *Local Economy*, vol. 7, no. 2, August, pp. 146-62.

Mansfield, E. (1988), 'The Speed and Cost of Industrial Innovation in Japan and the United States: External vs. Internal Technology', *Management Science*, vol. 34, no. 10, pp. 1157-168.

Marshall, A. (1920), *Industry and Trade,* Macmillan, London.

Maxwell, J. (1994), *Plastics in the automotive industry*, Woodhead Publishing, Cambridge (UK).

Millar, J. et al (1997), 'Trans-organizational Innovation: a Framework for Research,' *Technology Analysis and Strategic Management*, vol. 9, no. 4, pp. 399-418.

Miller, R. (1994), 'Global R&D Networks and Large-scale Innovations: The Case of the Automobile Industry', *Research Policy*, vol. 23, pp. 27-46.

Mowery, D. C. (1989), 'Collaborative Ventures between US and Foreign Manufacturing Firms,' *Research Policy*, vol. 18, pp. 19-32.

Mueller, F. (1993), 'Understanding Technological Leadership: Observations from the Automobile Industry,' *Technology Analysis and Strategic Management*, vol. 5, no. 1, pp. 15-26.

Office for National Statistics (ONS) (1998a), *Sector Review: Chemicals, Rubber and Plastics Products*, Quarter 3 1997, HMSO, London.

Office for National Statistics (1998b), *Sector Review: Vehicles and Other Transport*, HMSO, London.

Office for National Statistics (1999), *Annual Abstract of Statistics*, 135, The Stationery Office, London.

Office of Science and Technology (OST) (1995), *Technology Foresight. Progress Through Partnership 10: Materials*, OST, London.

Office of Science and Technology (1997), *Winning Through Foresight: Action for Materials*, OST, London.

Olian, J. D. et al (1998), 'Designing Management Training and Development for Competitive Advantage: Lessons from the Best', *Human Resource Planning*, vol. 21, no. 1, pp. 20-31.

Pike, A. (1998), 'Making Performance Plants from Branch Plants? In Situ Restructuring in the Automobile Industry in the United Kingdom', *Environment and Planning*, vol. 30, May, pp. 880- 900.

Ross, K. (1993), 'Training and Evaluation in SMEs: Manufacturing Enterprises in the West Midlands', *Local Economy*, vol. 8, no. 2, August, pp. 143-54.

Rycroft, R. W. and Kash, D. E. (1999), 'Managing Complex Networks – Key to 21st Century Innovation Success', *Research-Technology Management*, vol. 42, no. 3, pp.13-18.

Schrader, S. (1991), 'Informal Technology Transfer between Firms: Cooperation Through Information Trading', *Research Policy*, vol. 20, pp. 153-70.

Tilson, B. (1997), *Survey of Firms in the Plastics and Rubber Processing Sector in the West Midlands Region*, Confidential Report for the West Midlands Development Agency and its Consortium Partners, Centre for Urban and Regional Studies, University of Birmingham.

Tilson, B. (1998a), *Plastics and Rubber Processing: International Contexts, Industry Change and Implications for the West Midlands*, West Midlands Research Report 6, Centre for Urban and Regional Studies, University of Birmingham, Birmingham.

Tilson, B. (1998b), *The Drive for Change in the Automotive Components Sector and Implications for Suppliers in the West Midlands Region*, West Midlands Research Report 5, Centre for Urban and Regional Studies, University of Birmingham, Birmingham.

Tilson, B. (1999a), 'A Tidal Wave for Change: The Case of the Automotive Supply Chain in the West Midlands', *Local Economy*, vol. 13, no. 4, February, pp. 295-309.

Tilson, B. (1999b), *Innovation and Technology Trends in the Metals Sector*, Report for the Regional Innovation Strategy for the West Midlands, University of Birmingham Business School, Birmingham.

Tilson, B. (1999c), *Plastics and Rubber Processing: A Sector Update 1998,* Report for the West Midlands Development Agency, Centre for Urban and Regional Studies, University of Birmingham, Birmingham.

Utterback, J and Suárez, F. (1993), 'Innovation, Competition and Industry Structure', *Research Policy*, vol. 22, pp. 1-21.

Valpak (1999), *The Regulations*, Valpak web site: valpak.co.uk/regulationscontent, accessed 4 October 1999.

Wakasugi, R. (1992), 'Why are Japanese Firms so Innovative in Engineering Technology?', *Research Policy*, vol. 21, pp. 1-21.

Wells, P. (1992), 'European Foreign Direct Investment and Local Development: The Case of the Automotive Sector', *Local Economy*, vol. 7, no. 2, August, pp. 132-45.

West Midlands First (1999), *West Midlands Regional Innovation Strategy and Action Plan: Shaping our Future,* West Midlands First, Birmingham.

Wilhelmsson, L. and Mcqueen, D. (1999), 'Product Diversity and Performance: A Macro Study of 20 Large Swedish Industrial Corporations', Scandinavian Journal of Management, vol. 15, pp. 43-64.

Zahra, S. et al (1994), 'Technological Choices within Competitive Strategy Types: A Conceptual Integration', International *Journal of Technology Management*, vol. 9, no. 2, pp. 172-95.

8 Change and Development in the Business Services Sector: An Emerging Regional Agenda

MARGARETA DAHLSTRÖM

Introduction

The business services sector has recorded remarkable growth all over the industrialised world at least since the 1960s, but with a marked acceleration since the early 1980s (Keeble et al, 1991). Business services (here defined as professional business services and financial services) are the biggest source of direct job increases, with growth figures such as a 140% increase in US employment between 1971 and 1991, and a doubling of UK and French employment in the sector over the same period. More recently, employment in the sector increased by 50% in the UK between 1986 and 1994. In 1994, business and financial services together accounted for around 20% of employment in, for example, the UK, France and the Netherlands (Townsend, 1997). The business services sector accounts for 14% of employment, or over 3.2 million people, in Britain (Annual Employment Survey, 1997).

Business services can be defined in several different ways. The basic criterion that distinguishes business services from other services is, however, that they are sold to other producers, i.e. they provide input in the production of other services or goods. The input may be into companies in any economic sector, such as primary industries, manufacturing, other service companies or the public sector and administration. Business services, and especially advanced or professional business services, also tend to be 'information intensive or human capital intensive (or both) in nature' (Juleff-Tranter, 1996, p. 389). Business services is sometimes used as an 'all-embracing' concept that can include financial services as well. This chapter does not deal with financial services. The distinction between business services and financial services is not always clear-cut, however, and the distinction is getting increasingly blurred, as will be illustrated. Within business services, both advanced services (professional business services such as management consultancy) and routine

179

services (e.g. industrial cleaning), are included. This chapter deals with business services in this wider sense, but looks particularly at professional business services. Special attention will also be paid to call centres. These are workplaces that may provide services to other businesses as well as to private customers. Strictly speaking, they are not all business services. They are, however, of great interest because of their recent rapid growth, their spatial organisation, and the fact that they are the result of technological restructuring of service industries (Richardson and Marshall, 1999).

The long trend of growth in the business services sector and the way it has been identified as an engine of economic growth in, for example, the South East, renders an interest in business services, not least in a regional development perspective. Agglomeration and clusters are at the heart of this industry, with networks and linkages between companies being of great importance (Bennett et al, 1999). It is clear that a comprehensive understanding of business services in terms of what they are, their heterogeneity and their various trends is crucial for the successful elaboration of regional development policies and programmes.

Business services are produced in large multiple-site companies (including multinationals), in SMEs and increasingly in micro-businesses. A large share of companies are SMEs; in the UK more than 95% of business services firms belong to this category (O'Farrell and Wood, 1998).

This chapter begins by assessing the international outlook for business services. Three key drivers of change with regard to these services are introduced; technological development, globalisation and deregulation. Thereafter the geographical focus of the chapter concerns itself with business services in the UK, with the strong dominance of London and the South East, and then more particularly considers the West Midlands region. Two specific 'cases' are presented: firstly, a closer look at the professional business services and, secondly, an example of developments linked to technological change – the growth of call centres. The chapter concludes by examining the business services sector and the new regional agenda.

Drivers of Change and Development

The world economy is growing more and more specialised and the division of labour is ever-increasing. Crucial factors behind this movement include technological development (especially in relation to information and communication technologies), 'globalisation' and deregulation. These factors are also key drivers of change and development, and challenges, in the business services sector. The drivers are interconnected and mutually reinforcing, but the key elements in relation to business services are dealt with in turn below.

Technological Development

The rapid development of information and communication technologies has made it possible for many companies to become footloose. Back-office functions can now be conducted almost anywhere regardless of the geographical location of company headquarters. Non-stop international trade and 24-hour banking are also facilitated through advancements in ICT. Consumers are also increasingly happy to use telephones and computers to conduct business; the growth in e-commerce and interest in 'dotcom-companies' are examples of this. The rapid emergence of the call centre industry is also witness to this kind of change in business processes.

Data on call centres vary quite considerably between sources. This is partly as a result of how call centres are defined. In terms of employment, some estimates refer to 'agent positions' while others refer to number of employees. 'Agent position' is call centre terminology behind which can be hidden more than one member of staff. In many cases, there may be three staff working shifts for every agent (operator) position. In 1997, there were 428,000 agent positions in more than 10,000 call centres across Europe. It is estimated that there will be 737,000 agent positions in over 15,000 European call centres by the end of 2000 (Datamonitor, 1998). In terms of number of employees, almost 2 million people are expected to work in call centres in Western Europe by 2003 (Datamonitor, 1999a). The UK is the leading country in terms of employment, with over 37% of all European agent positions in 1998 (Datamonitor, 1999b). Other countries in Europe, for example Germany and Italy, are now reporting a faster growth of call centres and agent positions than the UK. Despite this, the UK is still expected to host at least one-third of all European call centres by the end of 2000 (Datamonitor, 1998). Datamonitor estimates that the number of agent positions in the UK will reach almost 250,000 in 2000, and will increase between 5 and 10% over the next couple of years (1999b).

Internationalisation and Globalisation

The continuous internationalisation of the world economy, increasingly called 'globalisation', is an important driver in relation to business services.

Growing international trade between companies and transactions within multinational companies, have contributed to an increase in demand for professional business services in the shape of expertise, for example in marketing, language and international business law. International trade in business services is not only an option for multinationals in the sector, such as PriceWaterhouseCoopers and Ernst and Young. Small and medium-sized business services firms are increasingly operating in the global business services market as well (O'Farrell and Wood, 1998).

Another effect of globalisation is the way in which regional crises transfer throughout the world economy. The recent turmoil in the South East Asian economy, and its ripple effects across the world, has also affected the business services sector. So far, the impact has been less severe than for the manufacturing sector, but the general decline in business confidence may come to affect the sector further over the longer term. On the other hand, it can be argued that some parts of the business services sector actually reap a degree of business gain from economic crises or recession. Law firms, for example, can expect an increase in insolvency cases in times of economic downturn.

Deregulation

International and national deregulation of the financial services sector has been important for the continuous internationalisation of markets, including those of business services firms. Deregulation of financial services has also resulted in a variety of firms adding banking, financial advice and insurance to their portfolio of services. Business services firms as well as supermarkets have expanded their trading to include financial services. Within the EU, reforms have been targeted at removing individual nations' regulation of financial structures, with the aim of creating an EU-wide financial system where financial services can move freely. The single European currency is an important element of this process.

Privatisation is another form of deregulation that affects the business services sector. A shift from monopoly markets of, for example, telecommunications and gas supplies to competitive markets generates demand for marketing, market research and other business services. Privatisation and other forms of deregulation also play an important role in the expansion of call centres. Competition in the telecommunications sector has, for example, led to dramatic falls in call charges, a factor that makes location less important for call centre activities. The World Bank estimates that the cost of a transatlantic voice call in the year 2000 will be 1% of what it was in 1987. Furthermore, it is estimated that you will be able to speak for one hour for 3 cents in 2010 (Dahlström, 1999a).

The International Context of the Business Services Sector

Business services is a growth sector across the industrialised world. With increasing interdependency, flexible specialisation, division of labour and complexity of the economy, there is a constant growth in demand for business services. It used to be argued that the growth in business services was related to servicing primarily the manufacturing industries. Research in recent years has, however, shown the manufacturing sector to be a less important client of professional business service companies than the service sector itself (Juleff-Tranter, 1996).

The increasing importance of business services worldwide can also be illustrated by the growing contribution of the sector to national output. In the US, for example, financial and business services together already accounted in 1987 for a quarter of GDP. By 1996, this figure had increased to almost 29%. The sector contributed with 26% to GDP in Australia in the same year, and for France the share was 23% in 1997 (OECD, 2000).

The Importance of the Business Services Sector in the UK

The business services sector in Britain has grown rapidly, and employed 3.2 million people in 1997 (Annual Employment Survey, 1997). The financial and business services sector contributed with over 22% of GDP in the UK in 1995 (OECD, 2000). The sector is very heterogeneous, and for data collection purposes has been divided into five sub-sectors (Table 8.1).

Regional Distribution of Business Services

The South East, and especially London, strongly dominates the business services sector in Britain (Figure 8.1). This is a long-standing pattern supported by other concentrations in the main conurbation areas, including Birmingham, Manchester, Glasgow and Cardiff (Bennett et al, 1999). Within the major conurbations, there is a trend of decentralisation of business services towards the accessible small towns and rural areas in the urban-rural fringe (Gillespie, 1999). This strong concentration of business service firms can be seen as an example of clustering.

Table 8.1 The business services sector (using SIC)

SIC	Sub-sector	Employees in GB, 1997
70	Real estate activities	277,874
71	Renting of machinery and equipment	134,498
72	Computer and related activities	351,825
73	Research and development	90,352
74	Other business services	2,350,277

Source: Annual Employment Survey data from 1997, Office of National Statistics, © Crown Copyright 2000.

   The role of industry clusters in regional economic development has a long tradition. In one form or another it can be traced to classic location theory dating back to Weber (1909) through the central place theories of Christaller (1933) and Lösch (1940), the growth pole ideas of Perroux (1955) and the notion of the spread-and-backwash effects posited by Myrdal (1957) and Hirschman (1958) (all cited in Smith, 1971) to today's rejuvenated interest in industrial districts and clusters (Porter, 1998). In terms of business services, clustering has often been argued as related to the need for face-to-face contact, especially in the case of non-standardised knowledge-based information exchange and the elements of trust involved in the production of these types of services (Coffey and Bailly, 1992; Daniels, 1993; Hermelin, 1997). Much attention has been paid to the industrial districts of the textile and clothing industry in Emilia Romagna and the computing and software industry in Silicon Valley (Piore and Sable, 1984; Morgan and Sayer, 1988). More recently, business services have also been studied in the context of industrial clusters and their role in economic development. A detailed British study has shown that, business services are exceptionally geographically clustered and that, despite having recorded a certain decentralisation from London and the South East, they remain fundamentally unevenly distributed and strongly concentrated in this area. This may seem a paradox since technological development in the ICT industries should theoretically allow for global sourcing and competition. It has, however, been argued that local clusters provide a check and balance

Figure 8.1 Share of employment in the business services sector by region and compared to Great Britain average, 1997

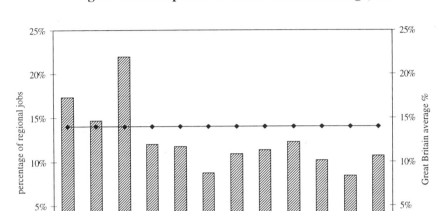

Source: Annual Employment Survey data from 1997, Office of National Statistics, © Crown Copyright 2000.

to the worst excesses of international competition, in that clusters, by developing intricate networks between firms located in the same area, can render local and regional economies more robust and sustainable.

Outside the South East, the major conurbations provide strong regional clusters of business services and also a focus for intra-regional decentralisation within the conurbations themselves (Bennett et al, 1999). There is also a discernible trend among business services companies to grow in accessible rural areas especially near large conurbations (Keeble and Tyler, 1995; Gillespie, 1999). The growth of especially small, professional business services companies in the urban-rural fringe of the Birmingham conurbation in the West Midlands is an illustration of this trend (Dahlström, 2000).

Professional Business Services

Professional business services are characterised by their high content of expertise. Staff producing these services are, in general, highly qualified

(Hermelin, 1997). The professional business services are also a heterogeneous selection of activities and comprise 10 sub-sectors (Table 8.2). London and the South East is even more dominant with regard to employment in professional business services than is the case with the larger business services sector.

As can be seen in Figure 8.2, professional business services account for almost 10% of employment (335,000) in London. That is considerably more than the entire manufacturing sector, which accounts for 8% of employment (284,000) (Annual Employment Survey, 1997).

The Relative Importance of the Business Services Sector in the West Midlands Region

The West Midlands is a classic example of an industrial heartland region. Here, because of the economic history of the region, the service sector has been comparatively poorly developed, even in the city of Birmingham itself. However, by the end of the 1990s, the industrial structure of the West Midlands region was much more similar to that of the national average despite the manufacturing sector being larger and the service sector still smaller than for the country as a whole. The service sector has played an important role in the restructuring of the West Midlands, but the manufacturing heritage has provided some constraints on this process. The skill level and educational level of the workforce restrict the development of parts of the service sector to its full potential. There are also signs that a 'cultural' heritage of negative views on service employment disadvantages further expansion of the service sector to some extent (Dahlström, 1999b). Key agents in the region are becoming more active in supporting regional development based on the service industries. The new regional development agency, Advantage West Midlands, has for example identified the tourism, leisure and creative industries sector as one of eight key sectors in the Regional Economic Strategy. These key sectors have been identified as having the best potential for job creation and for generating exports (Advantage West Midlands, 1999).

The business services sector, as defined above in Table 8.1, employed over 250,000 people in the West Midlands region in 1997, almost 12% of employment. It is a growth sector which recorded a 20% increase in employment from 1995 (Annual Employment Survey 1995 and 1997). Despite this growth, the business services sector is still under-represented in the West Midlands. The region has a lower share of employment in the sector than the national average (Figure 8.1).

Table 8.2 Sub-sectors of professional business services

SIC	Description
72.20	Software consultancy and supply
73	Research and experimental development
74.11	Legal activities
74.12	Accounting, book-keeping and auditing activities; tax consultancy
74.13	Market research and public opinion polling
74.14	Business and management consultancy activities
74.15	Management activities of holding companies
74.20	Architectural and engineering activities and related technical consultancy
74.30	Technical testing and analysis
74.40	Advertising

Source: Annual Employment survey (1997).

Figure 8.2 Share of employment in professional business services by region and compared to Great Britain average, 1997

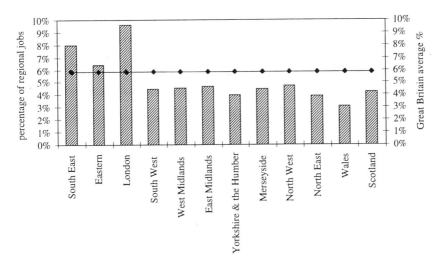

Source: Annual Employment Survey data from 1997, Office of National Statistics, © Crown Copyright 2000.

Employment Growth in the Professional Business Services

The West Midlands Region also has a lower share of the professional business services sector than the national average (Figure 8.2). In 1997, professional business services accounted for 4.5% of employment in the West Midlands region (Annual Employment Survey, 1997), which represents an increase from 1995 when the sector accounted for 4.2% of employment in the region (Annual Employment Survey, 1995). In absolute numbers, the professional business services employed 96,600 people in the region in 1997 (Annual Employment Survey, 1997). Compared with other regions in Britain, apart from the dominant South East, the West Midlands fares reasonably well in a 'middle group' of regions where the sector accounts for around 4.5% of employment and is ahead of Scotland, Yorkshire and the Humber, the North East and Wales.

Figure 8.3 below illustrates the change in employment between 1995 and 1997 for the sub-sectors of professional business services in the West Midlands region. All sub-sectors registered an increase in employment between the two years. The growth was particularly large in software consultancy and supply, with an increase of 5,000 employees (almost 50%). In relative terms, the largest growth was in research and experimental development, which more than doubled in size between the two years to reach over 4,000 employees in 1997 (Annual Employment Survey 1995; 1997).

Professional business services are growing increasingly in accessible rural areas and small towns on the outskirts of main conurbations. This pattern is driven by residential preferences held by many in the professional classes. Such intra-regional decentralisation has also been facilitated by developments in ICT. Laptop computers, e-mail and mobile phones assist home-working, either in the shape of micro-businesses or as a result of policies in larger companies. Some companies which employ staff who mainly work at customers' premises, have established company bases in easily accessible locations, such as near motorway junctions on the outskirts of conurbations. These offices allow mobile professionals to 'touch base' with their companies without having to travel into city centres (Gillespie, 1999).

This intra-regional pattern is also visible in the West Midlands. In 1995, for example, two of the top 20 districts in the country in terms of business services' contribution to total employment were West Midlands districts, both of them on the edge of the main Birmingham conurbation. Bromsgrove ranked 13th with 21.1% and Solihull 15th with 20.7% of total employment engaged in business services production.

In terms of home-working, the residential preferences of the professional classes are reflected further in a stronger presence of rural areas as important locations. The top 30 districts in terms of non-manual workers working from home, as a proportion of all workers, included four West Midlands districts: South Herefordshire, Leominster, South Shropshire, Malvern Hills. It is important to note that these data do not include farming but only service activities, albeit not only business services even though that type of service is likely to be significant (Gillespie, 1999). A small study into micro-businesses and home working in the urban-rural fringe of south Birmingham/North Worcestershire confirmed this picture (Dahlström, 2000).

Professional Business Services: The Accountancy Sector in the West Midlands

The accountancy sector is growing in the region. A few major changes have also taken place in the sector, presumably strengthening it further. On a macro scale, the merger between two of the 'Big Five' firms – PriceWaterhouse and Coopers and Lybrand, into the new PriceWaterhouseCoopers – has altered the situation among the key players of the sector. The new company has a network of 140,000 people across 152 countries (PriceWaterhouseCoopers, 1998) and a strong presence in the West Midlands.

Another major change is the tendency of the large accountancy firms to strengthen their corporate finance services side and thereby move even further towards being able to offer a one-stop shop for business **and** financial services. The large accountancy firms of the region are reportedly winning new business from investment banks because the accountancy firms are better connected locally at the same time as being part of global networks. Top professionals from the former merchant banks in the region and from law companies have moved into the larger accountancy firm (Dahlström, 1999a).

These new developments in the large accountancy firms can be described as a simultaneous strengthening of both the local and global level of their business operations. All the main players in the region stress that they focus their services on the local market, but because even smaller local companies are driven by international markets, the latter need help from companies which have international expertise and networks as well. Having said that, the main accountancy firms do have some very large international clients. Apart from the buying-in of local corporate finance expertise, the strengthening of the local level includes the development of industry-specific expertise, particularly in the form of the recruitment of automotive industry experts (Dahlström, 1999a).

Figure 8.3 Employment in professional business services* in the West Midlands region, 1995 and 1997

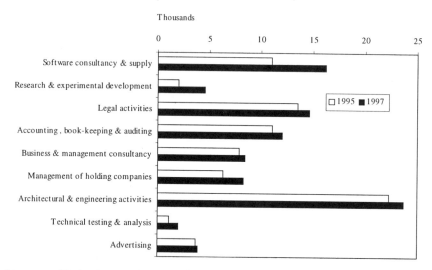

* because of faulty data, market research and public opinion polling has been excluded.

Source: Annual Employment Survey data from 1995 and 1997, Office of National Statistics, © Crown Copyright 2000.

The Call Centre Industry and Regional Development

Call centres, because of their potential footlooseness and fast growth, have generated interest from economic agencies trying to attract inward investment to regions (Richardson and Marshall, 1999). Almost a quarter of UK call centre employment is to be found in the South East. However, in relative terms, Yorkshire and Humberside and the North East are the most important call centre regions in the country (Figure 8.4). Leeds has the single largest concentration of call centre employment in the country with 10,000 people employed in the industry, the equivalent of 4% of the active working population. In neighbouring Bradford, about 5,000 people work in call centres. The sector is still growing in this call centre cluster (Heycock and Jones, 2000). The North East, another call centre stronghold, is an example of a region that has been more successful in attracting call centres than in generating this type of activity from indigenous growth (Richardson, 1998). The West Midlands, however, is under-represented in terms of call centre employment. Only Northern Ireland fares worse in terms of relative importance of the call centre sector.

Although the West Midlands has a relatively limited call centre sector, there are at least 200 call centres based in the region. Telford, a growth node within the region, hosts a number of call centres, including Sunlight Services, Claims Direct and Scoot (UK). The key locational attraction for Telford has been its young and fast-growing workforce, competitively priced land, buildings and labour costs; and local training facilities (Dahlström, 1999a).

What can be the reasons behind the rather limited call centre employment in the West Midlands compared with other former industrial regions such as the North East and Yorkshire? Popular myths may suggest that the 'Brummie' accent could prove a disadvantage for call centre employment in the West Midlands. However, the importance of accent for the call centre business is likely to be over-exaggerated. Banks running call centres state that accents rank low on the list of priorities when location decisions are taken (Dahlström, 1999a). Telecommunications infrastructure and services, the overall availability and cost of labour, and financial incentives are the most important locational factors for most call centres. Agglomeration factors have also been cited as important, so that companies would seem to prefer to locate in places where call centres already exist. The reason for this is that there can be a pool of appropriately trained and experienced labour – even if this situation also means the risk of local competition and wage inflation. There are documented examples of local competition driving up wages, for example near Sunderland in the North East. The concentration of call centres in this part of the country has also led to the creation of a micro labour market of its own (Dahlström, 1999a; Richardson and Marshall, 1999).

Significant investment has been made in Birmingham to overcome any negative perceptions in relation to the location of call centres. The West Midlands Development Agency, Birmingham City Council, Birmingham TEC and Birmingham Chamber of Commerce have come together to establish a centre of excellence for call centres. The aim of the centre is three-fold: to create an employers forum, to act as a technology forum and to provide specialist training. The call centre college, based at Birmingham's Aston Science Park, has been established in collaboration with Callscan, a company specialising in call centre management equipment (Dahlström, 1999a). Callscan, with its headquarters based in Birmingham, provides training programmes within the framework of National Vocational Qualifications for call centre agents as well as for supervisors and managers (Callscan Ltd, 2000).

Figure 8.4 Regional share of call-centre employment in the UK in 1997

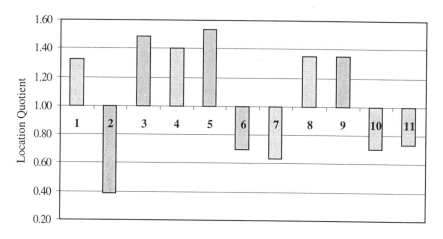

Regions:

1 Scotland	7 West Midlands
2 Northern Ireland	8 Wales ·
3 North East	9 East Anglia
4 North West	10 South East
5 Yorkshire & Humberside	11 South West
6 East Midlands	

Source: The Guardian, 1998; Regional Trends, 1998.

The Business Services Sector and the New Regional Agenda

A number of phenomena, including the 'regional renaissance' – an increased importance and focus on the regional level in policy-making, governance and regional development in recent years – have added to the interest in clusters based in economic geography thinking. In the case of England, a new key player in regional development was introduced with the establishment of the regional development agencies on 1st April 1999. These new agencies are charged with providing a Regional Economic Strategy aimed at sustainable regional development for all citizens within their regions (Jones and MacLeod, 1999). This new institutional development provides a special opportunity for this chapter to take a closer look at the regional and intra-regional role of business services. As indicated above, professional business services have shown strong growth in accessible rural areas and small towns on the urban-rural fringe of major conurbations. This is also the case in the West Midlands region.

The rise of intra-regional decentralisation and home-working make the clustering of business services more multi-faceted. The overall strong clustering of business services in the major conurbations partly hides the growth of business service activities based in the urban-rural fringe. Furthermore, the strong relative growth of business services employment in remoter rural areas may illustrate a deeper decentralisation of these activities in the long term (Gillespie, 1999). Behind these developments lie the opportunities related to ICT and the complexity of the business service products themselves. Since business services evolve through interactions between the producer and the client, they involve human factors such as personality and trust, which at least initially is best engendered in personal face-to-face contacts. However, other elements of the same service can be developed with the help of ICT or by individual work by the producer in the company's office, wherever that may be located (Hermelin, 1997).

In terms of call centre employment, technological developments that are underway may contribute to the decentralisation of these types of activities as well. Software developments have made it possible for the 'virtual' or 'distributed' call centre to emerge. Virtual call centres can be defined as 'several groups of agents, in geographically separate locations being treated as a single entity for call-handling, reporting, management and scheduling purposes' (Datamonitor, 1999c). British Telecom, for example, has already linked six call centres across the UK into one virtual call centre with 4,000 agent positions. New software can handle customer and sales enquiries both from the telephone and via the Internet (Dahlström, 1999a). Datamonitor (1999c) states that there is a very large growth potential for virtual call centres, and that the market has already taken off in the US. The annual growth rate for virtual call centres in Europe is estimated at over 40% up until the year 2003.

Technological change, globalisation and deregulation clearly provide huge challenges for policy-makers and strategists to identify opportunities and alleviate threats to robust regional development. Hitherto, there has been a tendency for agencies dealing with regional development to focus on the manufacturing sector, although increasingly with special interest in high-tech and knowledge-intensive industries. However, the business services sector is playing an increasingly important role in regional development and related strategies, and it is clear that a comprehensive understanding of these services and their various trends is crucial for the successful elaboration of regional development policies and programmes. The new regional development agencies provide an opportunity to promote pan-regional work with regard to the business services sector and its role in creating robust regions. It is early days yet, but Advantage West Midlands can take the lead in its region and help to make it happen.

References

Advantage West Midlands (1999), *Creating Advantage: The West Midlands Economic Strategy.* Advantage West Midlands, Birmingham.

Annual Employment Survey, (1995).

Annual Employment Survey, (1997).

Bennett, et al (1999), 'The Location and Concentration of Business in Britain: Business Clusters, Business Services, Market Coverage and Local Economic Development', *Transactions of the Institute of British Geographers*, vol. 24, no. 4, pp. 393-420.

Callscan Ltd (2000), http://www.callscan.com/

Coffey, W.J. and Bailly, A. (1992), 'Producer Services and Systems of Flexible Production', *Urban Studies*, vol. 29, pp. 857-68.

Dahlström, M. (1999a), Private Sector Services: Current Trends in The West Midlands Region, *West Midlands Research Report* No 8, Centre for Urban and Regional Studies, University of Birmingham, Birmingham.

Dahlström, M. (1999b), 'The Role of the Service Sector in the Restructuring of Old Industrial Regions – The Case of the West Midlands', Paper presented at 3rd Morovian Geographical Conference CONGEO '99, *Regional Prosperity and Sustainability*, Slavkov u Brna, Czech Republic, 6-10 September 1999.

Dahlström, M. (2000), *Urban-rural interdependencies - exploring 'Hidden' Employment in the Urban-Rural Fringe*, West Midlands Research Report No. 13, Centre for Urban and Regional Studies, Birmingham.

Daniels, P.W. (1993), *Service Industries in the World Economy*, Blackwell, Oxford.

Datamonitor (1998), *Call Centers in Europe,* 2nd edition, Description, http://www.datamonitor.com/

Datamonitor (1999a), *Call Center and CTI Markets in Europe: Perspective 2003*, Description, http://www.datamonitor.com/

Datamonitor (1999b), *Call Center Markets in the UK to 2003*, Description, http://www.datamonitor.com/

Datamonitor (1999c), *Virtual Call Centers*, Description, http://www.datamonitor.com/

Gillespie, A. (1999), 'The Changing Employment Geography of Britain', in M. Breheny, (ed), *The People? Where Will They Work?* Town and Country Planning Association, London.

The Guardian, (1998), ' Remote control of the High Street' The Guardian, 2nd June.

Hermelin, B. (1997), 'Professional Business Services. Conceptual Framework and a Swedish Case Study', *Geografiska Regionstudier*, no. 30, Kulturgeografiska Institutionen vid Uppsala Universitet, Uppsala.

Heycock, S. and Jones, B (2000), *The Local Economy and Call Centres; the Case of Bradford*, Paper presented at the 18th Annual International Labour Process Conference, University of Strathclyde, April 2000.

Jones, M. and MacLeod, G. (1999), 'Towards a Regional Renaissance? Reconfiguring and rescaling England's Economic Governance', *Transactions of the Institute of British Geographers*, vol. 24, no. 3, pp. 295-313.

Juleff-Tranter, L.E. (1996), 'Advanced Producer Services: Just a Service to Manufacturing?', *The Service Industries Journal*, vol. 16, no. 3, pp. 38-400.

Keeble et al (1991), 'Small Firms, Business Services Growth and Regional Development in the United Kingdom: Some Empirical Findings', *Regional Studies*, vol. 25, pp. 439-457.

Keeble, D. and Tyler, P. (1995), 'Enterprising Behaviour and the Urban-Rural Shift', *Urban Studies*, vol. 32, no. 6, pp. 975-97.

Morgan, K. and Sayer, A. (1988), *Microcircuits of Capital. "Sunrise" Industry and Uneven Development,* Polity Press, Cambridge.

O'Farrell, P.N. and Wood, P.A. (1998), 'Internationalisation by Business Service Firms: Towards a New Regionally Based Conceptual Framework, *Environment and Planning' A*, vol. 30, pp 109-28.

Organisation for Economic Co-operation and Development (2000), OECD, http:/www.oecd.org/

Piore, M. and Sabel, C. (1984), *The Second Industrial Divide*, Basic Books, New York.

Porter, M.E. (1998), 'Clusters and the New Economics of Competition', in *Harvard Business Review*, vol. 76, no. 6.

PriceWaterhouseCoopers (1998), Promotional material from the company.

Regional Trends (1998), vol. 33.

Richardson, R. (1998), *The Competitiveness Project. Developing the Call Centres Industry in the North East,* Centre for Urban and Regional Development Studies, University of Newcastle, Newcastle.

Richardson, R. and Marshall, J.N. (1999), 'Teleservices, Call Centres and Urban and Regional Development', *Service Industries Journal*, vol. 19, no. 2, pp. 96-116.

Smith, D. M. (1971), *Industrial Location. An Economic Geographical Analysis,* vol.19, no.1, John Wiley & Sons, New York.

Townsend, A.R. (1997), *Making a Living in Europe. Human Geographies of Economic Change*, Routledge, London and New York.

9 The ICT Industries: Corporate Behaviour and Regional Change

CHRIS COLLINGE AND ALAN SRBLJANIN

Introduction

The phrase 'information and communication technologies' refers to a diverse but converging set of activities, which share a common concern with the creation, storage, processing and transmission of information in a digital form. The pervasive nature of this technology reflects its generic character, its capacity to find application in almost all economic fields. But the present chapter is concerned with those parts of the economy that are involved in producing rather than using ICT. Hence it is concerned with sectors such as telecommunications and computing, rather than (say) automobiles, pharmaceuticals or financial services (each of which makes extensive use of ICT).

The ICT-producing industry is more diverse than many, reflecting the fact that it is currently converging from a group of previously distinct activities. One of the key challenges for any study of this industry is therefore to make sense of the diverse sectors it embraces, to identify their characteristics, to map their inter-relationships, and to understand their dynamics at both a corporate and an economy level. The present chapter will therefore suggest ways of categorising ICT, and will attempt to identify the dynamics at work in the emergence of this new industry. These dynamics need to be understood in order to identify the roots of change at the local or regional level, and to suggest an appropriate policy response in each case. It will in addition illustrate this process by reference to the development of ICT production in the urban core of the West Midlands, and will identify some specific issues that arise for ICT analysis and policy within regions.

Various ways of sub-dividing ICT products have been proposed. Hawkins et al (1997) identify a two-fold distinction between the transportation of content and the content itself, and between services and products. This provides a two-dimensional matrix in terms of which the different segments are arranged. The Harvard map of ITEC uses distinctions between products and services (tangibles and intangibles) and between form and substance (for example, between paper and books, or between disks and data). The Royal Institute of International Affairs also makes a distinction between 'medium' and 'content', but adds 'information handling' to this, with the different ICT products arranged in a triangular relationship (Cable and Distler, 1995). It is this last approach which comes closest to the method developed here.

Communications, Computers, Content

A broad distinction can be drawn between the *content* of a medium and the *communication* vehicle it is conveyed through (Figure 9.1). 'Content' includes text, data, sound, images, games, video, genres such as programmes, advertisements and interactive media, including e-commerce. It also includes what we might call 'second order' content such as web sites and internet portals. 'Communication vehicles' on the other hand are systems of capital equipment, and there are five main types of platform: fixed wire line, cable, terrestrial, satellite and mobile. The 'utility' character of these platforms, and the large investments they entail, is reflected in the fact that the companies involved have also in the first instance been the providers of platform services (such as telephone connections or TV channels). For various functional reasons, however, the laying out of infrastructure and the provision of platform services has generally been undertaken separately from the manufacture of, say, radio receivers or fibre optic cable. Also along this dimension is what we have called 'communications platform hardware', which refers to the different 'receivers' that are used by consumers. At present these include telephones, televisions, various players (such as CD, DVD, minidisk, tape, video) and the recordings they play.

The distinction between medium and message cannot be sustained so easily in reference to computers, however, and must be transposed into the distinction between data and data processing, or between *content* and *computing*. Computer services include specialist management consultancy and data warehousing activities as well as computer retailing. Computer hardware includes a number of distinct platforms, from palmtops and notebooks, through PCs and networked computers to mainframes and supercomputers. Software is a manufactured product lying between these two broad categories and is increasingly tied in with the provision of consultancy services.

The difficulty with sectoral classifications of economic activity is that they can become arbitrary and detached from real business processes such as

Figure 9.1 Dimensions for mapping ICT

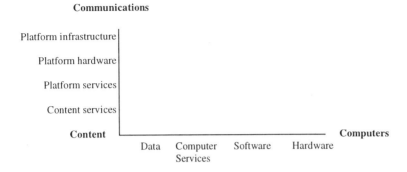

the pursuit of profit and market power. The primary role of sectoral classification is to identify contrasts or similarities between different kinds of products and services – in purpose, market, technology, construction – which can then be related to each other and to variables such as company behaviour or market structure. Products and services may be regarded as the 'pieces' used in the business 'game', while companies are the players that seek to develop and market these products in pursuit of corporate success (defined in various ways).

In traditional manufacturing a distinction is drawn between the components of a product and the product itself, which helps us to understand corporate linkages and *supply chain* dynamics. Likewise a distinction is drawn between *complementary products* (such as petrol, cars and roads) which must be combined in the process of consumption, and *competing products* (such as cars, motorcycles and taxis) which are alternatives to one another. The distinction in ICT between semiconductors, large computers and internet hubs is of the first variety and concerns products which are related in a *supply chain*. The distinction between TV programmes, TV channels, transmission equipment and TV sets is of the second kind, and identifies *complementary* products which are combined in delivering TV viewing. Finally, the distinction between fixed wire, cable, cellular and satellite communication is of the third kind, identifying alternative and perhaps *competing* product systems.

Despite these neat distinctions, individual companies will embrace several types of product and service according to their particular orientations. The value of a sectoral classification must lie in its contribution to the analysis of these orientations, to ways in which companies have sought to combine different kinds of products. It must also lie in the analysis of the ways in which companies have in aggregate distributed themselves across the industry, and established a de facto division of labour in which they are grouped into different ICT segments. For despite all the talk about 'convergence' it would be wrong to assume that all ICT firms will in future be doing everything. Particular companies, for example, tend to be committed to particular communication platforms and are likely to remain so. Figure 9.1 involves two axes which could in principle be used to plot the changing scope of any one company's product range and the changing distribution of companies between products. The next part of this chapter considers – very selectively – the main segments in the communications, computers and content dimensions of ICT.

Communications

Five main communication transmission platforms can be identified (fixed wire, cable, mobile, terrestrial TV and satellite) and while a distinction can be drawn in each case between communications infrastructure and services, generally the infrastructure and the services have in the past been provided by the same companies. At the time of writing, the world's largest telecommunications operators by turnover are NTT, Bell Atlantic-GTE, AT&T and MCI Worldcom-Sprint. Merger pressures in this industry derive from technological developments which have eroded market boundaries and increased competition between firms. They also derive from technological developments that have expanded capacity, reduced call charges and revenues, and increased investment costs (for example, in laying out fibre optic networks). The declining cost of phone calls is forcing operators to seek sales volumes in order to gain the economies that can restore profit margins. Finally, market boundaries have been eroded by ongoing deregulation, opening geographically separate markets to companies in other areas (for example, in the US the market between local and long-distance providers).

During a period in which capital concentration has been proceeding rapidly in other industries (such as airlines, oil and petroleum, automobiles), consolidation among telecommunications companies around the world has been held back by national regulatory frameworks. A bout of corporate consolidation has, however, been triggered recently which is all the more turbulent for being compressed into a short period. During 1998, both SBC Communications and Bell Atlantic undertook mergers that gave each approximately 30% of local telephone lines in the US. During 1999, SBC purchased Ameritech and Bell Atlantic has combined with GTE, creating two 'super-Bells'. We have also seen the merger between Telia of Sweden and Telenor of Norway, creating a Scandinavian champion. The purchase of IDC (the long-distance Japanese carrier) by Cable and Wireless Communications (CWC) breaks new ground in overcoming Japanese resistance to foreign takeovers.

While merger activity is continuing, new operators are also forming and the number of telecommunications companies is increasing every year. The first wave of new operators arrived in the mid-1980s with deregulation in the US and UK markets (firms included Sprint and WorldCom in the US and Mercury Communications in the UK). A more recent wave during the 1990s was based upon fibre optic networks and broadband technology (firms here included Qwest, Level 3, and Global Crossing in the US, and Colt and Energis in Europe). In the US, alternative local operators (CLECs – competitive local carriers such as Teligent and McLeodUSA) have also been establishing networks for business consumers.

Europe is still at an early and vulnerable stage in the consolidation of its industry. The European Union did not open markets in a consistent way to transnational competition until January 1st 1998. It is true that the large European operators (Deutsche Telekom, France Telecom, BT, Telecom Italia, and Telephonica) have all recently been involved in a range of acquisitions and alliances. But at the same time each of the big four US operators (AT&T, MCI WorldCom, SBC and Bell Atlantic) will want to acquire European operations in pursuit of global carrier status. AT&T already has close links with BT in the form of Concert, while MCI WorldCom is building a European network with MFS, and Bell Atlantic is involved with Omnitel (the Italian mobile operator).

The UK cable industry is now dominated by US corporations. In the early 1980s, the UK government awarded licences at a regional level to companies for the establishment of a cable TV network, and by 1993 there were 24 cable companies in operation. Subsequently, however, consolidation of the industry has been driven by ongoing losses, the search for sales volumes to compete with satellite and terrestrial platforms, and the need to move rapidly into broadband services. The most recent phase of consolidation was initiated by Cable and Wireless when it established Cable and Wireless Communications in October 1996. During 1999, NTL and France Telecom launched a joint bid for CWC, which had the effect of putting NTL in the dominant position in the UK cable industry and creating the largest domestic competitor to BT.

Cable is very effective as a medium for delivering bundled services including voice, data, fast internet, video-on-demand and digital TV, and has advantages over rival platforms such as satellite. Microsoft has acquired strategic holdings in a range of cable companies across the U.S. and Europe (including Comcast, NTL, and UPC in the Netherlands, Portugal Telecommunications, MediaOne and Nextel). It has an interest in the consolidation of the cable industry because this will increase the take-up of high-speed interactive services and strengthen the position of cable vis-à-vis satellite. In May 1999, Microsoft acquired a 29.9% stake in Telewest in the U.K. following its earlier acquisition of a 5% stake in NTL. This also ties in with the broader strategy of Microsoft to extend its dominance from PC operating systems to new media platforms utilising the internet, cable and wireless communications. The UK cable industry is ahead of others in introducing digital cable services, and it is likely that the operating system which establishes itself here will become the industry standard elsewhere.

Computers

A number of different computer platforms can be identified, including supercomputers, mainframes, mini-computers, PCs and networked computers as well as laptops, palmtops and other hand-held devices. Four principal eras of computer production have occurred since the 1950s, involving the mainframe (1950s-1970s), the PC (1980s), networked computing and the internet (1990s). It is only during the last of these that computers have come directly into competition with other communications platforms such as the telephone. Despite the large number of computers in use worldwide, computer hardware revenues have been growing more slowly than those from other more dynamic segments of the ICT market (such as IT services, e-commerce revenues, mobile services and consumer electronics). Indeed, for some time the industry has relied upon the replacement of existing systems and a declining product life-cycle to sustain demand, with a symbiotic relationship between hardware and software.

Although the market for personal computers has matured, and there is competition from other kinds of devices, the PC is likely to remain the most significant segment of the computer hardware industry for some time, and is evolving in several directions. Responding to the challenge of simple internet access devices (network computers being produced by Oracle and Sun Microsystems) firms such as Compaq are manufacturing low-cost internet PCs without floppy or compact disk drives. At the same time the growth in mobile communications is driving the development of palm-sized computers with internet and mobile phone capabilities. Furthermore, computer manufacturing is being restructured in order to drive down costs through outsourcing and inventory control.

The semiconductor industry is ferociously competitive at a global level, vulnerable to changes in its cost base, and subject to rapid product turnover and reducing life-cycles. The key technological pressure can be described as the race to produce ever thinner multiple system chips (which combine memory, logic and other circuits) with increasing speed and power. The market is divided into many different segments, from low-end commodity semiconductors (for PCs) to high-end application-specific semiconductors (for the defence and aerospace industries). Restructuring pressures mean that mergers and alliances between semiconductor firms in Japan, the US, Europe and South East Asia are now the norm and are likely to continue as firms seek to offset increased R&D costs. Toshiba and Fujitsu have collaborated on DRAM chip research and expect to launch a new generation of memory chips in 2002. Siemens of Germany and Motorola of the US are similarly collaborating on semiconductor chip research and development.

The maturity of hardware markets and the additional margins available elsewhere are reflected in changing corporate strategies. Many of the larger global entities (such as IBM) now secure approximately half of their revenue from computer support services and software. The largest 'vendors' of packaged software in 1998 were Microsoft, IBM, Computer Associates Inc, and SAPAG. Every year for the last decade Microsoft's share of the market for Intel-compatible PC operating systems has been above 90% (US Department of Justice, 2000). The focus of growth in software production has, however, shifted in recent years from packaged software to the integration of packages. Enterprise Resource Planning (ERP) systems, for example, are integrated suites of software that automate 'back office' operations for functions such as manufacturing, distribution, financial analysis, purchasing, sales and human resources. The complexity of systems that arises in some business mergers has led to the growth of Enterprise Application Integration (EAI) software (so called middleware) which replaces all the interconnections between different packages with a hub that provides an integrative architecture.

The EAI market was formed in the first instance by a number of small specialist companies (such as Active Software, Constellar, Neon and Template Software), but is now attracting the big operators, including IBM and Microsoft. The strategic focus of ERP and EAI firms is, with the growth of e-commerce, moving from internal to external systems integration, and this market looks set to merge with the supply chain and customer relations management (CRM) markets. At the time of writing, supply chain management software production is dominated by five big vendors: SAP, Oracle, PeopleSoft, J D Edwards and Baan.

The main challenge facing computer service companies is to shift focus from the maintenance and support of discrete data archives (so-called 'legacy' systems) towards the integration required by electronic commerce. The sector has responded by following an aggressive strategy of merger and acquisitions, buying up expertise and crossing the divide between software and services. Cap Gemini, for example, announced in March 2000 an alliance with Cisco Systems, the giant US network company, which will invest $835m to create a global internet consulting, integration and services company. The move follows Cisco's $1bn investment in KPMG Consulting in August 1999, and Novell's $100m investment in management consultants Whitman-Hart in September 1999. Having followed a pattern of acquisition in America, with the purchase of nearly 50 companies over 10 years; Cisco Systems recently paid £34.3m for UK high-technology firm Calista Incorporated.

Content

By 'content' we mean both the material communicated through media platforms and the material processed by computers, categories which are at present converging rapidly into a single form. It is important to remember that a significant example of content is provided by e-commerce. The early months of 2000 have seen a striking growth in web-based markets and product exchanges offering enhanced opportunities and reduced transaction costs, many of which have originated in the US. In February 2000, Ford, General Motors and Daimler Chrysler established a global automotive supply chain platform. At the same time, United Technologies and Honeywell set up an open internet-based exchange for aircraft parts. In March, Barclays announced B2B.com linking buyers of raw materials to their suppliers. Likewise, VerticalNet and Eastman Chemical formed a joint venture to create an online market for the paint and coatings industry. Boeing, Lockheed Martin, Raytheon and BAe Systems announced plans to set up a web-based trading exchange to place most of their $71bn in annual purchases.

Despite the large number of small companies which have been established on the basis of internet services over the past 12 months, this period has also seen a significant growth in merger activity among online companies. The most active firms in this context have been the large portals (such as Yahoo!, America Online (AOL) and Lycos which have been extending the range of services they provide (from search engines and directories to bulletin boards, auctions, instant messaging, calendars and voice services). The AOL purchase of Netscape was intended to combine the former's internet connection and the latter's range of online content services, as was the merger between AtHome (which gives access to the internet via cable TV) and Excite, something approaching 'vertical integration'. On the other hand, the purchase by Yahoo! of Broadcast.com and Geocities.com was intended to broaden the range of online services that Yahoo! already offers, approximating to 'horizontal integration'. The power of Amazon.com is being expressed directly through its purchases of smaller retailers and service companies, or of significant shareholdings in these (such as Drugstore.com and Pets.com). In the first instance most of these mergers were among on-line companies. Mergers between online and offline companies have been slower to develop; however, the recent acquisition of TimeWarner by AOL is one of the first and most significant mergers of this sort.

The oligopolistic nature of the TV market in America and the power of the big three networks (NBC, ABC and CBS) have been undermined by the expansion of cable and the internet. The big three, with a declining share of the viewing audience, are providing a broad range of programme contents, whereas cable channels are focusing on particular niches and so fragmenting the audience. At the same time, mergers between networks have been limited by regulation, so TV companies have responded by affiliating with production studios (hence Walt Disney has acquired ABC, while CBS and Viacom are merging) and by moving into cable (TimeWarner, for example, has now managed to combine both cable and broadcast interests) or the internet. Both Viacom and CBS have been moving into online service provision, taking stakes in e-commerce and entertainment firms. In the UK, the television group Flextech has recently merged with the cable operator Telewest. This merger represents a significant shift of strategy from what has been called 'platform neutrality', i.e. the separation of media content companies from media distribution (such as cable).

ICT Sector in Birmingham and Solihull

So far we have focused upon the dynamics of ICT development at a global or national level. But in the present context it is important to consider how these dynamics are expressed and refracted at a regional level, and what challenges are thereby produced for regional policy makers. This section of the chapter therefore considers the main characteristics, structure and composition of the ICT sector in Birmingham and Solihull. The West Midlands is geographically diverse, so it makes sense to focus on Birmingham as the main centre of the conurbation, and Solihull as another area that as provided an attractive location for ICT firms.

The problems facing a researcher investigating ICT at a regional level are partly conceptual and partly statistical. In the following discussion we will attempt to resolve the conceptual difficulties by adapting the definition of ICT set out above. As regards statistical difficulties, the Standard Industrial Classification should provide a comprehensive statistical basis for an analysis. However, the current system of SIC codes has not been substantially revised since 1992, and fails to take into account the rapid development of ICT. The approach adopted in the Birmingham and Solihull analysis was to take existing SIC codes and use them to generate figures for ICT as defined above. This approach allowed the creation of a proxy ICT SIC grouping involving the codes shown in Table 9.1.

Table 9.1 The ICT sector by SIC codes

2233	Reproduction of computer media
3002	Manufacture of computers and other information processing equipment
3210	Manufacture of electronic valves and tubes and other electronic components
3220/1	Manufacturing of telephone equipment
6420	Telecommunications
7210	Computer hardware consultancy
7220	Software consultancy and supply
7230	Data processing
7240	Database activities
7250	Maintenance and repair of office, accounting and computing machinery
7260	Other computer related activities
9220/2	Television activities

Having arrived at an operational definition of ICT, the first step was to determine how large the sector is compared to others. In 2000, the ICT sector in Birmingham and Solihull employs approximately 25,000 people, representing a little over 4% of total employment (Cambridge Econometrics/Institute for Employment Research, 2000). In absolute terms, then, ICT is one of the smaller sectors in the area by employment (Table 9.2). These figures should, however, be treated with some caution because they derive from two sources – the Birmingham Company Information System (BCIS) database, and the Cambridge Econometrics/Institute for Employment Research model.

**Table 9.2 Birmingham/Solihull economy: employment by selected
             sectors, 2000 (percentage)**

Sector	%
Public & Other Services	24.62
Financial & Business Services	22.21
Manufacturing	17.36
Logistics	11.14
Retail	8.49
Construction	5.87
Hospitality	4.97
ICT*	4.07
Primary & Utilities	1.26

Source: *BCIS; Birmingham & Solihull Economic Forecasting Model, Cambridge
Econometrics/Institute for Employment Research.

However, if we consider the rate of change of employment between
1997 and 2000, a rather different picture emerges. Over this period ICT activities
have contributed significantly to job creation, adding an extra 11,227 jobs from
a small base. While manufacturing (once considered the motor of the regional
economy) experienced a near 10% fall in employment, and financial and
business services (the fastest growing sectors in recent years) grew by 12%,
ICT increased in employment by almost 80% in this three-year period (Table
9.3). This phenomenal growth rate, and the pre-eminent performance of the
ICT sector compared to others, is however concealed by existing SIC
categories.

The next step was to consider the composition of the local ICT sector.
The BCIS database records 725 firms, 141 of which are recorded as having
ceased trading during the last year. The ICT population trading in 2000 is 584
firms, for which two SIC codes represent over 60% of the firms. The largest
activity within the sector in terms of number of companies, with a little over a
third (34%) of all trading firms, comes under the *other computer-related
activities* heading (SIC 7260). This is followed closely by *software consultancy
and supply* (SIC 7220) with a little under a third (29%) of all trading firms. As
regards employment, a little under three-quarters of all jobs in the ICT sector
are accounted for by three sub-sectors. The largest is *other computer-related
activities* (25.5%) followed by *telecommunications* (21.6%) (SIC 6420) and
software consultancy and supply (21.5%). The single largest ICT employer

Table 9.3 Birmingham/Solihull economy: relative growth of economic sectors 1997-2000

Sector	% change
ICT*	78.69
Financial & business services	12.27
Retail	11.27
Construction	8.07
Logistics	3.16
Public & other services	1.16
Hospitality	0.73
Primary & utilities	0.00
Manufacturing	-9.79

Source: Adapted from *BCIS; Birmingham and Solihull Economic Forecasting Model, Cambridge Econometrics/Institute for Employment Research.

in Birmingham and Solihull is Cap Gemini (UK) plc, with 1,720 jobs on two sites.

A measure of the volatility of the ICT sector can be seen in the number of firms recorded as 'ceased trading' during the current year. Of 725 firms recorded on the database, a little under 20% (141 firms) ceased trading in 1999/00, with a loss of 5,148 jobs. One firm, TSB Technology Ltd, accounted for 2,000 of the job losses and before it ceased trading was the largest employer in the ICT sector.

As regards employment change, three sub-sectors accounted for over three-quarters of all the jobs created during 1997/00: *other computer-related activities* with over a third of all new jobs (41.5%), *telecommunications* (28.2%) and *software consultancy and supply* (15.5%). The single biggest individual employment gain during this period was 1,400 jobs created by Cap Gemini UK Plc (SIC 7260), while the largest individual employment fall was 950 jobs lost from BBC Birmingham (SIC 92202, *television activities*).

Turning to the (average) size distribution of firms within ICT, the sub-sectors with the largest firms by employment are the *manufacture of telecommunications equipment*, and the *reproduction of* computer *media*. On the other hand, the smallest firms are concerned with *data processing* and *database activities* (Table 9.4).

Despite the presence of Cap Gemini, most firms in the sector are small in employment terms. Of the 584 ICT businesses in 2000, 353 (60%) fall into the five or fewer employees category, and 416 (71%) in the 10 or fewer category.

Table 9.4 Average size of ICT companies in Birmingham and Solihull by employment

SIC code		Average no. of employees
2233	Reproduction of computer media	148
3002	Manufacture of computers and other information processing equipment	13
3210	Manufacture of electronic valves, tubes and other electronic components	70
3220/1	Manufacturing of telephone equipment	187
6420	Telecommunications	80
7210	Computer hardware consultancy	50
7220	Software consultancy and supply	25
7230	Data processing	10
7240	Database activities	10
7250	Maintenance & repair of office, accounting and computing machinery	25
7260	Other computer-related activities	25
9220/2	Television activities	34

Source: BCIS database 2000.

On the other hand, despite the significance of small firms, just 13 of the 584 firms account for 50% of all ICT employment (Table 9.5).

The Birmingham and Solihull economy has a small but dynamic ICT sector that is at present exhibiting rapid employment growth. As might be expected, the sector is strongly polarised between a small number of major employers (many of them multinational companies) and a very large number of small firms. The strength of the ICT sector in this area is therefore as much a function of decision-making by large corporations as it is of the start-up and survival rate of small firms. The volatility of employment in both of these groups is evident from the fact that one employer can lose 2,000 jobs while another can gain 1,500, all in a sector that contains only a little over 20,000 jobs in total. The bifurcated nature of ICT activity in this region, which is divided between very large and very small companies, leads us to suggest that this sector comprises a dual economy, serving different products to different markets with radically different structures.

Dynamics of ICT Development

It is tempting to seek an explanation for the current burgeoning of ICT in one single factor such as technological breakthrough, state deregulation, or market

Table 9.5   Companies employing 50% of ICT workforce in Birmingham and Solihull

	Company name	No. of jobs	Cumulative %
1	Cap Gemini (UK) plc	1,720	8
2	British Telecom plc	1,400	15
3	ITnet Ltd	800	19
4	Lucas Aerospace	750	23
5	Fujitsu Telecommunication Europe Ltd	700	26
6	Vodaphone Call Centre	700	30
7	Birmingham Cable Communications Consumer Services	670	33
8	JBA Software Products Ltd	650	36
9	Sema Group	600	39
10	Severn Trent Systems Ltd	550	42
11	Specialist Computer Services Ltd	550	45
12	AG Solutions	500	47
13	Guild Television	470	50

Source: 584 currently trading businesses – adapted from BCIS, 2000.

change. Since the late 1970s, the telecommunications industry has of course benefited from deregulation, from the opening of domestic markets to foreign competition and the privatisation of national champions. But it can be argued that deregulation, and the consequential erosion of national boundaries, was itself a response by politicians to the new business logic introduced through concurrent market and technological changes. On the other hand, while technological breakthroughs have permitted new products and constrained corporate goals, companies do not always take up the technologies that have been invented, and frequently take them up in different ways. Finally, the demand for ever-increasing bandwidth to support data transmission and the mobile phone business has certainly been a significant factor driving forward change. But the market for ICT cannot be taken for granted and depends on the imagination of designers and the education of the public. There is, then, a complex interplay between public policy, technological change, demand and supply conditions, and corporate objectives. Effects at a regional level are produced through the interaction of this interplay with the existing spatial division of labour.

Corporate Orientations

At various stages over the last 20 years, scholars have put forward models for interpreting economic change by reference to corporate behaviour or strategy. Massey and Meegan, for example, refer to three forms of production reorganisation – *rationalisation, intensification,* and investment in *technological change* – in order to explain the process of restructuring in the 1970s and 1980s (Massey and Meegan, 1982). Friedman for his part refers to 'managerial strategies', and suggests that typically there are some which give greater autonomy to the workforce, and some which involve exercising greater control over the workforce (Friedman, 1986).

Of course these approaches have certain important limitations. They emphasise corporate attempts to reorganise the labour process and as such focus on the relationship between capital and labour, whereas company behaviours concern a range of other matters too, not least the competitive struggle between capital and capital. There is also the relationship between the activities of companies and their consequences for the wider economy. To some extent the activities of different companies will tend to interact, perhaps dovetailing, perhaps representing sequential moves in a game. The changing pattern of a regional or national economy must be seen as the emergent effect of the interaction between corporate orientations and environmental opportunities and constraints (including those afforded by other firms), in which the interaction process is one of 'learning'. The process of adaptation or learning is operative both through changes in corporate practices and orientations, and differential failure (or assimilation) rates between different types of companies. In moving from the company to the economy level it is necessary to combine an understanding of corporate behaviour with an understanding of the selective pressures upon this behaviour from the economic environment, and the degrees to which firms are able to learn from these pressures (Collinge, 1999).

Nevertheless, in order to build an explanation of sectoral change, the identification and classification of corporate behaviours and competitive manoeuvres is an essential first step. The evidence presented above identifies a variety of orientations on the part of ICT firms, which can be classified as follows:

1. Restructuring

Some companies are engaged in defensive consolidation, corporate restructuring, process innovation and even market exit in response to declining revenue streams and rising investment costs affecting their main product range. Various different circumstances are occasioning this response, including diminishing revenue streams from fixed line telephone services as other platforms – cable, the internet and mobile phones – become available. Relatively low sales and margins, high investment costs and competition from other platforms have fuelled ongoing consolidation in the UK cable industry.

2. Market Control

Some companies have pursued sales growth and the defence of market share in their existing markets by seeking to build monopoly positions, eliminate or assimilate rivals, and control outlets. Vertical integration, by buying into downstream outlets for products, can be used to guarantee access to customers, and to avoid reliance on competitors for this access. This strategy has been pursued by Microsoft in relation to cable, digital TV and set-top boxes. Many mergers and alliances are intended to ensure that companies are able to lock in their technology as the industry standard, or at least to avoid being locked out through the establishment of some other technology with which they cannot work. This is the case, for example, with Microsoft in its dealings with AT&T.

3. Territorial Expansion

Frequently, expansion across territorial borders is a way of entering new marketplaces with existing products, and is a response to the attenuation of revenues in existing markets. Territorial expansion typically involves participants in relatively mature regional or national markets (such as the US) looking for new outlets and opportunities in, for example, Europe and Asia. But it also involves the recognition that survival may depend upon having a strong presence in key markets such as the US.

4. Product Diversification

Diversification is especially apparent within ICT as companies seek to compete across old market boundaries. Mergers between new telecommunications companies and old-style public service operators (for example between Qwest and USWest) are intended to guarantee traffic to use the enormous capacity provided by the new fibre optic infrastructure.

AT&T is attempting to cross the boundary between telephone and cable services and is aiming to establish high speed internet and interactive TV access alongside its telephone service.

5. The Shift Towards Content

It is possible to detect an overall shift among ICT firms from hardware or software production towards service provision, and from routine services towards high value-added services rich in content. Sony is changing its emphasis by investing more in the production of entertainments and services, interactive games and educational software. Cable and telecommunications companies, to avoid being left managing delivery mechanisms, are raising their role in content through (for example) internet portals. Marconi, the telecommunications hardware company, is moving into telephone service provision as a contractor on behalf of governments and public service providers. Compaq, the internet hardware company, is set to become a major e-commerce player via its electronics web site.

6. Market Entry

On the basis of novel technology, improved market access or a new business model, new companies may form to enter a market while established ones may attempt to diversify into it. This is illustrated by the new wave of telecommunications operators in the 1980s (Sprint, WorldCom, Mercury) and more recently a second new wave (Qwest, Level 3, Vodafone, Global Crossing, Mannesmann). Likewise in hardware, the US glass company Corning has converted itself into the world's largest fibre optic filament and optical cable producer.

In practice several of the above orientations will be combined, with companies (for example) seeking both market control and territorial expansion, or restructuring and product diversification. However, each of the approaches outlined may be the prime focus for any particular company. It should also be noted that the same kinds of tactics might be involved in each case. Corporate tactics may include mergers and acquisitions, strategic alliances, process innovation and product innovation. Process innovation includes a changed approach to the 'spatial division of labour' within companies – the way in which different functions are assigned to different places according to the requirements of the functions and the characteristics of the places.

It is through the pursuit of these orientations in the context of other firms doing the same, and against a background of changing markets, technological and regulatory conditions that the ICT sector has developed at different spatial scales. To understand the characteristics of ICT in particular regional economies such as the West Midlands it is therefore necessary to examine these particular dynamics, and their interaction with the existing position of the region in the spatial division of labour.

Conclusions

The development of information and communication technologies over the last five years, and perhaps over the next five years, is bringing with it the most fundamental generic change in the economic system since the introduction of electricity and the internal combustion engine. Of course, the impact of electricity in particular took many years to mature, and expanded from electric lighting in the 1890s to the electric motor. Likewise the computer and the telephone have lived separate lives since the 1950s. But the merging of these industries is having a huge impact on the opportunities available to companies. For those who apply ICT there are benefits in the form of greater efficiency, reduced transaction costs and greater control, for example in gathering and collating market data or in organising design and communications.

Nevertheless ICT cannot be treated as one amorphous activity, and within this broad range of sectors there are different circumstances for different companies, reflecting different market structures and regulatory environments. As always in newer industries we see a combination of the emergence of new small companies and the merger of large powerful ones. But it is particularly striking to note the resurgence of the corporate predation which was so familiar in the 1960s and 1970s, with companies seeking to enhance their opportunities or defend established positions through horizontal and vertical integration. Despite the importance of new small firms in ICT, the consolidation of businesses in the ICT industries represents a considerable departure from the 1980s orthodoxy of 'small is beautiful' and 'vertical disintegration'. It is this reality with which policy-makers in the regions must come to terms.

Against this complex background the challenge for regional policymakers seeking to stimulate ICT production is indeed considerable. To begin with they must overcome the limitations of existing data, involving outdated standard industrial clarifications, if they are to establish even the most basic description of ICT activity. Secondly, they must focus their attention on both the behaviour of large global companies and small local ones, and attempt to gain an understanding of the goals and adaptations of each. Thirdly, on the basis of such an understanding they should strive for a policy which strikes an appropriate balance between inward investment and indigenous development.

References

Booz-Allen (2000), *The Competitiveness of Europe's ICT Markets,* A report prepared by Booz-Allen & Hamilton and commissioned by the Ministry of Economic Affairs of the Netherlands for the EU Ministerial Conference, 9th-10th March 2000, Portugal.

Cable, V. and Distler, C. (1995), *Global Superhighways: The Future of International Telecommunications Policy*, Royal Institute of International Affairs, International Economics Programme, London.

Cambridge Econometrics (2000), *Regional Economic Prospects. Analysis and Forecasts to the Year 2010 for the Regions of the UK,* February.

Collinge, C. (1999), 'Self-organisation of Society by Scale: A Spatial Reworking of Regulation Theory', *Environment and Planning D: Society and Space*, vol. 17, no. 5, pp. 557-74.

Friedman, C (1986), 'Developing the Managerial Strategies Approach to the Labour Process', *Class*, no.30, pp. 97-124.

Hawkins, R. W. et al (1997), *Mapping and Measuring the Information Technology, Electronics and Communications Sector in the United Kingdom*, prepared for the Office of Science and Technology, Technology Foresight Panel on Information Technology, Communications and Electronics, London.

Houghton, J.W et al (1996), *Mapping the Information Industries*, Australian Government Publishing Service.

Massey, D. and Meegan, R. (1982), *The Anatomy of Job Loss: The How, Why and Where of Employment Decline*, Methuen, London.

Robins, K. (ed) (1992), *Understanding Information Business, Technology and Geography*, Bellhaven Press, London.

US Department of Justice (2000), *Court's Finding of Facts: USA v Microsoft Corporation*, para.35, http://www.usdoj.gov/atr/cases/ f3800/msjudgex.htm.

CONCLUSION

10 Some Critical Issues for Regional Development Agencies in England

GILL BENTLEY AND JOHN GIBNEY

At the start of the 21st century, the foundations are being set in place for a very different form of regional economic governance in England. For the regional development agenda, significant progress has been achieved with the creation of the RDAs. Nevertheless, considerable political uncertainty still surrounds the English 'regional project' and this raises a number of questions about the longer-term prospects for the agencies themselves.

For some time the English regions have lagged behind the 'leading edge' experience of Wales, Scotland and other mainland European regions in terms of their regional development agency experience (Mawson, chapter 2). The establishment of the new English RDAs may go some way towards offsetting what has generally come to be regarded, rightly or wrongly, as a degree of competitive disadvantage within the UK. However, coherent organisational arrangements are only one part of the increasingly complex regional economic development equation. Moreover, inadequate, poorly conceived, undemocratic or misdirected RDAs may in some ways do more damage than good. We are not suggesting here that this is the case currently in England, but progress with the creation of the RDAs has not been without its problems. Those observing the process could be forgiven for thinking that the debate around the nature and role of the English RDAs in the first year of their operation has been dominated more by concerns of a constitutional and political nature than by questions about regional economic development per se. According to Derek Mapp, Chair of the East Midlands RDA, responsible until recently for co-ordinating all RDA links with government, apparent uncertainty at the heart of Whitehall early in 2000 regarding the approach to be taken on the more general question of English devolution is not helping the RDA boards to tread the delicate path between politics and executive action:

It is perfectly understandable for the government to take an evolutionary approach to English regional devolution. But what is not so acceptable is for different versions of the evolutionary approach to be in operation at the same time...The continuing uncertainty does not help our attempts to unite regional interests around shared strategies.[1]

In looking to understand better the style and nature of the strategic processes at work it is instructive to note the timetable for the preparation of the first round of regional economic strategies. Driven by political imperative, Whitehall imposed an overly compressed timetable on the RDAs through what became known as the 'summer of consultation' by allowing only three months or so between July and September 1999 for intra-regional consultation over the draft RES approach. Although provision is made in the RES arrangements for the review of design and delivery of economic development activity, this initial timetable arguably led to the preparation of 'rushed' regional economic strategies for the English regions. At the very least, it can be suggested that because of these time constraints, there may not have been the opportunity for a full and considered assessment by local consultees of all the economic development options or scenarios on offer. That central government should appear to place concerns over the legal and political form of the RDAs and related institutional matters before RES procedure and content is not wholly unsurprising at the beginning of a new administrative venture of this kind. It is, however, a worrying sign for the future inasmuch as it is an indication of Whitehall's decision-making being driven by short-term political considerations which can override the longer-term needs and aspirations of the English regions. This is a habit which will need to be broken if the RDA project is to succeed in the long term. Bearing this strategic political context in mind, we now move on to set out and discuss a number of more practical themes and features impinging on the day-to-day activities of the RDAs.

Some Critical Issues

Notwithstanding the constitutional and political imperatives of central government vis-à-vis the English RDA project, and echoing Boland and Lovering in chapter 5 of this book, there is always the danger that longstanding views and deep-rooted partisan expectations may tend to come to dominate discussions about the possible scenarios and choices for the regional economy. In these circumstances it becomes difficult to advance new ideas or ways of thinking about either the problems faced by regional economies or their possible solutions. Clearly, there are limits at any given time to the number of new policies or programmes which can be adopted within a given region without provoking 'initiative fatigue'. Although there is a need for appropriate organisational structures if regional development is to succeed in England, there is also a need for innovative thinking and catalytic behaviour if regional economies are to be helped to plan for and deal with radical change in the local business environment.

The chapters in Part II above (by Bentley, Tilson, Dahlstrom, Smith, Collinge and Srbljanin), which concern themselves with shift and transition in key sectors of the West Midlands economy, demonstrate the breadth of issues to be tackled. Most of the concerns raised are critical to the success of a regional economy such as the West Midlands. Increasingly, although perhaps unfairly, RDAs are expected to facilitate almost everything from improvements in skills and competencies at a time of increasing business complexity through to enhancing regional innovation capacity, while sustaining and increasing the regional share of foreign direct investment; securing urban and rural regeneration and so on. The RDAs themselves are attempting to play down local expectations. But there is nevertheless the very real danger of an extensive, confused and undeliverable 'wish list' developing over time as these new organisations find themselves caught between the sometimes conflicting political and policy aspirations of Whitehall and the regions around the broader issue of English devolution.

Moreover, in the contemporary and complex regional economies of England, it is certainly true that many areas of economic development activity are increasingly interconnected. For Shutt (chapter 4), each of the English RDAs faces the unenviable task of addressing a range of increasingly cross-cutting issues which will require deft handling in both policy and managerial terms. Unless reconciled, 'policy conflict' between Whitehall and the regions over the pace and scope of the English regional project, when coupled with the challenge of ever more complex regional economic scenarios, could threaten to induce apprehensive indecision across the RDAs and the headlong pursuit of the safest option.

Enhancing regional economic performance will mean looking for synergy between economic programmes and a more 'joined up' approach overall to both strategic and inter-organisational processes and day-to-day management of RDA business (Roberts and Shutt, chapters 3 and 4). Herein lies yet another worrying paradox, namely the extent to which a cross-cutting approach to regional economic development can be effectively delivered in what Roberts (chapter 3) considers to be an already institutionally congested and confused 'regional platform'. Achieving this 'joined up' approach to the regional economy would be in many ways one of the most visible 'success factors' for a RDA since it is increasingly being seen as *the* new component of regional economic development. How the RDAs are evaluated is critical (Shutt, chapter 4). There is already a tendency for classic performance indicators to be quoted as evidence of their impact pertaining to the numbers of jobs created, value of inward investment, value of the financial contribution to projects and programmes, numbers of task forces and partnership arrangements set up and so forth. The challenge for the RDAs is to get the right balance between quality and quantity of activity undertaken. At a simplistic level, two well-performing business task groups will no doubt provide better value for money than two dozen poorly performing ones. It may be that more thinking is required about complementary performance indicators which can tease out the 'softer' essence of the innovative and value-added 'joined up' economic development activity alluded to above.

Effective political and organisational co-operation at regional level (between the RDAs and other business support organisations) and at local level (including with local authorities, which are charged to varying degrees with designing and delivering economic development initiatives) is essential. Making new value-added connections between once seemingly discrete and disparate economic activities is core to the notion of generating original thinking in economic development. In looking to the future of the RDA project, however, there is likely to be more than one fly in the ointment. Leaving aside important questions around RDAs' transparency and accountability, a number of critical operational issues have surfaced in the preceding chapters around the following themes:

- vested interests and 'creative space';
- integration and co-operation;
- core functions and human resources;
- financial resources.

Let us now move to discuss each of these in turn.

Vested Interests

Firstly, local vested interest as evidenced by the signs of political tribalism and the competitive positioning of organisations has tended to determine the early economic agendas of the RDAs through the first round of regional economic strategies. Clearly, the various regional stakeholders across the public and private sectors represent considerable and legitimate constituencies, and they need to have their views heard and considered as part of the process of regional democratisation. The ideas around the creation of directly elected regional chambers in England will – if ultimately enabled – promote local democracy, but they can offer no guarantee of regional economic success in themselves. 'Different container same content' is no credible way forward for the English regional project in the long term.

Moreover, effectively organised and vociferous regional lobbies may have a downside if they ignore the wider comparative dimension of regional circumstances and serve simply to reinforce the established political landscape. It will always be tempting for policymakers and practitioners at regional level to fall into the trap of proposing only 'safe' consensus options, or become driven by imperatives arising from a new form of parochial regional 'realpolitik'. Providing for the institutionalisation of strategic preconceptions must be avoided (Boland and Lovering on lessons from Wales, chapter 5). Instead, the RDAs need to stimulate a more broadly informed notion of regional economic development which, while acknowledging the concerns of longstanding interests, is capable of transcending political, organisational and spatial closed-mindedness.

Without doubt, at the outset of this new venture there is a very real opportunity for the RDAs to promote and encourage new and original thinking and behaviour. However, this will mean making time and space for genuinely open and independent reflection on future options for the regional economy. How and in relation to which issues RDAs manage to avoid the temptation to settle for short-term partisan consensus and seek to bring about new and longer-term vision remains to be seen. Critically, if this is to be achieved, it will be important for the RDAs to encourage and fund unconstrained and genuinely reflective research on the regional economy over the long term.

Integration and Co-operation

Secondly, in relation to integration and co-operation, Mawson reminds us at the start of this book that local and regional structures must be based firmly on partnership. Much of the added value of the RDAs will come from stimulating a new generation of partnership working within the regions. Maintaining regular and genuinely non-prejudicial communication and discussion is an important facet of joint working. The task will not be easy, for as Roberts points out in chapter 3, the RDAs did not land in an 'institutional desert' when they were created in 1999. The institutional environment is extremely complex at regional level in England, with a significant range of strategic work going on at any one time. There is already anecdotal and research-based evidence of lack of co-ordination and competitive positioning occurring among RDAs, local authorities, business interests and so on, in spite of the joint working mechanism of the RES exercises.[2]

Undoubtedly, even in the 'good practice' areas of the country a degree of confusion, misunderstanding and downright suspicion is always likely to be present given the number of organisations now involved in parallel economic development activity in the English regions. Recent changes in administrative boundaries in England have further complicated the task of joint working. Individual RDA managers may be able to ensure openness and coherence on a project-by-project basis with their opposite numbers in other local bodies, but they will need to generate extensive goodwill and trust between individuals before 'intelligence' or 'knowledge' sharing happens as a matter of course. Most importantly, as Roberts observes, without some form of over-arching strategic guidance on regional development policy, RDAs are unlikely on their own to be able to ensure any significant degree of integration or coherence at the policy level.

Core Functions and Human Resources

Thirdly, and in respect specifically of their core activities, the organisation and staffing of the executive functions within the RDAs will need to reflect the process of continued change in the economy.

It is clear from the overview of business sectors in Part II of this book that many aspects of economic development at regional level are interactive and interdependent in terms of their local and global dynamics (e.g. Tilson, chapter 7). The more complex the challenges posed by the economy, the more critical organisational and human resource capacity and calibre become. Rather than be content with their initial internal structures, the RDAs will need to reconfigure their organisational arrangements on an almost ongoing basis in order to accommodate a variety of threats and opportunities. Operating with suppleness and fluidity in a complex technical environment at both regional and sub-regional levels, the RDAs will similarly be faced with all-round management challenges in terms of their internal and external duties. Their day-to-day work will be multifaceted and will involve seamlessly connecting the work of sub-regional teams with cross-cutting regional strategic activity – and all of this in public/private-sector partnership mode (Shutt, chapter 4).

RDA managers and project officers will need to be dextrous administrators, advisors and motivators with highly developed 'softer' diplomatic, networking and political skills. In professional terms, joined-up professional training may come to underpin joined-up government at regional level. Unlike France, for example, with its much longer history of regional councils and their associated regional development agencies, there is no regional development 'corps' in England.

Even closer to home, it is true to say that the eight individual English regions have varied and differing levels of regional development experience. It may be that a 'regional development professional' will evolve over time, and in some ways the role and scope of the RDAs may take staff far beyond the often very localised experience of English economic development and require them to learn new mixes of skills and talents. Most crucially, while obligated to manage the delivery of predetermined central government programmes, which is essentially a question of administration, the RDAs must resist becoming hide-bound bureaucratic entities and must focus on developing core functions and people who can respond creatively and with insight to the complex requirements of their respective regional economies.

Financial Resources

Fourthly, and over the longer term, the issue of resources in the broader sense is key to the success of the RDA project. It is true to say that the model envisaged for the RDAs has always been as much about co-ordination and influence as about direct implementation. The need for an economic development catalyst at regional level in England is clear. But unless RDAs have sufficient 'resource credibility', their capacity to exercise a genuinely catalytic role at regional level will be seriously limited. Over and above the largely earmarked financial resources for mainstream programmes, only scarce additional government funding has been made available to the RDAs, and they presently operate within the parameters of existing powers and responsibilities transferred from central government (Mawson, chapter 2).

Extrapolating from the complexity of the economic challenges facing business sectors in the West Midlands, as depicted in Part II of this book, it is questionable whether the RDAs will have the necessary resources to make a real impact. Partnership working and better integration of public programmes bearing on economic development will go some way towards assisting with the delivery of the sophisticated regional action plans which are emerging. Yet there is the real risk that limited staff and financial resources will not enable the RDAs to achieve the ambitious range of tasks and targets which are presently being set for them (Shutt, chapter 4). The scope for innovative public policy in economic development at regional level will rely heavily on the ability of the RDAs to use government funding streams more flexibly than is allowable under present central government constraints. The English regions will have very different problems, needs and solutions to address. What is right for the West Midlands may not be right for the South West, for instance. There is a good case for the RDAs to be allowed much greater discretion over their spending priorities than at present.

The West Midlands Case Example

What, then, does all this mean for the West Midlands? The story of the regional economy over recent times is one of continuing change, challenge and on occasion the totally unexpected (Smith and Collinge, preface to Part II). In spite of the best efforts of local and regional economic actors over the past two decades, the prospects for the economy remain mixed and are inextricably bound to the evermore interwoven local/global dynamic of capital, labour, technology and know-how. In the certainty that doing nothing is not a credible option, the advent of Advantage West Midlands could present local and regional communities with a valuable set of tools and resources for improving the odds of securing economic advantage from the cycle of business change.

However, as the chapters in Part I of this book show, the RDAs are not constituted to carry out all the tasks necessary to secure regional economic development. Instead they must rely on partnership working with other agencies to implement the RES. Nonetheless, while the chapters in Part II of the book show the economic realities with which the RDAs must contend, it is clear that the RDAs have a catalytic role. This is well illustrated by chapter 6 (Bentley) on the automotive industry. The Rover Task Force might not have been set up and able to take a *regional* perspective had Advantage West Midlands not been in place. AWM clearly rallied agencies and individuals to examine the consequences and take action about the impending possible closure of Rover. AWM has also stepped into the role of steering the development of the regional innovation strategy on behalf of the regional partners. Tilson (chapter 7) identifies some of the issues that the RDA will face in fostering innovation in the plastics and rubber industries.

Moreover, for AWM, promoting and funding a better understanding of business change and development in the regional economy is not an abstract luxury, rather a prerequisite of effective intervention and mediation. Dahlstrom (chapter 8) and Collinge and Srbljanin (chapter 9) reinforce this point, in their chapters on the business services sector and the ICT industries.

The advent of the English RDAs holds promise, but it is far too soon to definitively evaluate their performance. Assuming they survive over the longer term, their involvement at the forefront of economic development work will call for further research into their impact on policy and practice.

Notes

1 Derek Mapp quoted in a Financial Times survey, *England's Regional Development Agencies*, Thursday 11 May 2000.

2 For a more in-depth assessment of the micro-politics of regional working in the West Midlands see a conference paper presented by S. Ayres and P. Davis (2000) to the Fourth International Research Symposium on Public Management. *Welcome to the Party? Inclusion, Mutuality and Difference in the West Midlands Regional Development Agency Network in the UK.* Public Services Management Research Centre, Aston Business School, Aston University, Birmingham.

Appendix:
West Midlands Region -
History Sources

BARBARA SMITH

The following references have been chosen to reflect the different research bodies and reports relevant to the state of the regional economy and policy development towards it. They are in chronological order, with brief annotations.

1940s

West Midland Group on Postwar Reconstruction and Planning (1948), *Conurbation. A Planning Survey of Birmingham and the Black Country*, Architectural Press, London.

   Famous private/academic study; argued for containing the conurbation at its present level (i.e. 2 million) plus natural increase so no need for overspill (the study had underestimated the population, in the absence of postwar data). Conurbation with its 'diversified but closely linked industries' vital to whole country, so argued that it should retain its character.

Ministry of Town and Country Planning (1948), *West Midlands Plan* by Patrick Abercrombie and H. Jackson, unpublished (because of paper shortage).

   Discusses containment and overspill to surrounding towns (needed because the population of Birmingham was known to have gone up).

1960s

Department of Economic Affairs (1965), *The West Midlands. A Regional Study,* HMSO, London.

   Overspill need was estimated at 507,000 people (107,000 dwellings), of whom 357,000 were covered in existing schemes and infilling; critical of region's economic performance (p. 24).

West Midlands Economic Planning Council (WMEPC) (1967), *The West Midlands: Patterns of Growth*, A first report by the West Midlands Economic Planning Council, HMSO, London.

Overspill was now up to 590,000 people of whom 60,000 were to go to Chelmsley Wood and 50,000 to North East Worcestershire. In 1967, 227,000 people were to move out of the conurbation by 1981; they needed 115,000 jobs of which 62,000 were to be in manufacturing (see sources for 1970s, Smith, 1972, p. 7).

1970s

West Midlands Economic Planning Council (1971), *The West Midlands. An Economic Appraisal*, HMSO, London.

Important study. First to point out serious state of the regional economy, with manufacturing employment declining.

West Midlands Planning Authorities Conference (WMPAC) (1971), *West Midlands Regional Study: 1971. A Developing Strategy for the West Midlands (The Blue Book)*.

Joint regional, local and central study. 'Option' population 1 million by 2001 to be located outside the conurbation, mainly by 1981 (300,000 before 1981). Manufacturing employment already started to decline, but service growth expected. Expected 24,000 - 43,000 manufacturing jobs to move out of conurbation into region between 1967 and 1981.

Smith, B. (1972), *The Administration of Industrial Overspill: The Institutional Framework Relevant to Industrial Overspill in the West Midlands*, Occasional Paper 22, Centre for Urban and Regional Studies, University of Birmingham, Birmingham.

West Midlands Planning Authorities Conference (1972), *Report of the West Midlands Planning Authorities Conference* (included in *The Orange Book*).

Planning outcome of the 1971 *Blue Book*. Since 1966, unemployment and job losses up sharply in the 'shake-out' (p. 8). Population estimates falling because of lower birth-rates and out-migration (p. 11); said this must be monitored.

West Midlands Planning Authorities Conference (1973), *Addendum to the Conference Report*, (included in *The Orange Book*).

Regional and local study. Option population cut to 250,000 and industrial job movement to 25,000; some population to go to Sutton Coldfield and Solihull.

West Midlands Planning Authorities Conference (1974) *Letter from Secretary of State for the Environment*, George Rippon (included in *The Orange Book*).

As regional policy has top priority and as industrial mobility low, 20,000 - 35,000 jobs only likely to move; option population now to be 250,000, by 1986; much movement close in.

West Midlands County Council (WMCC) (1975), *Time for Action. Economic and Social Trends in the West Midlands*, WMCC, Birmingham.

Important report indicating serious decline in regional economy. David Liggins was one driving force. County Council produced annual reports and sector studies, among other reports (see also sources for 1980s, Spencer et al).

Joint Monitoring Steering Group (1975), *A Developing Strategy for the West Midlands. West Midlands Regional Study. The First Annual Report of the Joint Monitoring Steering Group* and Joint Monitoring Steering Group (1976), *A Developing Strategy for the West Midlands. West Midlands Regional Study. The Second Annual Report of the Joint Monitoring Steering Group.*

Regional and tripartite (WMEPC, WMCC and WMPAC) work. The West Midlands Economic Planning Council was abolished in 1979; tripartite thereafter equals West Midlands Economic Planning Board, West Midlands Planning Authorities Conference (the Regional Study team and local authorities) and government departments.

Wood, P. (1976), *The West Midlands*, David and Charles, Newton Abbott.

Joyce, F. (ed) (1977), *Metropolitan Development and Change. The West Midlands: A Policy Review*, University of Aston and Teakfield, Birmingham.

Prepared for 139th meeting of Association for the Advancement of Science; chapters by civil servants, local government officers and academics.

West Midlands Planning Authorities Conference (1979), *A Developing Strategy for the West Midlands. Updating and Rolling Forward of the Regional Strategy to 1991. Report of Joint Monitoring Steering Group. (The Green Book).*

Regional tripartite work supporting physical plan.

West Midlands Planning Authorities Conference (1979), *The Regional Economy. Problems and Proposals. West Midlands Regional Study* (companion volume but without DoE support).

Economic study by WMPAC and WMEPC presenting four policy options. Central government unwilling to accept decline of the economy.

1980s

West Midlands County Council (1982), *Action for the Eighties*, WMCC, Birmingham.

The 1982 structure plan. Annual statement of the WMCC.

West Midlands County Council and 'Managing the Metropolis' Working Party (1982), *West Midlands. Futures Study*, WMCC, Birmingham.

Presents four possible scenarios. Includes notes of economic, social and other issues. Two determinants seen as the state of the economy in terms of output and jobs, and the attitudes and responses of people and organisations both national and local. A third was the integration between the local and national economies re indigenous development, inward investment and trade. Much driven by David Thew.

West Midlands Forum of County Councils, *Annual reports for 1983; 1984 and 1985.*

From the West Midlands Regional Study team.

West Midlands Forum of County Councils (1984), *West Midlands Region. Economy and Employment. Indicators of change.*

The work of the West Midlands Regional Study team.

West Midlands County Council, Economic Development Committee (1984), *Action in the Local Economy. Progress Report. Campaign for Jobs*, WMCC, Birmingham.

West Midlands Forum of County Councils (1985), *Regenerating the Region: A Strategy for the West Midlands. West Midlands Regional Strategy Review.*

The work of the West Midlands Regional Study team inter alia for 1991 to 2001. Substantially an advocacy document seeking the necessary resources and policies from central government (and the private sector) to implement regeneration priorities, namely: strengthening the region's economic base; improving living conditions in older urban areas, especially the inner areas of the conurbation; and improving the environment and image of the region, particularly its urban areas.

Birmingham City Council, City Planning Office (1985), *An Economic Strategy and Development Programme for Birmingham. Birmingham, the Business City.*

West Midlands County Council (1985), *Strategic Planning in Action. A Situation Report: April 1985.*
    1984 annual statement by A.A. Cave, county planner.

Smith, B. (1985), *Alternative Explanations for Economic Change in a Local Economy and their Applicability to the West Midlands County Council Area*, Working Paper 18 in Economic and Social Research Council (ESRC) Inner Cities in Context Research Programme, Centre for Urban and Regional Studies, The University of Birmingham, Birmingham.
    Tests each of nine 'popular' explanations against West Midlands data.

West Midlands Enterprise Board (WMEB) (1986), *Priorities for Economic Regeneration in the West Midlands. The Future Role of the West Midlands Enterprise Board Ltd Group of Companies.*
    Paper presented by chair Councillor Geoff Edge to Board of Directors in January.

West Midlands Enterprise Board, *Enterprise.*
    Newsletters, each about four pages. Issue 2 January 1986; Issue 3 May 1986; Issue 4 September 1986.

West Midlands Enterprise Board (1986), seminar on 'What's Happening to Enterprise Boards', June 25.
    Includes paper by John Mawson entitled 'Towards a Regional Development Agency: West Midlands Enterprise Board'.

West Midlands County Council (1986), *Strategic Planning in the West Midlands Metropolitan Area. Current and Future Approaches,* Discussion paper of a working group to Royal Society of Arts/Royal Town Planning Institute (RTPI) at the University of Birmingham, 6 March.

Spencer, K. et al (1986), *Crisis in the Industrial Heartland. A Study of the West Midlands*, Clarendon, Oxford.

Report was part of ESRC 'Inner Cities in Context' research programme.

Flynn, N. and Taylor, A. (1986), 'Inside the Rust Belt: an Analysis of the Decline of the West Midlands Economy. 1 Corporate Strategies and Economic Change. 2 International and National Economic Conditions', *Environment and Planning A*, vol. 18, pp. 865-900 and pp. 999-1028.

Analysis takes Massey and Meagan's theory (see Massey, D. and Meagan, R. (1982), *The Anatomy of Job Loss: The How, Why and Where of Employment Decline*, Methuen, London and New York.) to examine recent economic history of West Midlands; developed out of work for ESRC 'Inner Cities in Context' research programme (see Spencer, K. et al above, 1986, chapter 5). Flynn was then in Institute of Local Government Studies (ILGS) and Taylor in CURS at the University of Birmingham.

Field, P. and Press, M. (1988), *Rover into the 90s: The Local Government Response. A Report Prepared for the Motor Industry Local Authority Network,* The Research Partnership, Stoke.

MILAN was a discussion group meeting at ILGS initiated by John Benington et al.

Department of the Environment (1988), *Strategic Planning Guidance for the West Midlands*, HMSO, London.

Hesse, J.J. (ed) (1988), *Regional Structural Change and Industrial Policy in International Perspective*: *United States, Great Britain, France, Federal Republic of Germany*, Nomos Verlagsgesellschaft, Baden-Baden.

Comparison of West Midlands region with Ruhr, Pittsburg and Pas de Calais, with chapters by Ken Young, 'Regional Structural Change in the West Midlands', pp. 161-195; Barbara Smith, 'The Economic and Social History of the West Midlands Region 1966-1986: Experience and Response to Structural Change and Manufacturing Decline', pp. 197-269; and Ken Spencer, 'Public Policy and Industrial Decline in the West Midlands Region of the United Kingdom', pp. 271-324.

West Midlands Regional Forum (of County Councils and Metropolitan Counties) (1989), *The West Midlands. 1989 Report*.

Hirst, P. and Zeitlin, J. (eds) (1989), *Reversing Industrial Decline? Industrial Structure and Policy in Britain and Her Competitors*, Berg, Oxford.

Includes a chapter by David Elliott and Michael Marshall, 'Sector Strategy in the West Midlands', pp. 191-223. At the time of writing, they were principal economists at the West Midlands Enterprise Board.

Tilson, B. (ed) (1989), *Made in Birmingham. Design and Industry 1889-1989*, Brewin Books, Studley.

Has 22 chapters, including ones on Lucas, bicycles, cars, jewellery and motorcycles, among others.

1990s

West Midlands Enterprise Board (1990), *Quarterly Economic Commentary*, February 1990; July 1990, 12pp each, WMEB, Birmingham.

Refers to WMEB's *Automotive Sector Review: Vehicle Manufacturers*, published January 1990 and reports on power plant sector (June 1889); aerospace sector (February 1989); steel sector (January 1989); new engineering materials sector (November 1988) with motor vehicles components sector then forthcoming.

Shaylor, G. (1990), *Draft Birmingham Unitary Development Plan. Public Consultation Document,* Birmingham City Council, Birmingham.

On Birmingham, but includes chapter 3 on the economy.

Townroe, P. and Martin, R. (eds) (1992), *Regional Development in the 1990s. The British Isles in Transition*, Regional Studies Association and Jessica Kingsley, London.

Includes profile of 'The West Midlands' by Michael Marshall, pp. 59-67.

Smith, B. (1993), *The West Midlands Economy and Labour Market in the 1980s and 1990s*. A talk, typescript, unpublished.

West Midlands Regional Forum of Local Authorities (1993), *The West Midlands Region. European Development Strategy. Partners in Europe*.

Comprises nine documents. Document 1 is 'The Regional Strategy'; documents 2-8 are 'The Sub-Regional Strategies' defined by European aid programmes; and document 9, the Appendix. Initiated by John Jones; many academics and officers met and prepared papers at preceding discussions at CURS and elsewhere.

Gerrard, A. and Slater, T. (eds) (1996), *Managing a Conurbation: Birmingham and its Region*, Brewin Books, Studley.

Prepared mainly by the Geography Department at the University of Birmingham to follow tradition, for the Association for the Advancement of Science meeting (see Joyce, F. (ed), 1977, above). Includes J. Bryson et al, ' From widgets to where? The Birmingham Economy in the 1990s', pp. 156-68 and R. Gwynne, 'From Craft to Lean: Technological Change and the Motor Vehicle Industry in the West Midlands', pp. 169-86, and chapters by M. Beazley and B. Nevin (with P. Loftman).

Government Office for the West Midlands (1998), *Working to Win. A Framework for Competitiveness in the West Midlands*. Regional Economic Consortium, Birmingham.

West Midlands Development Agency (1999), *Opportunity West Midlands. Understanding Business Change in the Regional Economy*, WMDA, Birmingham.

Overview and sector studies prepared by the Centre for Urban and Regional Studies, the University of Birmingham, in 1998.

Advantage West Midlands (1999), *Creating Advantage. The West Midlands Economic Strategy*, AWM, Birmingham.

The regional economic strategy for the West Midlands, produced by the new regional development agency, AWM.

Regional Economic Forecasts

Northern Ireland Economic Research Centre and Oxford Economic Forecasting (1992), *Regional Economic Outlook. Analysis and Forecasts to the Year 2000 for Standard Planning Regions of the UK.*

John Mawson and Barbara Smith wrote chapter 4 on the West Midlands in January 1992, which appeared as chapter 4, pp. 91-102, in the longer volume.

Cambridge Econometrics (1993 and sequence), *Regional Economic Prospects. Analysis and Forecasts to the year 2005 for the Standard Planning Regions of the UK. Main report.*

John Mawson, Barbara Smith (from CURS) and Martyn Booth (from West Midlands Enterprise Board) wrote these reports on the West Midlands until John left CURS. His place was taken by Chris Collinge. Figures are provided back for 20 years and forward to 2010 for GDP, employment and investment, with some given for earnings and housebuilding, among other variables, as well as comparative figures for the UK. Back figures are adjusted each year, so a complete series back to 1971 cannot be derived easily.

Government Office for the West Midlands (1996), *West Midlands Labour Market and Skill Trends. Nineteen Ninety Six; Nineteen Ninety Seven*, GOWM, Birmingham.
There have been other issues before and since.

PriceWaterhouse, Birmingham, Warwick Business School and University of Wolverhampton Business School (1997 and sequence), *The West Midlands Business Survey, Autumn 1997.*
Biannual in autumn and spring. In spring 2000, Wolverhampton Business School was replaced by The Nottingham Trent University.

West Midlands Regional Group of Chambers (of Commerce) (2000, quarterly) *2000. Economic Survey*, sponsored by KPMG.
See also Birmingham Chamber of Commerce, *Quarterly Economic Survey 2000*, for the Birmingham area.

Index